Women and Men Police Officers

Status, Gender, and Personality

Gwendolyn L. Gerber

Westport, Connecticut
London

Library of Congress Cataloging-in-Publication Data

Gerber, Gwendolyn L.
  Women and men police officers : status, gender, and personality /
  Gwendolyn L. Gerber.
    p. cm.
  Includes bibliographical references and index.
  ISBN 0-275-96749-2 (alk. paper)
    1. Police—Professional relationships—New York (State)—New York. 2.
Policewomen—Professional relationships—New York (State)—New York. 3.
Sex role in the work environment. 4. Police—New York (State)—New York—
Social conditions. I. Title.

HV8009.G47 2001
363.2'09747'1—dc21   00-049170

British Library Cataloguing in Publication Data is available.

Library of Congress Catalog Card Number: 00-049170
ISBN: 0-275-96749-2

First published in 2001

Praeger Publishers, 88 Post Road West, Westport, CT 06881
An imprint of Greenwood Publishing Group, Inc.
www.praeger.com

Printed in the United States of America

The paper used in this book complies with the
Permanent Paper Standard issued by the National
Information Standards Organization (Z39.48-1984).

10 9 8 7 6 5 4 3 2 1

To Brent and Brooke

Contents

Preface   ix

Introduction: Women and Men in Policing   xiii

1. The Status Model of Gender Stereotyping   1

2. Status Characteristics Theory and the Gender-Stereotyped
   Personality Traits   17

3. Description of the Study: The Sample of Police Partners
   and Measures   29

4. Status and Personality: The Dominating, Instrumental, and
   Expressive Traits   39

5. Coping with Low Status: The Verbal-Aggressive and
   Submissive Traits   53

6. Police Officers Who Violate Gender Norms:
   The Bipolar Traits   65

7. Self-Esteem: The Impact of Status and Personality Traits   83

8. The Patterning of Traits Within Individual Personality   99

9. Status, Gender, and Personality: Toward an Integrated
   Theory   119

10. Implications for Policing   141

Appendix A. Procedure   155

Appendix B. Development of Measures   159

Appendix C. Further Statistical Analyses   167

Notes   185

References   201

Name Index   215

Subject Index   221

Preface

When I started the research on which this book is based, I was concerned about the problems women officers have working in the highly masculine-typed field of policing. I wanted to understand better the difficulties they face in being accepted as fully competent police officers. Because women police officers are often perceived as having different personality traits from male officers—as being more accommodating and more concerned about others' feelings—many people question whether women could be assertive enough to enforce the law effectively.

My earlier research on gender stereotyping had suggested that women may appear to be more accommodating than men because they have less power and lower status. If so, then women police officers who have equal status with male officers would be seen as equally self-assertive—and presumably as equally competent in enforcing the law.

The beliefs about male and female police officers' personality traits are similar to stereotypes that are held within the larger society in which men are viewed as assertive or "instrumental" and women are seen as accommodating or "expressive." These characteristics, which reflect stereotypes about the two sexes, are known as the "gender-stereotyped personality traits."

The relationship between police partners is particularly relevant to studying whether the so-called gender-stereotyped traits relate to status. Because women police officers generally have the lower status when they work with a male partner, I expected that they would be viewed as having more accommodating or expressive personality traits. By the same token, a less-experienced male officer who works with a male partner would have lower status than his partner and, according to my hypothesis, would also be seen as more expressive.

That is how the research project started. As it evolved, I decided to expand the study to include less extensively researched personality traits, such as the verbal-aggressive and submissive traits that are used to stereotype women. I hypothesized that all of the gender-stereotyped personality traits function as "status-related" personality traits. Because men have higher status than women in our society, "male-typed" personality traits are characteristics associated with higher-status positions, and "female-typed" traits are characteristics associated with lower-status positions.

According to my hypothesis, sex or gender no longer would be central to our implicit theories of personality; it would become one part—certainly an important part but only one aspect—of the more general status processes that take place in interactions. By focusing on the interconnections between status processes that take place in interactions and the personality attributions that result from these processes, we could understand what appears to be gender stereotyping by using basic psychological and sociological principles. The instrumental and expressive traits, for example, no longer would be viewed as the exclusive purview of one or the other sex; they would be seen as status-related traits that emerge from interactions, including interactions between members of the same sex. When two female police officers work together as partners, for example, the higher-status woman would be characterized as having more instrumental personality traits, and the lower-status woman would be characterized by more expressive personality traits.

Further, by focusing on status, I could expand my original focus on the issues faced by women police officers to include those of men police officers. The status-related expectations that govern police organizations, as well as other work organizations, promote the smooth and predictable functioning of the organization as a whole. The happiness and work satisfaction of the men and women who work within this organizational structure are secondary to this overall goal. By studying how status processes affect different types of police partnerships—all-male, male–female, and all-female partnerships—I could delineate some of the impact that status-related expectations have on both women and men officers.

Much of the research on "police personality" has assumed that a modal personality characterizes all police officers regardless of their experience, their role, or even their nationality. By contrast, the status approach assumes that police officers are affected by the same processes that occur in other kinds of occupational groups. It emphasizes the similarities between police officers who work as partners and members of other kinds of work groups; the status processes that operate in interactions would have similar effects on their perceptions of personality traits. This approach views police officers as individuals, similar to those in other occupations, who respond to particular situational demands involving status.

In developing the theoretical underpinnings of the study, I employed status characteristics theory. I extended the theory, which has focused primarily on the behaviors that take place in task-oriented groups, to deal with social cognition—the way interaction partners perceive one another's personality attributes. In doing so, I drew on other theoretical work in social cognition and personality. This made it possible to examine additional issues in status and personality—the factors that affect police officers' self-esteem and the way traits are organized within personality.

This is truly an interdisciplinary book. The issues it concerns cut across the fields of criminal justice, psychology, sociology, and gender. By studying police officers who work as partners, I have been able to explore some basic questions involving status, gender, and personality. The answers, I hope, will expand our understanding and help us find ways to ameliorate the stress experienced by women and men who work in policing and other masculine-typed occupational fields, helping them to function more effectively.

This book and the research project it describes would not have been possible without the help and support of many people. First, I would like to express my deep appreciation to the New York City Police Department, which provided very tangible help and support in collecting the research data with police partners. The assistance of the NYPD made this research project possible. I also want to express my deep-felt gratitude to the men and women of the NYPD who participated in the research.

I am particularly indebted to Joseph Berger for his support, encouragement, and suggestions throughout the duration of the project and for his thoughtful comments on the final manuscript. I would like to thank Edwin Hollander and Florence Denmark, whose unwavering encouragement and belief in my ideas helped sustain me throughout.

A number of generous colleagues read various chapters and provided reactions and helpful criticism; I would like to express my gratitude to them: Murray Webster, Martha Foschi, Nancy Jurik, Abraham Fenster, and Maureen O'Conner. And special thanks to my sister, Carolyn LeVasseur, for her careful editorial comments and suggestions on the manuscript. Thanks also to individuals who provided valuable help and suggestions for carrying out the research: Robert Mealia, Nancy Jacobs, Maria Volpe, and Robert Louden. And to my friends and colleagues—Joan Einwohner, Joanne Lifshin, Marianne Jackson, and Patricia Hollander—my appreciation for their unfailing inspiration and encouragement throughout the project.

Finally, I would like to thank my research assistants and students, some of whom are police officers, for their dedication and assistance with various parts of the project: Karen Dunaif, Christine Fortune, Diana Soto, Dennis Kelly, Mark Aguila, Frank Valluzzi, Dorothy Fiske, Shaneequia Singletarry, Laureen Rybacki, Cory Bee, and Susan Fuller.

The research was supported by grants from The City University of New York PSC-CUNY Research Award Program, as well as by Faculty Research Awards from the Criminal Justice Center and the Graduate Studies Program at John Jay College of Criminal Justice. My thanks also to the Forty-Five Foundation, which provided support for the project for several years.

Introduction: Women and Men in Policing

> When you're in uniform and you're a man, people see a cop. If you're a woman and you're in uniform, people don't see a cop, they see a woman.
>
> —*Female officer in an all-female police team*

The changes in traditional gender roles now taking place in our society have made it possible for women to enter traditionally masculine-typed fields, such as police work. But despite numerous research findings that show women police officers perform their job as effectively as men, men are still believed to be more competent (Lunneborg, 1989; Martin, 1990). Men are thought to have more of the directive, assertive personality traits necessary for the job of police officer. Women, who are thought to possess more accommodating personality traits, are believed to be less effective as police officers.

These beliefs about men's and women's personalities reflect stereotypes that are held within the larger society. Despite the social changes of recent years, particularly in women's occupational roles, people still believe that women and men have different personality traits (Spence, Deaux, & Helmreich, 1985).

This book proposes that men and women only appear to have different personalities because men have higher status than women. These status differences would be particularly evident when a man and a woman work together as police partners. The higher-status man would act as leader in the partnership and would appear to have more assertive or "instrumental" personality traits. By contrast, the lower-status woman would play the role of follower, thereby appearing to have more accommodating or "expressive" traits.

According to this formulation, status is the primary factor that affects personality. Sex is simply one of many ways in which status can be designated.[1] It can also be designated by work experience, so that when two men or two women police officers work together, the officer with more experience takes charge. As a result, the more-experienced officer appears to have more instrumental traits and the less-experienced officer seems to have more expressive traits.

In the research project described in the book, we will study different types of police partnerships—those in which two men or two women work together and those in which a woman works with a man. In doing so, we will be able to determine whether differences in the status of men's and women's roles lead to apparent sex differences in personality. Women and men police officers typically play different roles when they interact with one another; this may explain why they appear to have dissimilar personality traits.

This difference is a critical issue within policing; if women truly have different personality traits than men, they may never be able to function effectively as police officers—they may never be able to manifest the highly assertive characteristics necessary for the job of police officer. However, if women's apparent personality traits result from situational forces, namely, their low status within policing, this opens up a variety of possibilities for change.

The research described in the book focuses on this question: Do male and female police officers appear to have different personality traits because men have higher status than women? To answer this question, we need to explore basic issues involving gender and people's stereotypes about gender, as well as the way status affects people's perceptions of their personality traits.

THE RELATIONSHIP BETWEEN POLICE PARTNERS

The relationship between police officers who work together as partners has been portrayed extensively in television and in movies. Although this relationship has caught the fancy of the public, it rarely has been studied empirically. This book is concerned with examining the relationship between police partners and, in particular, the way the relationship affects the individual officers.

Police officers who work as partners have an unusually intensive work relationship. They work closely together five days a week, often for more than two years.[2] Not only must they cooperate with one another in order to perform their job effectively; they also are dependent on one another for their very life and safety.

An intensive relationship such as this can have a major impact on the individual officers. This book explores how the relationship affects the officers' sense of self—the images they have of themselves and their personality traits. In addition, it explores how the relationship affects the officers' perceptions of their partner's personality traits and other issues related to status, gender, and personality. These issues not only have important implications for men and women in policing but also for men and women within society as a whole.

The major part of the research project was carried out with the help of the New York City Police Department (NYPD) and included all-male, male–female, and all-female police teams. Both members of each team completed an extensive questionnaire in which they described themselves, their partners, and their relationships. These empirical findings were then supplemented with interview data from an additional sample of female and male police officers.

STATUS IN POLICE PARTNERSHIPS

Researchers who have studied work relationships have found that when two people work together, the individual who is believed to be more competent generally is given higher status and exercises greater influence (Berger, Fisek, Norman, & Zelditch, 1977). Hence, when two men or two women work together as police partners, seniority would be of primary importance in determining their relative status. The officer with more experience in policing would be perceived as being better able to perform the job effectively, and so he or she would be given higher status.

When two male police officers work together, for example, the man with more experience would be in the superior status position. This is illustrated in the following quotation from a member of an all-male police team. Asked who makes the final decisions in the partnership, the officer says it is his more-experienced partner. Implicit in his answer is the expectation that, as junior officer, he is expected to be accommodating: "It's an unwritten rule that if you're the new man, the senior officer calls all the shots and makes all of the decisions." In another all-male partnership, the officer with more seniority explains how he exercises influence:

> It's not a question of getting my partner to do what I want. It's explaining to him, for example, why it's better to do it this way or what could be the outcome if we don't do it this way. If I say, "Listen, we have to go to the Bronx," obviously there's a reason why we have to go there.

As is evident from these interviews, there is general agreement that status is based on seniority in all-male police teams. When two women work together as partners, status is designated in a similar way. Members of these teams take it as an "unwritten rule" that the more-experienced officer has higher status and the right to make most of the decisions; the less-experienced officer has lower status and is expected to accommodate.

By contrast, when a man and a woman work together as partners, status is almost always determined by the officers' sex category. Because policing is one of the most masculine-typed of all occupations and men far outnumber women, men are expected to perform more capably than women, regardless of seniority. As a result, when a man and a woman officer work together, the man is given higher status and has greater influence. This is described in an article by a woman police officer (Higbie, 1995, p. A30): "Male police officers are usually the ones who set the rules for policewomen, who are almost always the subordinates."

For example, a male officer relates in an interview how he made more decisions than his female partner even though they both had exactly the same amount of seniority.[3] Most of the time he did so by talking with her first, but in the following incident he took action without any discussion or explanation. He describes what happened after he and his partner responded to a radio call about an auto stripping that was taking place:

> When we arrived at the scene, we both agreed it was minor because the guy didn't have any major parts from the car, so we sent him on his way. Then the person that had called 911 came over and pointed out other parts the guy had taken off the vehicle.
>
> I decided—without asking my partner—that if I could catch up to the guy we just let go, he was going to jail that evening. I got in the radio car, took off, and caught the guy and 'cuffed him. Then I saw the other perpetrator. I told my partner to stay with the first prisoner and caught the second guy after a short chase.

In this incident, both the male and female partners agreed to let the perpetrator go when they first arrived at the scene. Then, without any discussion, the male officer decided to "take off" after the perpetrator. He relates how he caught the "bad guys" single-handedly and goes on to describe in the interview how he left his partner with two arrests to process—an extremely time-consuming task that required her to work overtime. He then explains to the interviewer that he had been unable to process either of the two arrests because he had a previous commitment for that evening.

These examples illustrate the ways in which status is generally designated in different types of police teams. When two men or two women work as partners, the more senior officer has higher status and makes more of the decisions. But when a man and woman work as partners, the man has higher status regardless of their relative seniority. Even though individuals sometimes experience discomfort as a result of their status-defined roles, most partnerships follow these implicitly accepted guidelines.

POLICE PERSONALITY

We have seen from these illustrations that status affects the behaviors of police officers who work as partners: the high-status officer acts in a more dominant way, and the low-status officer acts in a more accommodating manner. The goal of the present research project is to test whether these behaviors also affect the way the officers perceive their personality characteristics—both their own and their partner's—so that the high-status officer is seen as having more instrumental or assertive traits and the low-status officer is perceived as having more expressive or accommodating traits.

This is very different from the traditional approach to studying "police personality," which assumes a "modal police personality" that characterizes all police officers and distinguishes them from other occupational groups. According to the traditional approach, all police officers have the same personality traits because initial selection processes determine what kinds of people become police officers (Burbeck & Furnham, 1985). Certain types of individuals are attracted to the field of police work, and the extensive screening procedures used by police departments select for particular kinds of candidates. In addition, strong socialization pressures affect individuals after they become police officers, modifying and shaping their personality attributes (McNamara, 1999; Niederhoffer, 1967; Skolnick, 1994).

By contrast, the present research project proposes that police officers who work as partners are affected by the same kinds of status processes as are members of other task-oriented groups and that these processes affect their perceptions of their personality traits. Consequently, there is no such thing as a modal police personality. As in other types of work groups, police officers' perceptions of their personality traits are affected by their status.[4]

Much of the previous research on police personality has focused on a small subset of personality characteristics: authoritarianism, cynicism, and overall psychological health. This research has been concerned primarily with men. In Niederhoffer's (1967) classic work, he proposed that police officers are characterized by authoritarianism, which includes aggressive, rigid behavior in which people are seen as either good or bad, friends or enemies (Adorno, 1950). Because of the nature of their work, police officers constantly are faced with keeping people in line. To do so, they need to anticipate that most people intend to break the law. As a result, police officers become cynical and develop the idea that all people are motivated by evil and selfishness. They come to mistrust the people they are charged to protect and, as a result, "lose faith in people, society and, eventually, in themselves. In their Hobbesian view, the world becomes a jungle in which crime, corruption, and brutality are normal features of the terrain" (Niederhoffer, 1967, p. 9).

Certainly, the notion that people are affected by their occupational choices is reasonable, as is the assumption that the police officer's "working personality" is altered by the danger and need to exercise authority that characterize the task of policing (Skolnick, 1994). Yet empirical research has failed to support the idea that male police officers are characterized by either authoritarianism or cynicism. Furthermore, it has failed to show them to be less psychologically healthy than other occupational or civilian groups (Burbeck & Furnham, 1985; Fenster, Wiedemann, & Locke, 1978; Langworthy, 1987; Lefkowitz, 1975). On the contrary, some studies have found that male officers are lower in authoritarianism than other groups and are also psychologically healthier (Fenster et al., 1978; Lefkowitz, 1975).

Despite the lack of support from empirical research, the idea that police officers can develop authoritarian traits and cynical attitudes because of the nature of their work persists throughout the literature on policing (McNamara, 1999; Skolnick, 1994; Wilson & Braithwaite, 1995). Equally troubling is another observation that appears throughout the literature—namely, that as male police officers become more experienced and gain greater self-confidence in their abilities, they nevertheless can have problems with low self-esteem. Reports indicate that experienced officers sometimes feel dissatisfied with the kind of person they find they have become (Adlam, 1982; Doerner, 1985; Lefkowitz, 1975). Perhaps by taking a closer look at the forces within the organizational structure of policing that affect police officers and their personality traits, we might find conditions under which a subset of male officers would develop more authoritarian attitudes and experience a loss of faith in themselves.

Female Police Officers' Personality Traits

Research on the personality of police officers generally has involved men, but as more women have entered policing, the research has been extended to include women. Some of this research has been concerned with the cluster of "masculine-typed" personality traits, including authoritarianism, assertiveness, and cynicism, that have been the focus of research with men. However, too few empirical studies have been done to draw any conclusions about the personality traits that characterize women (see Lunneborg, 1989, for a review). Despite the paucity of empirical studies, women police officers are often described as being less authoritarian and less assertive than men (Austin & O'Neill, 1985; Sherman, 1973).[5] The present formulation suggests that if women officers are less authoritative and less assertive in comparison to men, it is due to their lower status within policing.

A concern expressed throughout the literature on the "woman police officer personality" is that women need to be "defeminized" and manifest masculine-typed personality traits in order to be successful in police work (Berg & Budnick, 1986; Jurik & Martin, 2000; Kennedy & Homant, 1981). But other studies have suggested that women officers need to exhibit some feminine-typed qualities in order to be considered competent (Hunt, 1984; Jacobs, 1987). These conflicting reports raise some important questions, which will be explored in the present study: What personal qualities are necessary for women police officers to be evaluated as competent? Are women officers required to manifest stereotypically "masculine" attributes, or are there pressures on them to demonstrate that they meet cultural standards for "femininity"?

STRESSES ON MEN AND WOMEN IN POLICE PARTNERSHIPS

Police work can be stressful both for women and for men (Norvell, Hills, & Murrin, 1993; Terry, 1981; Violanti, Marshall, & Howe, 1985; Wexler & Logan, 1983). However, research has rarely studied the stresses associated with police partnerships. One of the goals of this project is to understand better the stresses that affect different kinds of police partnerships, including all-male, male–female, and all-female police teams.

Implicit status guidelines impose fewer restrictions on the behaviors and opportunities available to men than on those available to women. When two men work together, status is determined primarily by seniority. Because the overwhelming majority of patrol teams are male, men have an opportunity to enact both high- and low-status roles.[6]

For women, however, the situation is quite different. Women still comprise a small minority of patrol officers—only 10 percent of the members of patrol teams are women.[7] Because of the resistance to allowing two women to work together as a team, many women patrol with a male partner. In male–female partnerships, the male has higher status than the female. No matter how much experience a woman has—even if she has more experience than her male partner—she cannot be openly acknowledged as the higher-status leader in the relationship.[8] This can be a source of continuing frustration for her, especially as she gains more experience as a police officer.

For example, a woman police officer describes her dissatisfaction with her male partner and the low-status role he expects her to play:

> He just comes out and says, "So I think we're going to arrest," or "Let's give him another chance." He says all that "we" and "us" stuff, but it's really him making the decisions. Even if I attempt to add something or give my own opinions, he'll listen, but then he'll convince me to do things his way.

Strong sanctions are often imposed on members of male–female teams who violate status expectations. A man who does not assume his expected leadership role can be teased by other male officers about being "hen-pecked," and a woman who does not comply with her expected follower role can be the target of hostility and sexual innuendos designed to "put her in her place" (Martin, 1990; Wexler & Logan, 1983). These pressures can be so extreme that women officers describe them as their greatest source of job-related stress (Morash & Haar, 1995; Wexler & Logan, 1983).

The restriction of women to low-status roles whenever they work with a male partner may have other consequences. According to the formulation proposed here, it affects the way their personality traits are perceived. In their role of follower, women police officers are expected to be highly accommodating and therefore to manifest characteristics believed to be stereotypic of women. When people observe a woman officer acting in an accommodating way, they assume that she is doing so because she is female. They are unaware that she is simply enacting the role she is expected to play with her male partner. On the basis of their observations, people conclude that their stereotypes are correct and that women—even policewomen—are naturally more accommodating than men. These stereotypes are then used as part of the rationale that restricts women to the lower-status follower role whenever they patrol with a man.

Although the overwhelming majority of teams within policing are ones in which two men work together, research rarely has looked at the problems that affect the officers in these teams—in particular, how these problems relate to an officer's status within the partnership. Studies have shown that male officers can sometimes lose faith in themselves and other people as they gain in seniority (Dorsey & Giacopassi, 1987; Niederhoffer, 1967). Other serious problems are faced by many men who are police officers, including marital difficulties, divorce, alcoholism, and even suicide (Bonifacio, 1991; Niederhoffer, 1967; Terry, 1985). The high-status role expected of many male police officers may contribute to these problems.

One aspect of the male officer's high-status role that can create stress is the expectation that he always appear confident and sure of himself and his actions. Further, male officers are not expected to show any emotion, even though many of the situations they confront can be extremely distressing. For example, a male officer describes in an interview how the need to always appear sure of oneself and one's decisions can cause personal distress:

> Doing your job places you in an awkward position at times, and you wonder whether you're doing the right thing or not. I don't think you really feel satisfied with yourself after any arrest situation. I know I don't because you're taking away someone's freedom.

He goes on to describe how the requirement that male officers be nonemotional can also cause stress: "You're supposed to be like a robot and have no feelings. People fail to recognize that cops are just like ordinary people. We have feelings and we're subject to emotion just like everyone else."

One of the most distressing experiences for male officers can occur at the point at which they would expect to feel most satisfied with themselves. As male officers gain experience and feel more self-confident in their work, they can find that they experience intense dissatisfaction with the kind of person they have become (Adlam, 1982; Doerner, 1985; Niederhoffer, 1967). For example, a male officer describes in an autobiographical account how he changed in ways he had not anticipated as he became more experienced. As he gained an increased sense of pride and competence as a police officer, he found himself acting in ways that were disruptive to his personal life, particularly with his wife (Doerner, 1985, p. 398):

> Gradually my strength increased and I became more proficient at handling myself. . . . Now I was cockier, more assertive, more arrogant, and less fearful on the street. . . . Instead of asking my wife to do something, I would order it to be done. If the question of why arose, the inevitable response was "Because I said so." . . . My "self" had become an extension of the uniform.

Not only are such experiences distressing to male police officers, they are perplexing as well. As male officers gain in competence, thereby meeting their own and others' expectations for a "good police officer," they sometimes find that, paradoxically, they do not feel good about themselves. Thus, it is important to explore whether aspects of the high-status role expected of many men leads them to form a poor opinion of themselves.

Because all-female teams are still relatively new within the police department, there has been little examination of the problems confronting the women in these teams. One apparent problem is that some supervisors perceive women as unsuited to police work and so are reluctant to let them work as a team. This is exemplified in an interview with a woman police officer who was a member of the first all-female team permitted to work in one of the New York City precincts:

> One sergeant was behind the two of us working together despite the fact that we were both women. He was very supportive and had confidence in both of us.
>
> On the other hand, another sergeant would say, "You're going to let those two little girls work together? They could get themselves killed out there; this isn't Kansas."
>
> The [first] sergeant would reply, "Yes, I am. They're both good cops."

As we can see from this interview excerpt, one supervisor perceives the women officers as "little girls" who require protection; the other supervisor sees them as "good cops" who are effective out on the street. The more supportive supervisor prevails, and the women police officers are permitted to work as partners. But such conflicting perceptions of women officers by people in authority, whether as little girls or as good cops, must have some impact on the officers who work in these teams. The special problems faced by members of all-female teams are explored in the present study.

STATUS, GENDER, AND PERSONALITY

This book hypothesizes that police partnerships are subject to the same processes that take place in other kinds of task-oriented groups. A considerable body of research has shown that when two people work together on a task, one person generally develops higher status than the other (Berger, Wagner, & Zelditch, 1985). This earlier research focused on behavior and found that higher-status individuals behave in a more assertive, directive way and lower-status individuals behave in a more accommodating way. The present study extends this research to look at personality and postulates that the status relation between police partners affects each individual's sense of self—the way each officer perceives his or her own personality traits. The study also examines the way each officer perceives the partner's personality traits.

This differs from previous approaches to studying the police that have focused on police officers' uniqueness in comparison to people in other occupations. For example, research on "police personality" has described a cluster of personality traits believed to typify police officers and differentiate them from other occupational groups (Balch, 1972). In contrast, the present study takes the view that the relationship between police officers who work as partners is similar to relationships between workers in other task groups. The status processes that affect the personalities of police partners are similar to those that affect workers in other occupational groups.

By exploring these status processes, we can appreciate some of the pressures that operate on female and male police officers. In addition, we can see ways in which the larger organizational system of the police department and the status expectations governing that system help to maintain distinctions between the sexes—how they help to perpetuate seeming gender differences in personality.

These critical issues within policing also have implications for our understanding of basic issues regarding gender and personality throughout society. The following chapter provides the foundation for the study because it presents an overview of the issues involving status, gender, and personality to be explored throughout the book. Chapters 2 through 8 describe the theoretical background, the methodology of the study, and the results from the research with police officers who work as partners. The last two chapters integrate the various findings and discuss their implications for the study of gender and personality and for policing.

The Status Model of Gender Stereotyping

Males are more domineering; they act like men—sure and assertive. Females use their female abilities—like I might sometimes smile or lightly joke to make the situation a little less tense.
—*Female officer in a male–female police team*

Once at the station house, a boss said to me, "You're going to stay inside today. . . . I need someone to type." . . . You see, women are *born* with typing skills. Isn't that convenient?
—*Police Officer Dana Higbie, in* New York Newsday

Do men and women have different personality traits? Most people believe that they do. They think that men are more assertive and decisive and that women are more accommodating and considerate of others (S. L. Bem, 1974; Spence, Helmreich, & Stapp, 1975). People often assume that such personality differences stem from differences in biology or the ways women and men are socialized in their early years (Bohan, 1993). According to this explanation, the two sexes have essentially different natures, which they manifest in all situations. Even women who work in highly masculine-typed occupations such as policing are thought to have uniquely "feminine" qualities such as warmth, concern, and accommodation to others.

This book proposes an alternate explanation that involves status (see Berger, Rosenholtz, & Zelditch, 1980). According to the "status model," instrumental or assertive traits are associated with high status, and expressive or accommodating traits are associated with low status. Therefore, men and women appear to have different personality traits, but only because men have higher status than women. If, because of the situation, a woman had higher status, she would manifest instrumental traits.

The status model focuses on the processes in interactions that give rise to apparent sex differences in personality (James, 1997; Worell, 1996), going beyond issues related specifically to gender to deal with a larger issue—how status processes in interactions affect people's perceptions of their personality traits (Morgan & Schwalbe, 1990; Stryker, 1987). The basic premise of the status model is that the instrumental and expressive personality traits reflect status processes in ongoing interactions between people. We can extend this premise to include other gender-stereotyped traits, such as the verbal-aggressive traits. Because men are overrepresented in positions of high status in our society, "male-typed" traits reflect processes associated with high status; because women are overrepresented in positions of low status, "female-typed" traits reflect processes associated with low status (see Eagly & Wood, 1982; Heilman, 1995; Lorber, 1994).

In this book, we test the status model of gender stereotyping by examining the instrumental and expressive traits that have been the focus of most theoretical and empirical work (Spence, Helmreich, & Holahan, 1979). In addition, we examine other, less-researched gender-stereotyped traits, such as the verbal-aggressive traits. Finally, we explore more general issues in personality trait theory and research as they relate to status.

Police officers who work together as partners participated in the research project, making it possible to examine these issues in a natural setting. The project included police partnerships in which two women or two men worked together and partnerships in which a woman worked with a man.

THE STATUS MODEL VERSUS THE
GENDER-SPECIFIC MODEL

The present study tests two explanations for the apparent differences in women's and men's personality traits: one based on the "gender-specific" model of gender stereotyping and the other based on the status model. According to the gender-specific model, men and women have dissimilar personality traits because of basic differences in their biology or in their early socialization experiences; these differences are specifically related to gender, not to any other factors (Bohan, 1993; Maccoby & Jacklin, 1974; Reinisch, Rosenblum, Rubin, & Schulsinger, 1997).[1] This model views gender as being an essential part of the individual; it involves fundamental attributes that are internal, persistent, and separate from the ongoing experiences of daily life (Bohan, 1993).

The status model is based on status characteristics theory (Berger, Fisek, Norman, & Zelditch, 1977). It extends the theory, which has focused primarily on behavior, to deal with "personality"—how one's own and others' personality attributes are perceived (Wyer & Lambert, 1994).[2] According to the status model, men have higher status than women in our society, thus when a man and woman work together, the higher-status man assumes a more directive role and behaves in an assertive way. By contrast, the lower-status woman enacts a more supportive role and behaves in an accommodating way (Berger, Rosenholtz, & Zelditch, 1980). When people observe these behaviors, they infer that the man has more assertive or instrumental traits and the woman has more accommodating or expressive traits (Gerber, 1993).

People repeatedly observe interactions such as these in the course of their daily lives. For example, in families the husband generally has higher status than the wife, and in work situations male employees usually have higher status than female employees (Heilman, 1995; Hollander, 1985; Scanzoni, 1979). Based on these repeated observations, people develop stereotypes about men's and women's personalities; they conclude that men have more instrumental qualities and women have more expressive qualities (McCauley, Stitt, & Segal, 1980). [3]

The status model postulates that *status* is the primary factor that organizes interactions. Sex is simply one of many variables, such as work experience or seniority, used by members of interactions to designate status (Ridgeway & Smith-Lovin, 1999). For example, when a man and a woman work together, sex category would be highly salient and would be used to designate their relative status.[4] As a result, the man would have higher status than the woman. But when two men work together, work experience would be salient and would be used to designate status; the man with more experience would have higher status and would appear to have more instrumental qualities, and the man with less experience would have lower status and would seem to have more expressive qualities (Bales & Slater, 1955; Berger et al., 1977).

Hence, the gender-specific and status models give very different answers to the question: Why do men and women appear to have different personality traits? The gender-specific model states that these are real differences, stemming from fundamental differences between the sexes. By contrast, the status model postulates that these are only *apparent* differences, determined by differences between men's and women's status (see Bohan, 1993; Hare-Mustin & Marecek, 1990; James, 1997).

The gender-specific and status models conceptualize "personality" in very different ways. The gender-specific model is consistent with the traditional view of personality as relatively stable and unchanging regardless of the situational context; consequently, women's and men's personality traits would remain constant in different situations (see Epstein, 1988; Pervin, 1990). By contrast, the status model proposed here describes how people's perceptions of their personality traits would vary across different situations according to their status (Mischel, 1990; Morgan & Schwalbe, 1990; Stryker, 1987). For example, men would sometimes be characterized by instrumental traits and sometimes by expressive traits, depending on their status. We test these differing predictions in the present study with police partners.

THE STUDY OF POLICE PARTNERS

More and more women have entered policing over the past twenty years, but police work remains a highly masculine-typed occupation in which men far outnumber women (Martin, 1990).[5] In sex-typed occupational fields, such as policing, sex category and gender are extremely salient (Heilman, 1995; Kanter, 1977). As a result, we would expect strong pressures on men and women to manifest sex-typed behaviors and personality traits. Under these circumstances, a finding that status was the primary determinant of men's and women's perceived personality traits would provide strong support for the status model of gender stereotyping.

The relationship between police officers who work as partners is especially suited for testing hypotheses derived from the status model. The status model specifically deals with the behaviors—and personality traits—that emerge when people such as police partners work together on common tasks (Berger et al., 1977; Foschi, 1997). Further, the changes in the perceptions of people's personality traits predicted by the status model are most likely to occur in the long-term relationships that develop between police partners—as compared to the short-term interactions between people in laboratory settings examined in most research (Berger et al., 1977; Buss & Craik, 1984).[6] Police partners work together every day, often for a year or longer.[7] As a result, they have numerous opportunities to observe one another's behaviors in a wide variety of situations. They would be expected to make inferences from these observations about their own personality traits as well as their partner's traits (D. J. Bem, 1972; Jones & Davis, 1965).

Most important, by studying police partners, we are able to separate out the effects of status and sex category on personality. In many occupations, it is difficult to disentangle such effects, because men frequently hold positions of high status and women are in positions of low status (Heilman, 1995; Kanter, 1977). Within policing, however, officers work together in different types of partnerships—all-male, male–female, and all-female partnerships. Since the status model predicts that an informal status order will be established between the officers in each of these partnership types (Berger et al., 1977), men and women will both be in high-status positions and in low ones. By comparing the personality traits associated with men and women who are in the same status position, we can determine which model best accounts for the data—the status model or the gender-specific model.

The critical test of the status model concerns the same-sex partnerships. Here, the status model predicts that only one officer will be perceived as having conventionally stereotyped personality attributes; the other officer's attributes will go counter to the stereotypes. In the all-male partnership, the lower-status man will be perceived as having the expressive qualities associated with women; in the all-female partnership, the higher-status woman will be seen as having the instrumental qualities associated with men.

But if, instead, the gender-specific model is supported by the data, we would simply expect that all officers would be perceived in traditionally stereotyped ways; all the male officers would be perceived as having instrumental traits and all the female officers would be perceived as having expressive traits.

As we have seen, the status model proposed in the present study with police partners shifts the focus from the study of gender per se to the study of task-oriented interactions between people. To understand this development better, we need to examine some of the previous research on gender stereotyping.

RESEARCH ON THE GENDER-STEREOTYPED PERSONALITY TRAITS

The empirical research during the past thirty years has furthered our understanding of gender and the gender-stereotyped personality traits and in doing so, it has challenged many assumptions about gender. During the course of this research, it has become increasingly evident that gender is not a central determinant of personality; other factors are more important.

Only recently have studies focused on issues of status. Before this could occur, it was necessary to develop measuring scales for the gender-stereotyped traits that freed them from unsubstantiated assumptions about gender and personality. Another issue involved the construct of "personality" itself. Instead of construing the personality traits that make up the self-concept as essentially constant throughout the adult years, it was necessary to see that these perceived personality traits can change as people interact in different situations (Stryker, 1987).

Development of Measures

Originally, many implicit assumptions about gender were hidden and embedded in the very scales intended to measure the gender-stereotyped personality traits (Spence et al., 1985). In order to test these assumptions, it was necessary to develop new, more refined scales to measure these attributes.

The earliest scales were based on the belief that masculinity and femininity represented opposite extremes of a single continuum (Constantinople, 1973; Lewin, 1984a). On these bipolar scales, it was impossible for an individual to be rated as having characteristics associated with masculinity as well as femininity—an individual had to be rated as either "masculine" or "feminine."

A major breakthrough occurred when new scales were developed that measured "femininity" and "masculinity" as independent constructs (S. L. Bem, 1974; Spence et al., 1975). The new scales could then be used to test the assumption that masculinity and femininity were at opposite ends of a single continuum. If so, then people who described themselves as high on the masculine traits would also describe themselves as low on the feminine traits, and vice versa. However, the empirical research showed that this was not the case. The masculine and feminine traits were essentially uncorrelated, or orthogonal to one another (S. L. Bem, 1974; Spence et al., 1975).

Another belief was that a person's self-ratings on these scales were highly correlated with other "masculine" and "feminine" characteristics and could be used as an index of that person's underlying gender identity. Again, research provided little support for this belief (Deaux & Lewis, 1984; Spence & Sawin, 1985). Further, it was demonstrated that men's and women's ratings of their instrumental and expressive qualities had little to do with their ratings of their own masculinity or femininity (Pedhazur & Tetenbaum, 1979). When it became evident that the so-called gender-stereotyped traits could not be used as an index of an individual's gender identity, the scales were renamed to reflect this new understanding. The masculine characteristics were relabeled the "instrumental" traits, and the feminine characteristics were relabeled the "expressive" traits (Spence et al., 1985).[8]

But there remained some unanswered questions: If the gender-stereotyped traits were unrelated to gender identity, why were the two sexes perceived as different on these characteristics? Was it because the expressive traits enhanced the psychological functioning of women and the instrumental traits enhanced the functioning of men? Results from various studies showed that this was not the case—the instrumental and expressive traits were valuable for both sexes. The instrumental traits were correlated with self-esteem in both sexes (Spence et al., 1979; Whitley, 1983);[9] the expressive traits were associated with satisfaction in relationships with others (Antill, 1983).

Most of the research and theory had focused on the instrumental and expressive traits, which are socially desirable characteristics. However, subsequent studies found that other traits are associated with the two sexes as well, many of which are socially *undesirable* (Kelly, Caudill, Hathorn, & O'Brien, 1977; Spence et al., 1979). The measuring instruments were then broadened to include negative as well as positive characteristics. The Extended Personal Attributes Questionnaire used in the present study includes scales for expressiveness as well as for the positive and negative aspects of instrumentality (instrumental and dominating traits). In addition, it contains scales for other less-researched gender-stereotyped characteristics: the verbal-aggressive and submissive traits associated with women, and the bipolar traits that measure qualities associated with the ideal female versus the ideal male (Spence et al., 1979).

Despite these new developments, however, research on gender and personality continued to be limited by its focus on individual factors, such as psychological adjustment, instead of the larger social factors involving status that were being studied in other areas of research.

Gender Stereotypes and Status

Remarkable advances were taking place in our understanding of gender in relation to a variety of verbal and nonverbal behaviors. It was becoming increasingly clear that many behaviors that previously had been viewed as gender-based were, instead, determined by social factors involving the status relation between the sexes. A number of behaviors that characterize men were found to be typical of individuals in high-status positions, and those that characterize women were found to be typical of subordinates (Eagly & Wood, 1985; Epstein, 1988; Henley, 1977; Kanter, 1977). This meant that a male subordinate, for example, generally would manifest the same kinds of verbal and nonverbal behaviors that previously had been thought to be unique to women.

Despite the advances in other areas, research on gender and personality rarely focused on power and the larger social structure (Deaux, 1985). It is difficult to understand why there were so few studies in this area. However, it may have been due to the notion, prevalent in psychology, that an individual's personality essentially was established early in life; once an individual reached adulthood, his or her personality was unlikely to vary much across different social situations (see Epstein, 1988; Pervin, 1990). It was acknowledged that people could assume roles that required the enactment of new and different behaviors. For example, a women who assumed a managerial role would necessarily act assertively with her subordinates. However, her basic underlying personality was viewed as fixed and unchanged.

Another problem involved the instrumental and expressive dispositions themselves. When one examines the traits that comprise instrumentality, it is apparent that the capacity to be assertive, independent, and decisive would probably be related to power and status. However, the connection between the expressive traits and power is less obvious. On the face of it, one finds it difficult to comprehend how characteristics such as warmth, helpfulness, and the capacity to understand others' feelings could be associated with status.

To understand how the expressive traits are related to status, we cannot simply focus on a single individual, as most of the research on stereotyping and social cognition has done (Howard, 1990; Stryker & Gottlieb, 1981). We must widen the focus to include both members of an interaction (Berger et al., 1977; Gerber 1973, 1993). When two people interact, the low-status person is expected to exercise less power and accommodate to the high-status partner's directives. To do so, the low-status person needs to be closely attuned and reactive to the partner; therefore, he or she would appear to be helpful, warm, and understanding—in other words, more expressive.

According to this formulation, the stereotypes about men's and women's personalities are determined by their implicit assumptions concerning the power relation between the sexes. If so, it should be possible to override these implicit assumptions with specific information involving power. As research has shown, people use stereotypes in the absence of other information. But when they are given specific information about an individual, they use that information to make judgments instead of using the stereotypes (Locksley, Borgida, Brekke, & Hepburn, 1980). This implies that if one were to reverse the power relation between the sexes to describe a relationship in which the woman has more power than the man, the stereotypes would be reversed as well.

A study by Geis, Brown, Jennings, and Corrado-Taylor (1984) suggested this might be the case. These investigators used the earlier bipolar scale to measure "masculinity–femininity" and found that women and men in high-status roles were rated toward the masculine pole of the scale and that those in low-status roles were rated toward the feminine pole. However, as discussed previously, the problem with bipolar scales is that they measure masculinity and femininity as opposite ends of a single continuum. As a result, one cannot determine whether one or both traits relate to status. In addition, the global masculinity–femininity scale used here includes a variety of traits, not just the instrumental and expressive traits that are the focus of the present study.[10] To determine whether the instrumental traits characterize people in high-status positions and the expressive traits characterize people in low-status positions, it is necessary to measure these traits as independent constructs.

Subsequent studies measured these traits as independent constructs and provided strong support for the hypothesis; these studies showed that the instrumental and expressive traits are associated with power, not sex category. A powerful person of either sex is perceived as high on the instrumental traits, and a nonpowerful person of either sex is seen as high on the expressive traits (Gerber, 1987, 1988). Not only does information about power affect the socially desirable aspects of instrumentality and expressiveness, but it affects the undesirable aspects as well (Gerber, 1991). Thus, a powerful person of either sex is perceived as having many positive instrumental traits, such as assertiveness, as well as negative instrumental traits, such as dominance.

Further research showed, as status characteristics theory would predict, that differences in occupational status between members of a hypothetical married couple lead to assumptions about their relative power that, in turn, affect their perceived instrumentality and expressiveness (Smoreda, 1995). Within work settings as well, hypothetical individuals with high status are characterized as being instrumental, and those with low status are characterized as being expressive (Conway, Pizzamiglio, & Mount, 1996).

These studies are important because they provide support for the hypothesis that status and power differences underlie people's stereotypes about men's and women's personality attributes. However, they explain only one component of gender stereotyping—people's belief that typical women and men have different personality attributes.

Another essential component of gender stereotyping needs to be explained: actual men's and women's ratings of their own personalities (Spence et al., 1985). Research has shown that men rate themselves higher on the instrumental traits and women rate themselves higher on the expressive traits (S. L. Bem, 1974; Spence et al., 1975). To explain gender stereotyping fully, one must show that these self-ratings are also determined by status.

An additional issue in gender stereotyping that has received less attention involves the way *other* persons are perceived in interactions. The present study with police partners explores how members of long-term, close work relationships perceive the interaction partner with regard to the instrumental and expressive traits. It examines whether male and female interaction partners are perceived in conventionally gender-stereotyped ways or whether these perceptions are also determined by status.

IMPLICATIONS OF THE STATUS MODEL FOR OTHER GENDER-STEREOTYPED TRAITS

Verbal-Aggressive and Submissive Traits

The basic premise of the status model is that the gender-stereotyped traits and the behaviors they reflect relate to status processes that occur in interactions. The verbal-aggressive and submissive traits are linked with women. Because women are overrepresented in low-status positions in our society (Eagly & Wood, 1982; Heilman, 1995; Lorber, 1994), the status model proposes that these "female-typed" traits reflect processes associated with low status. Instead of focusing on issues of sex and gender, the status model poses a more general question that relates to status (see Wagner & Berger, 1997): Why are these traits associated with individuals, such as women, who often occupy low-status positions? What functions would these traits serve within interactions?

Studies of interacting groups have indicated that characteristics such as submission can serve important functions (Wagner & Berger, 1997). On the face of it, submissiveness appears to reflect a self-abasing acceptance of one's powerlessness, but it can actually serve to enhance an individual's power. As shown by research, low-status individuals who accompany their assertive acts with other behaviors that are submissive are able to gain in power and influence (Carli, 1990).

The verbal-aggressive traits, which involve characteristics such as complaining and nagging, are especially interesting in this regard. They may serve as an indirect way of exercising influence from a low-status position while at the same time acknowledging that the interaction partner has the right to make the final decision (Johnson, 1976).

This discussion highlights the way in which the status model takes a fresh approach to the study of gender stereotyping. It proposes that all of the so-called gender-stereotyped traits relate in some way to status. This issue will be explored with respect to the verbal-aggressive and submissive traits in our sample of police partners.

Bipolar Traits: The Ideal Woman Versus the Ideal Man

The bipolar traits are especially interesting because they differ from all of the other gender-stereotyped traits included in the Extended Personal Attributes Questionnaire used in the present study (Spence et al., 1979). This questionnaire, the most comprehensive instrument available for measuring different kinds of gender-stereotyped traits, includes six different scales. On all of the scales, with the exception of the bipolar scale, the same pole is socially desirable for *both* sexes. For example, even though women are stereotyped as being more expressive than men, expressiveness is perceived as being desirable for both sexes. By contrast, on the bipolar traits, the desirable characteristics associated with women are directly opposite those associated with men. For example, on the "home-oriented" versus "worldly" bipolar item, the ideal woman is rated as home-oriented, whereas the ideal man is rated as worldly.

Because the bipolar traits are the only characteristics on which the two sexes are seen as "opposite" one another and as having mutually exclusive attributes, these traits and the behaviors they reflect might serve a special function within interactions. They might serve as "displays" of an individual's identity as a man or woman (Goffman, 1976).

Essentially in any situation, one's sex can be relevant, and one's performance as a member of that category can be subjected to evaluation by others (West & Zimmerman, 1987). For example, a woman who manifests the expressive characteristics associated with females would be evaluated favorably, as "feminine." However, a woman who appears dominating and assertive would be evaluated unfavorably, as "unfeminine" (Gerber, 1990).

Research has shown that individuals who manifest characteristics deviating from gender-related norms are evaluated unfavorably by observers in other ways as well—they are seen as unlikeable and, most important for work relationships, as less competent (Costrich, Feinstein, Kidder, & Maracek, 1975; Falbo, Hazen, & Linimon, 1982). This poses a critical question for status characteristics theory, on which the status model is based. What happens when the behaviors (and traits) associated with an individual's status position conflict with observers' expectations about "gender-appropriate" behaviors (and traits)?

Status characteristics theory postulates that when people work together to perform various tasks, one person generally enacts a higher-status role and engages in more instrumental behaviors, and the other person plays a lower-status role and manifests more expressive behaviors. A considerable body of research has demonstrated that this takes place in all types of interactions, including interactions between two women or two men (Berger et al., 1977; Berger, Wagner, & Zelditch, 1985).

But what happens when these status-related behaviors conflict with observers' expectations about what is appropriate for each sex? Within an all-female police partnership, for example, the more-experienced woman generally assumes a higher-status role and behaves more instrumentally than her partner. Does the fact that her behavior deviates from gender norms affect the way she is perceived by others? Most important, does it affect perceptions of her competence? By the same token, how do people perceive the less-experienced man in an all-male police partnership? According to the theory, he generally assumes a low-status role and behaves more expressively than his partner. Do other people penalize him for his atypical behavior by seeing him as ineffective in his work?

Behaviors such as these, which deviate from gender norms, occur in most interacting dyads. Consequently, it would be advantageous if individuals could avoid the sanctions that frequently are imposed. This raises another, even more important question: Can the bipolar traits and the behaviors they reflect serve as "gender displays" that enable individuals in nontraditional gender roles to counter the negative impressions that otherwise might be associated with their roles (see Meeker & Weitzel-O'Neill, 1977; Ridgeway, 1982)? Gender displays such as these would be especially important when individuals have their competence in work settings evaluated by an outside observer. The present study will explore whether self-ratings on the bipolar traits by police officers who are in roles that deviate from gender norms affect the way their competence is evaluated by their immediate supervisor.

Thus far, our focus has been on the implications of the status model for each of the gender-stereotyped personality traits, including those that have received less research attention. Our premise has been that all of these traits and the behaviors they reflect relate in some way to status and interactions. We have explored some of the functions that each of these traits may serve. We now turn to more general issues in personality trait theory and research.

ISSUES IN PERSONALITY TRAIT THEORY AND RESEARCH

Status characteristics theory, originally developed to explain people's behaviors in task-oriented interactions, has been extended here to include people's perceptions of their personality traits. With this extended theory, it becomes possible to explore crucial issues in personality trait theory and research—issues that have also been a focus in research on the gender-stereotyped personality traits: (1) the role of personality traits in self-evaluations and (2) the organization of traits within individual personality (Pervin, 1990; Spence et al., 1985; Wyer & Lambert, 1994). As we examine these issues in relation to status, we can gain a further understanding of some perplexing findings that relate to gender and the gender-stereotyped traits.

Role of Personality Traits in Self-Evaluations

According to personality trait theory, the self-concept has two related components: a descriptive component that refers to one's perceptions of one's personality traits and an evaluative component that refers to one's self-esteem or sense of self-worth (Wyer & Lambert, 1994). These descriptive and evaluative components of self are assumed to be related in that people use their personality traits as bases for their own self-evaluations. In other words, people who perceive themselves as having desirable attributes are assumed to evaluate themselves positively as well.

This raises a question about some puzzling findings involving women's and men's self-esteem. Because men have higher status than women in our society and are perceived as having more valued task-related attributes, it often has been assumed that they would have higher self-esteem. Yet research does not support this assumption. Most studies find that men and women are very similar in their level of self-esteem (Kristen, Hyde, Showers, & Buswell, 1999; Maccoby & Jacklin, 1974; Major, Barr, Zubek, & Babey, 1999).

One way of reconciling these findings with personality trait theory might be to shift the focus away from gender and ask a more general question that involves status: How do status and the personality traits associated with status relate to self-esteem? Based on personality trait theory (Wyer & Srull, 1989), status may play a role in self-evaluations, but only an indirect role. The critical factor would involve the social desirability of the traits linked with status. If high-status persons see themselves as having desirable traits, they would be expected to evaluate themselves favorably; but if they see themselves as having undesirable traits, they would be expected to evaluate themselves unfavorably.

This formulation would help explain why women and men have similar self-esteem. As we have hypothesized here, status differences between the sexes would affect the *kinds* of traits they attribute to themselves—higher-status men would perceive themselves as having more instrumental or task-related attributes, and lower-status women would see themselves as having more expressive attributes. However, because the instrumental traits and the expressive traits are both considered socially desirable, men and women would both perceive themselves as having desirable traits and would be expected to have similar levels of self-esteem.[11] To gain a better understanding of this issue, we will explore how status and personality traits relate to self-esteem in the sample of police officers.

Organization of Traits in Individual Personality

Another long-standing issue in personality theory involves the question: How are the elements or traits that constitute the basic building blocks of personality organized into higher-order dimensions of personality (Pervin, 1990)? This issue also has been of critical importance in research on the gender-stereotyped personality traits. Originally, it was believed that the instrumental and expressive traits were organized into a "masculine–feminine" dimension. Individuals who were at the "masculine" pole of this dimension were thought to perceive themselves as being high on the instrumental traits and low on the expressive traits; those at the "feminine" pole were thought to manifest the opposite pattern.

Contrary to this belief, studies showed that the instrumental and expressive traits essentially were uncorrelated within individual personality (Spence et al., 1985). Instead, when the measuring instruments were expanded to include desirable as well as undesirable characteristics, other kinds of intercorrelations were found among the attributes known as the gender-stereotyped traits. The dominating and expressive traits were found to be correlated negatively, as were the instrumental and submissive traits (Spence et al., 1979), suggesting that the so-called gender-stereotyped traits are organized into two dimensions within individual personality.

The question raised by these results is: What do these two dimensions represent? According to some theories of social cognition, the social structure is represented in the cognitive systems of individual actors (Howard, 1995; Morgan & Schwalbe, 1990; Stryker, 1989). Therefore, because the status model postulates that status plays a major role in determining the personality traits *between* people who work together, it also may play a major role in organizing the dimensions *within* an individual's personality. The personality traits with which the self is perceived may be organized along dimensions that relate to status and power. In the present study, we will develop this conceptualization further and explore whether the same kinds of intercorrelations among traits found in previous research are found for police officers who enact high- and low-status roles.

OVERVIEW OF THE BOOK

This book asks a fundamental question about gender stereotyping: Why do men and women appear to have different personality traits? According to the status model of gender stereotyping proposed here, they do so because men have higher status than women.

The status model of gender stereotyping deals with people's perceptions of their personality traits. It extends status characteristics theory, which was originally developed to explain people's behaviors in task-oriented interactions, to include people's perceptions of personality traits in themselves and others. Once the theory is extended, we are able to explore additional, more global issues involving gender and personality in relation to status—issues involving self-esteem and the organization of traits within individual personality.

The following two chapters present an overview of the theory and the research with police partners. In Chapter 2, status characteristics theory is extended and the process by which status affects dyad members' perceptions of their personality traits is explained. Chapter 3 provides a description of the study—the procedure for selecting matched samples of all-male, all-female, and male–female police teams and the scales that were used.

The next chapter focuses on our central question: Does status determine police officers' perceptions of themselves and others regarding the expressive traits and the socially desirable and undesirable instrumental traits? The analyses described in Chapter 4 provide a critical test of the status model of gender stereotyping.

The basic premise of the status model is that all of the gender-stereotyped traits relate in some way to status processes in interactions. Chapters 5 and 6 explore other, less extensively researched gender-stereotyped traits and the functions they might serve in interactions. In Chapter 5, the focus is on the verbal-aggressive and submissive traits: Are these traits used by low-status individuals, such as women police officers, to gain influence and cope more effectively with the established status structure? In Chapter 6, the concern is with the bipolar traits—the only traits that form a continuum with idealized feminine and masculine qualities at opposite poles. We examine whether police officers' self-ratings on the bipolar traits affect how they are perceived by an observer—in this case, their immediate supervisor.

The next two chapters explore more global issues involving gender and personality. In Chapter 7, we examine some intriguing theoretical and empirical questions about the factors that contribute to self-esteem: Is self-esteem determined by status per se or by the traits associated with status? This question is explored with the sample of police officers. Chapter 8 addresses another issue with a long-standing tradition in personality theory—the way traits are organized within individual personality. Previous research suggests that the "gender-stereotyped" traits are organized into two dimensions within individual personality. This chapter explores whether the same two dimensions are found for individuals of differing statuses. Furthermore, it draws on personality theory and research to formulate how these two dimensions within individual personality would relate to status and power.

The final chapters consolidate the various findings and discuss their implications. Chapter 9 presents an overview of the theory and discusses the implications of the results for our understanding of gender stereotyping and for broader issues involving the status processes in

interactions that shape people's perceptions of their personality attributes. With this new understanding, we are able to integrate the study
of the gender-stereotyped personality traits into the broader framework
of social interaction. Chapter 10 discusses the implications of the findings for police work, proposing ways police organizations can change
to enable women and men police officers—and their supervisors—to
work more effectively.

Status Characteristics Theory and the Gender-Stereotyped Personality Traits

Question: In a disagreement between you and your partner, who usually gives in?
Answer: It's usually me. I really don't know the reason for this.
—*Female officer in a male–female police team*

I wouldn't ask my partner; I would just say, "Pull over that car." And he wouldn't hesitate; he would just agree with me.
—*Senior officer in an all-male police team*

Status characteristics theory focuses primarily on the way status affects the behaviors that take place in interactions (Berger, Fisek, Norman, & Zelditch, 1977). To understand why men and women are stereotyped as having different personality traits, we need to extend the theory to describe how status would affect perceptions of their personality traits.

To illustrate the process by which this would occur, suppose two male police officers have worked as partners for more than a year. According to the theory, the officer with more experience would have higher status; consequently he would behave more assertively than his partner and make most of the decisions. Upon observing his own behavior in a variety of situations, he would infer that he has more instrumental or assertive personality traits. By contrast, the less-experienced officer would have lower status; consequently, he would behave in a more supportive and accommodating way. Upon observing his own behaviors, the lower-status officer would infer that he has more expressive or accommodating traits.

According to this formulation, differences in status lead to differences in instrumental and expressive behaviors, which in turn lead to inferences about personality attributes. People make inferences about their own personality traits by observing their overt behaviors; they make inferences about other people's personality traits in a similar way (D. J. Bem, 1972). For example, the junior officer in an all-male police team who observes himself engaging in many expressive behaviors would infer that he has many expressive personality traits. His partner, who also observes his expressive behaviors, would make the same inference and would also perceive him as having many expressive traits.

HOW IS STATUS DETERMINED?

When people work together on a task, they develop expectations about one another's ability. These expectations are based on information about their "status characteristics"—attributes such as work experience and sex that are assumed to be related to one's competence in performing a task (Wagner & Berger, 1997; Webster & Foschi, 1988).

There are two types of status characteristics, "diffuse" and "specific." Diffuse status characteristics refer to socially recognized distinctions, such as sex category or race, that most people believe to have wide-ranging implications for performance. For example, sex category serves as a diffuse status characteristic and refers to the cultural belief that men can perform most tasks, particularly masculine-typed tasks, better than women (Balkwell, 1994). By contrast, specific status characteristics refer to attributes that are related to particular tasks. For example, one's experience working as a police officer is believed to be related to one's competence, and so an officer with more seniority would be expected to be more competent than one who has less seniority. Both types of status characteristics refer to cultural beliefs that may or may not be objectively true (Balkwell, 1994). The theory simply says that if people believe something to be true, they will act in accordance with that belief, thereby bringing about the expected consequences.

In all-male or all-female police partnerships, previous work experience would be a salient status characteristic (Berger, Rosenholtz, & Zelditch, 1980). The more-experienced officer would be expected to be more competent and, as a result, he or she would be seen as having higher status than the less-experienced partner. This is illustrated in the following interview with the junior officer in an all-male team. The junior officer acknowledges that the senior partner is far more knowledgable because he has more extensive experience: "My partner has had more time on the street and he knows a lot more than I do."

According to status characteristics theory, behavior is affected by the type of task that is performed. If the task is identified as male, men are seen as more competent than women and engage in behaviors that reflect their high status (Eagly & Karau, 1991; Martin, 1990; Wagner & Berger, 1997). Policing is an extremely masculine-typed occupation and so when a male and female officer work together, the man would be expected to outperform the woman regardless of seniority. Thus, in a male–female police partnership, the most salient status characteristic would be sex category, and the man would have the superior status (Berger et al., 1980; Lockheed & Hall, 1976).[1]

The salience of sex category is illustrated in an interview with a woman police officer who works with a male partner. Even though her male partner has only one more year of experience than she, the woman officer maintains that he is more competent: "My [male] partner is an experienced police officer, and his tactics are safe for both of us." In another interview—this time with the *male* officer in a male–female team—the officer states, "I think the decisions I made were well thought out and designed to avoid problems and maximize safety." However, he does not give any evidence to support that assumption. On the contrary, he goes on to describe a situation in which his female partner wanted to check out a "strange looking, beat-up looking car with darked-out windows." He overrules her and maintains he made the correct decision even though they never checked out the car. The male officer's assumption that he has the right to make the final decision is particularly striking because his female partner has several years more experience than he.

According to the theory, initial status differences lead to differences in dyad members' behaviors: the person with higher status engages in more task-related behaviors, which include giving opinions, suggestions, and direction.[2] By contrast, the person with lower status engages in more accommodating behaviors, which include asking for suggestions and communicating approval of the partner's performance.

Studies of group behavior have supported the theory by showing that these behavioral differences generally occur in same-sex as well as mixed-sex groups (Bales & Slater, 1955; Berger et al., 1977; Dion, 1985; Ridgeway & Diekama, 1992; Strodtbeck, 1951). Such findings are critical because they demonstrate that status can be determined in different ways—by work experience in same-sex groups and by sex category in mixed-sex groups. Regardless of the way status is designated, however, different kinds of status characteristics have the same effect on behavior.

These findings are important for the present study because they suggest that a woman who has higher status than her partner would be expected to manifest the same kinds of instrumental or assertive behaviors as would a higher-status, more-experienced man. By the same token, male and female officers who have lower status in comparison to their partners would be expected to manifest the same kinds of expressive behaviors.

FROM BEHAVIORS TO TRAITS

Attribution theorists agree that after observing one another's behaviors, people make inferences about one another's personality traits (D. J. Bem, 1972; Jones & Davis, 1965). In doing so, people generally need to observe a large number of specific behaviors (Buss & Craik, 1984). Status characteristics theory has described the kinds of behaviors that would lead to inferences about the instrumental personality traits. When we observe a person engaging in numerous task-related behaviors by giving opinions and suggestions across many situations (Berger et al., 1977), we infer that the person has an instrumental or self-assertive disposition. Because high-status dyad members engage in more task-related behaviors than low-status dyad members, we expect that they are characterized by more instrumental traits.

The connection between status and the expressive traits is less clear. Status characteristics theory has focused on instrumental, task-related behaviors, not the more "social" behaviors that are reflected in the expressive personality traits (Ridgeway & Diekema, 1992). In his seminal research studies, Bales (1951, pp. 178–182) described a variety of expressive behaviors, which include acting friendly, congenial, and empathic or telling someone, "You've done a good job." Status characteristics theory points to similar behaviors and calls them "positive reward actions" and "expressive task cues" (Berger & Conner, 1974; Berger, Webster, Ridgeway, & Rosenholtz, 1986). Positive reward actions are behaviors in which an individual evaluates the other person's task contributions positively through agreement or praise—for example, by saying "That's a great idea." Expressive status cues refer to behaviors such as using a soft voice and less-direct gaze. We would expect that these positive reward actions and expressive status cues would become summarized as a global expressive disposition (Buss & Craik, 1984) that reflects the extent to which an individual is perceived as warm, accommodating, and supportive toward others—and hence more expressive.

Studies have shown that low-status dyad members communicate more "positive reward actions" and manifest more "expressive status cues" than high-status dyad members (Berger & Conner, 1974; Berger, Webster, Ridgeway, & Rosenholtz, 1986). Thus, we would expect that low-status dyad members would be characterized by more expressive personality traits as well.

The present research with police partners provides an opportunity to test the predictions about the instrumental and expressive personality traits in a natural setting. According to the theory, the partners will evolve the same kind of status order as do other kinds of interacting dyads: one partner will be high status and the other partner will be low status. Because high- and low-status partners are expected to behave differently when they interact with one another, we are predicting that they also will attribute dissimilar personality traits to one another. This will affect the officers' perceptions of themselves as well as their perceptions of the partner (Berger, Wagner, & Zelditch, 1985; Johnston, 1985).

A STATUS EXPLANATION OF GENDER STEREOTYPING

The instrumental and expressive traits are personal attributes that most people associate with the two sexes—the gender-stereotyped personality traits (S. L. Bem, 1974; Spence, Helmreich, & Stapp, 1975). People believe that men are characterized by a more instrumental disposition and women by a more expressive disposition.

According to the status model of gender stereotyping, these stereotyped beliefs are based on men's higher status in relation to women. Because people frequently observe men and women interacting together in an established power order (Deaux, 1985; Eagly, 1987; Hollander, 1985), they assume the two sexes are characterized by the dispositions associated with that order (Gerber, 1987, 1988, 1991).

In support of the status argument, studies have shown that instrumental and expressive behaviors are not restricted to interactions between men and women. They are far more general and are manifested by members of same-sex groups as well (Bales & Slater, 1955). Within same-sex police teams, for example, differences in work experience would be expected to lead to some of the same behaviors as would sex category. The more-experienced officer's behavior would be more instrumental, and the less-experienced officer's would be more expressive. Because of their differing behaviors, we would expect that the officers would infer that their personality traits are dissimilar as well.

According to this formulation, the instrumental and expressive traits reflect status processes that are based on sex as well as "non-sex" status characteristics, such as work experience. If this is the case, we need to ask why the instrumental and expressive traits have become associated with sex but not with the other non-sex status characteristics.

To answer this question within the framework of status characteristics theory, we need to look at the way sex functions as a status characteristic in comparison with other non-sex status characteristics (Gerber, 1993). Sex has only two categories: "male" and "female." This means that whenever a man and woman interact and the only salient information involves sex, the man has high status, and the women has low status. After repeatedly observing interactions such as these, people learn to associate the instrumental attributes with men and the expressive attributes with women.

By contrast, non-sex status characteristics, such as work experience, generally vary along a continuum—they are not restricted to just two categories as is sex. Because of this, people are not able to associate personality traits with any given level of the non-sex status characteristics. For instance, let us take work experience: a male police officer with a five-year level of work experience could have either high or low status. If he works with a male partner with only one year of experience, his status will be high, but if he works with a male partner with ten years of experience, his status will be low.[3] Hence, people could not associate particular personality traits with a given level of work experience.

Additional differences exist between sex and the non-sex status characteristics. An individual's sex is readily observable, in contrast to many non-sex status characteristics such as seniority or education, making it easier for people to associate specific personality attributes with either men or women. Further, people repeatedly observe men and women interacting together to perform various tasks—within families, husbands and wives carry out daily chores that are necessary for the maintenance of the family, and within occupational settings, traditionally, a male boss interacts with a female subordinate (Blood & Wolfe, 1960; Kanter, 1977; Parsons & Bales, 1955). By contrast, situations in which people with differing non-sex status characteristics work together on a task are far less common. For example, an individual with a college degree might work collaboratively with someone who did not complete high school, but this would occur much less frequently.

According to this formulation, the instrumental and expressive personality traits have become associated with sex because people have observed numerous interactions in the past in which men have higher status than women (Gerber, 1993). As a result, people form stereotypes of men as being instrumental and women as being expressive.

Given that people have stereotypes about women's and men's personality traits, we need to address a further issue: Would these stereotypes affect the way people perceive one another's personality traits in actual ongoing interactions such as the ones between police partners? The answer is: No. In ongoing interactions, we would not expect people's impressions to be affected by these previously formed stereo-types. Research has shown that stereotypes are used to form impressions only when other information is absent. When specific information about an individual's behavior is provided, people use that information to make judgments instead of basing their impressions on stereotypes (Locksley, Borgida, Brekke, & Hepburn, 1980). Thus, we would expect that the police partners in the present study will use the information that is currently available and salient to them to form impressions of their personality traits (D. J. Bem, 1972; Jones & Davis, 1965). In other words, police officers who work as partners are expected to base their impressions of one another's personality traits on their observations of their current behaviors.

INDIVIDUAL STATUS AND GROUP STATUS

Status characteristics theory has focused on the status order that evolves within an interacting dyad. Based on a comparison of the dyad members' status characteristics, one person is perceived as having high status, and the other person is seen as having low status. I call this type of status ordering "individual status."

In addition to the ranking of individuals within a dyad, the entire dyad can also be ranked within the larger organization of which it is a part (Gerber & Kaswan, 1971; Hogg & Abrams, 1988; Tajfel, 1982). Thus, we can extend the theory to include the status ordering of the group as a unit. I call this kind of status ranking "group status."

The status order of the group as a whole is based on the averaged statuses of the individuals who comprise the group. For example, a group of men would have higher status than a group of women, and by the same token, an all-white group would have superior status to a group of blacks.

Group members develop expectations about the performance of individuals within a group based on their individual status (Berger et al., 1977): Individuals with high status are thought to be more capable than those with low status. In a parallel fashion, they would develop expectations about the performance of the group *as a unit* based on its group status: Groups with high status would be expected to outperform groups with low status, which would affect the behaviors and perceived personality traits of all group members.

The concept of group status is new, but results from previous research on group behavior are consistent with this formulation (Dion, 1985; Ridgeway, 1988). All-male groups, which would have a high group status, engage in more instrumental behavior than do all-female groups. By comparison, all-female groups, which would have a low group status, engage in more expressive behavior. Groups with a mixture of female and male participants, which would have an intermediate group status, engage in intermediate levels of both types of behaviors.

Because policing is such a masculine-typed occupation, sex category is an extremely salient status characteristic (Martin, 1990).[4] Thus, the proportions of men and women in the different partnerships would be critical in determining the partnership's group status (Kanter, 1977).[5] The all-male partnership would be *highest* in group status because both officers are male, and men have higher status than women within the larger organization of the police department. The all-female partnership would be *lowest* in group status because both officers are female, and women have lower status than men within the police department. The male–female partnership would be *intermediate* in group status because one officer is a high-status male and the other officer is a low-status female, giving an intermediate status ranking to the partnership as a whole.

Based on previous research (Dion, 1985; Ridgeway, 1988), we would expect that group status would affect the personality traits (and behaviors) of both police team members. As an officer in one of the all-male police teams says during an interview, "When you're with your regular partner, you have a way of doing things together. It's two cops, but they think like one person." Officers in the highest status all-male team would view themselves as having the most instrumental traits and the fewest expressive traits in comparison to officers in other partnerships. Officers in the intermediate-status male–female team would perceive themselves as having intermediate levels of the instrumental and expressive traits. In addition, officers in the lowest-status all-female team would see themselves as having the fewest instrumental traits and the most expressive traits in comparison with officers in other partnerships.

During the interviews that were conducted as part of this study, many officers expressed the opinion that all-male police teams are given more respect than other kinds of police teams, both within the police department and from the public at large. A male officer, who had worked in both an all-male and a male–female team, describes the greater mutual respect he felt with his male partner: "We had pretty much about the same experience. We came from the same station house, and there was a mutual respect—they call it comradery. I felt a little more secure with him [than with my female partner]."

The more aggressive behavior that goes along with the high group status associated with all-male teams is illustrated in the following interview with a senior male police officer. He describes working as a team with his partner: "I like the fact that he's also aggressive. When I say aggressive, I mean not afraid to tackle something or get into some-thing. He thinks on the same level as me." Another male officer says, "You have to be forceful, and you have to be strict. That's why a lot of people might say that cops are rude. But sometimes we have to be because when we pull someone over, we don't know who we're dealing with. This person may have just killed somebody."

By comparison, male–female and all-female police teams are given a lower group status ranking. This means they are given less respect, and it is considered less desirable to be a member of one of these teams. The quotes from the following interviews show how both the public and the officers themselves perceive an all-female team as having lower group status than a male–female team. Both of these women officers had had experience working in both types of teams. The first woman officer describes the public's negative reaction to an all-female police team as compared to a male–female team:

> I didn't feel two women coming on the scene get the same respect as a man and a woman. People won't accept it, and you can sense it. Two women [did not represent] the authority figures that the public calls 911 for; they want someone who is going to come there and *know*. A man and a woman works great, but two women—I don't know; it just doesn't seem right.

Another woman police officer who had a very brief experience work-ing with a female partner before going back with her male partner concurs: "When we [my female partner and myself] showed up at a situation like a car stop, I don't feel that people felt as intimidated as if I was with my male partner."

Research has shown that people identify with their role within a group, as well as with the group as a whole (Gerber & Kaswan, 1971; Hogg & Abrams, 1988; Tajfel, 1982). Hence, we would expect that both types of status—individual status and group status—would affect people's behavior and personality attributions. In other words, in the present study, we expect differences in the personality traits attributed to high- and low-status police officers *within* each type of police team. In addition, we predict overall differences in personality attributions *between* different types of teams. For example, an all-male team would be expected to be more instrumental than a male–female team (group status). In addition, within each of these teams, the roles of the individ-ual partners would be differentiated so that the high-status officer would be more instrumental than the low-status officer (individual status).

In summary, police officers are expected to identify with their indi-vidual roles within the partnership as well as with the partnership as a whole. Thus, it is expected that their personality attributions will be affected by two types of status orderings—individual status and group status. These are independent variables that would have separate and independent effects on personality attributions.[6]

SOCIALLY DESIRABLE AND UNDESIRABLE PERSONALITY TRAITS

Instrumentally oriented personality attributes include two kinds of traits: the socially *desirable* and the socially *undesirable* personality traits (Spence, Helmreich, & Holahan, 1979). The desirable attributes are called the "instrumental" traits and include characteristics such as decisive, active, and independent; the undesirable attributes are called the "dominating" traits and include characteristics such as dictatorial, arrogant, and egotistical.

Status characteristics theory does not differentiate between instrumental behaviors that are perceived as positive and others that are seen as negative (Berger et al., 1977), even though research has shown that some instrumental behaviors are viewed negatively by others (Bales, 1958).[7] Because the theory does not distinguish between desirable and undesirable instrumental characteristics, the predictions in the present study refer to both types of instrumentality. The expressive traits that are also the focus of the present research are considered to be socially desirable.

Thus, the hypotheses for individual status can be restated as: The high-status officer within each partnership will be perceived as having more instrumentally oriented (dominating and instrumental) traits than the low-status officer; the low-status officer will be perceived as having more expressive traits. With respect to group status, members of higher-status partnerships are expected to perceive themselves as having more instrumentally oriented (dominating and instrumental) traits, as well as fewer expressive traits, than members of lower-status partnerships.

These hypotheses refer to the perceptions of both the self and the partner. In the present study, high- and low-status officers in all-male, male–female, and all-female police teams were asked to describe their own personality dispositions (self-perceptions). In addition, each officer was described by the partner (partner-perceptions). In general, the effects of status on the self- and partner-perceptions are expected to be similar because individuals usually make inferences about their own dispositions as do observers—by observing their overt behaviors (D. J. Bem, 1972). Under some circumstances, however, individuals can perceive themselves differently than do observers (Jones & Nisbett, 1972). Because of this, we may find some differences between the effects of status on the self-perceptions and on the partner-perceptions, and this will be explored.

STATUS CHARACTERISTICS THEORY AND SOCIAL COGNITION

The "basic status argument" is that many task-related behaviors that people have interpreted as reflecting gender differences actually reflect underlying status differences (see Wagner & Berger, 1997, for a review). The argument is extended here to include personality attributes—how dyad members perceive one another on the so-called gender-stereo-typed traits. According to the present formulation, the expressive and instrumentally oriented traits are not related specifically to gender; instead, they reflect more general status differences.

The present chapter has focused on the expressive and instrumentally oriented (dominating and instrumental) attributes that have been the topic of most theoretical and experimental work. As hypothesized here, these traits stem directly from the status processes that take place in interactions. In addition, there are other gender-stereotyped attributes—the verbally aggressive, submissive, and bipolar traits. The proposition that will be explored throughout the following chapters is that all of the gender-stereotyped traits, including those that are less well known and less extensively researched, relate in some way to the status processes that take place in interactions. In subsequent chapters, we develop theoretical arguments to explain how these less well-known gender-stereotyped attributes relate to status and test these propositions with our sample of police partners. We will explore the proposition put forth by Wagner and Berger (1997) that some gender-stereotyped behaviors (and traits) reflect attempts by low-status team members to cope more effectively with their inferior status position.

As we extend status characteristics theory to include social cognition, we need to keep in mind that the theory was developed originally to explain behavior. We are able to use the theory to make predictions about social cognition because most of the time personality traits directly reflect behavior and serve as behavioral summaries (D. J. Bem, 1972; Buss & Craik, 1984; Jones & Davis, 1965). Sometimes, however, personality traits are affected by processes and biases that relate exclusively to social perception (Fiske & Taylor, 1991; Jones & Nisbett, 1972). As we develop an integrated theory that explains social perception as well as behavior, these cognitive processes will need to be taken into account.

Throughout subsequent chapters, we will also explore issues that have been of concern to social cognition and to personality trait theory and research. For example: What factors determine an individual's self-esteem? How are the traits that comprise individual personality organized? As we address these issues in subsequent chapters, we integrate theoretical and empirical work in social cognition and personality with status characteristics theory.

Description of the Study: The Sample of Police Partners and Measures

> When you want someone as a partner you don't just say, "I want this person as a partner." There's got to be some kind of bond between you before you even start working together—even if you've just met for the first time.
>
> *—Male officer in an all-male police team*

The procedures for carrying out the research and the measures used are described in this chapter. Members of all-male, male–female, and all-female police teams participated in the study and filled out a questionnaire describing themselves, their partner, and their relationship with the partner. The immediate supervisor also filled out a questionnaire evaluating the team's job performance. Following the completion of the study, interviews were conducted with an additional sample of officers who worked in police partnerships.

The police officers who participated in the study were steady partners who worked together in radio motor patrol cars. This is an unusually intense work relationship because most partners are together five days a week, often for more than two years. They are supposed to stay together on the job because it might be dangerous for them to separate, and so most partners work with one another all day and have lunch or dinner together during their shift.

The immediate supervising officer for each police team was generally a sergeant. The supervisor works closely with a small number of police teams. As a result, he[1] generally is well acquainted with them and has an opportunity to observe them in a variety of contexts—in the station house as well as in various work situations, such as making an arrest.

This chapter also describes the measures used in the research. These include several scales that were developed especially for this study: the Self-Evaluation Scale, which measures self-esteem, and the Police Decision Scale, which measures police partners' perceptions of their influence over the decisions made in the partnership.

PROCEDURE

The Sample of Police Teams

The New York City Police Department surveyed every police team throughout the 75 precincts of New York City, and teams were selected by means of this initial survey. Three types of police teams were chosen for the study: all-male, male–female, and all-female teams. The groups of teams were matched as closely as possible on the length of time the partners had worked together, the tour or shift they worked, and their precinct.

Because all-female teams were numerically few, all of these teams were selected for the study. This group of all-female teams was then matched with the groups of male–female and all-male teams on the critical variables. The final sample included 154 police teams—66 were all-male, 59 were male–female, and 29 were all-female. A complete description of the procedure for selecting police teams is provided in Appendix A.

Police partners' questionnaire. Members of each police team who were currently working together when the questionnaires were distributed were invited to participate in the study. Participation was voluntary, and all information was kept anonymous and confidential. Team members were given time on the job to fill out a questionnaire in which they each rated themselves, their partner, and their relationship with one another on various scales. Demographic data and information about the partnership were also obtained.

The operations coordinator (ranking officer in charge of operations) at each precinct supervised the administration of the questionnaires, thus ensuring that confidentiality was maintained. Each partner sealed his or her completed questionnaire in an envelope that was then sealed in a larger envelope and returned to me through Police Headquarters.

The response rate was extremely high—90 percent of the police teams who were asked to participate in the study agreed to do so.

Supervisor's questionnaire. The immediate supervising officer (sergeant) of each police team filled out a questionnaire that included demographic and partnership information, in addition to evaluations of the team's work performance.

Because the partners' and supervisor's questionnaires had been filled out at different times and were both anonymous, it was necessary to match them using the demographic and partnership information that had been obtained. Three of my research assistants and I worked together in pairs to do the matching. The overall initial agreement between pairs was 94 percent, and differences were resolved through discussion. By using this procedure, we were able to match partners' and supervisors' questionnaires for 125 teams.[2]

The Interview Sample

Following the analysis of the data, interviews were conducted with an additional sample of police officers who worked in police partnerships. The purpose of these interviews was to explore the results from the empirical study from the perspective of the officers themselves. Police officers volunteered to be interviewed, and all information was anonymous. Each interview lasted approximately one hour. Officers were asked a series of structured questions and filled out a brief questionnaire that included ratings of the self and partner on selected scales from the larger study, as well as demographic and partnership information. All interviews were tape-recorded and transcribed.

Whenever possible, both members of a partnership were interviewed. Of the 37 interviews conducted, 16 were with officers who worked in the same team. In the remaining interviews, only one member of the team was able to participate. In the interview sample, 22 officers worked in all-male teams, 13 worked in male–female teams, and 2 worked in all-female teams. Interviews were conducted by me and by four female and male research assistants, two of whom were themselves police officers. Quotes from the interview data are used throughout the book to supplement the empirical findings by illustrating the way police officers themselves describe their experiences.

DESIGNATING STATUS

The relative status of the officers in each police team (individual status) and the status ranking of each police team in relation to other teams (group status) were designated as follows.

Individual Status

Individual status refers to the status order that evolves between police officers who work together as partners. A primary purpose of the research was to compare high- and low-status officers in different types of police teams—male–female, all-male, and all-female teams. To do so, it was necessary to categorize the members of each type of police team into high- and low-status officers.[3]

In the male–female team, the categorization process was quite simple. Sex is a highly salient status characteristic in policing and generally overrides all other status characteristics (Martin, 1990). Even when a female officer has more seniority or education than her partner, the male officer still is viewed as having higher status. Consequently, in the male–female teams, the male was designated as the high-status officer and the female as the low-status officer.

In same-sex police teams, seniority is an extremely salient status characteristic that usually overrides other status characteristics (Niederhoffer, 1967). Consequently, in the all-male and all-female police teams, the officer with more seniority was designated high status, and the officer with less seniority was designated low status.

In some cases, both partners had the same amount of seniority, and education was used to designate status. Most patrol officers only consider education relevant to status when there are no differences in seniority (Blumberg, 1985; Niederhoffer, 1967). Thus, when the partners had the same amount of seniority, the officer with more education was designated as having higher status. For example, an officer who had completed college had higher status than an officer who had only finished high school.

Last, if both partners had the same amount of seniority and education, age was used to determine status. Age is not considered relevant in determining status unless there are no differences in seniority and education (Niederhoffer, 1967; Sherman, 1985). Thus, when both partners had the same amount of seniority and education, the older person was designated as having the superior status.[4]

For the majority of same-sex police teams, the individual status of the officers was determined by experience (69 percent in both all-male and all-female teams). In a minority of teams, as we would expect, individual status was designated by education (18 percent in all-male teams and 21 percent in all-female teams) or age (13 percent in all-male teams and 10 percent in all-female teams).[5]

Group Status

Group status refers to the status ranking of each partnership in relation to other kinds of partnerships within the larger organization of the police department. It is based on the averaged statuses of the individuals who are in the partnership.[6]

Because sex category is a highly salient status characteristic in policing, the *proportion* of men and women in the different partnerships was
used to designate group status. Because men have higher status than
women, partnerships with a higher proportion of males in comparison
to females have a higher group status. Thus the all-male partnership
(with 100 percent men) has the highest group status, the male–female
partnership (with 50 percent men and 50 percent women) has intermediate group status, and the all-female partnership (with 100 percent
women) has the lowest group status.

MEASURES

Police Partners' Ratings

Extended Personal Attributes Questionnaire. Each officer rated his or her
perception of the self, as well as the perception of the partner, on the
Extended Personal Attributes Questionnaire (EPAQ), a widely used
scale for measuring the gender-stereotyped personality traits (Spence,
Helmreich, & Holahan, 1979; Spence, Helmreich, & Stapp, 1974, 1975).

The questionnaire consists of a series of traits that are associated
more with one sex than the other (see Table 3.1).[7] Not only do people
stereotype the two sexes as having differing personality attributes,
but men and women also rate themselves as having dissimilar
attributes (Spence et al., 1975, 1979). With the exception of one scale
(the bipolar scale), the traits on the EPAQ have been judged either
to be socially desirable or socially undesirable for both sexes. For
example, even though the expressive traits are associated with women
more than men, expressiveness is considered to be desirable for both
sexes.

There are two types of instrumentally oriented attributes—the socially desirable "instrumental traits" and the socially undesirable
"dominating traits." Both these attributes are believed to be more
typical of men than of women. The instrumental traits consist of
self-assertive, agentic, or goal-oriented attributes, such as decisive,
active, and independent. The dominating traits consist of instrumental,
goal-oriented, dominating attributes—for example, dictatorial, arrogant, and egotistical.

The "expressive traits" are socially desirable attributes that are believed to be more typical of women than of men. These are interpersonally oriented, communal, or accommodating attributes, such as helpful
to others, aware of others' feelings, and warm.

The EPAQ includes two kinds of socially undesirable attributes that
are believed to be more typical of women than men. The "verbal-
aggressive traits" consist of verbally aggressive qualities, such as com-

TABLE 3.1
The Gender-Stereotyped Personality Traits

Personality Traits	Definition
Instrumentally Oriented and Expressive Traits	
Instrumental	Socially desirable, self-assertive, agentic, or goal-oriented characteristics that are more typical of men than women, for example, decisive, active, independent.
Dominating	Socially undesirable, instrumental, or dominating characteristics that are more typical of men than women, for example, dictatorial, arrogant, egotistical.
Expressive	Interpersonally oriented, communal, or accommodating characteristics that are more typical of women than men, for example, helpful to others, aware of others' feelings, warm.
Other Gender-Stereotyped Traits	
Verbal-Agressive	Verbally aggressive qualities that are more typical of women than men, for example, complaining, nagging
Submissive	Characteristics reflecting submissiveness and a lack of sense of self that are more typical of women than men, for example, subordinating self to others, servile.
Bipolar	Characteristics for which one pole is believed to be ideal for women (a low score), and the other pole is believed to be ideal for men (a high score), for example, home-oriented (female pole)—worldly (male pole).

plaining and nagging. The "submissive traits" include attributes reflecting submissiveness and a lack of sense of self—for example, subordinating self to others and servile.

The "bipolar traits" include items on which one pole is desirable for women and the other pole is desirable for men.[3] Examples of these items are: cries very easily (feminine pole)—never cries (masculine pole); very home-oriented (feminine pole)—very worldly (masculine pole). When these items are scored, the feminine pole is given a low score and the masculine pole is given a high score.

Each set of traits consists of eight items, except for the submissive and the verbal-aggressive traits, which consist of four items each. Following Spence et al. (1979), each item is rated on a five-point scale ranging from 0 to 4; summed scores are then computed for each set of traits.

Self-Evaluation Scale. The Self-Evaluation Scale measures self-esteem or the evaluative component of the self—the degree to which one prizes, values, approves, or likes oneself (Blascovich & Tomaka, 1991). Self-esteem can be based on a variety of factors that include one's sense of competence and mastery in the performance of tasks, as well as one's capacity to be supportive and helpful toward other people (Rosenberg, 1979/1986).

Some of the self-esteem measures used in previous research have been flawed because they overemphasized task-related competence (or instrumentality) in determining self-esteem (Nicholls, Licht, & Pearl, 1982). In some cases, there is an actual overlap in items between scales designed to measure self-esteem and those designed to measure instrumentality.

To remedy this problem, the Self-Evaluation Scale was developed especially for this study. Unlike some other measures of self-esteem (Nicholls et al., 1982), it was designed to be a "gender-neutral" measure of self-esteem that gives equal weight to both the competence and the interpersonal-relatedness components of self-esteem.

The scale includes 14 items—half of which are high in social desirability and half of which are low (Edwards, 1964). Each item is rated from "not at all" to "very" on seven-point scales, and ratings on these items are averaged to obtain a self-esteem score. Examples of the items are: fair-minded, responsible, dull, and pessimistic. In addition to rating themselves on the Self-Evaluation Scale, officers also rated their perception of the partner.

A low score indicates that one perceives oneself (or the partner) as having low self-esteem; a high score indicates that one sees oneself (or the partner) as having high self-esteem. The internal consistency of the scale (coefficient alpha = .78) was found to be satisfactory. (See Appendix B for a description of the earlier study in which this scale was developed and a list of all the items included in the scale.)

Police Decision Scale. The Police Decision Scale measures the relative influence of each officer over the decisions made in the partnership. It was developed especially for this study in earlier research with police officers (see Appendix B). In relationships between people, such as the one between police partners, it is important to have a measure of *relative* influence that is provided by the participants themselves (Blood & Wolfe, 1960). The decisions included in the scale are ones that police officers themselves consider to be: (a) important, (b) made by most partners in the course of their work, and (c) impacting the partnership as a whole (Blood & Wolfe, 1960).

Each officer indicated who made the final decision in 11 different areas—for example, whether or not to arrest someone and the tactics to use in a life-threatening situation. Ratings are made as follows: 1 = myself always, 2 = myself more than my partner, 3 = myself and my partner exactly the same, 4 = my partner more than myself, 5 = my partner always (Blood & Wolfe 1960).

Ratings on the items are averaged to obtain a relative decision score. A low score indicates that the *self* is perceived as making more of the decisions than the partner; a high score indicates that the *partner* is perceived as making more of the decisions. The internal consistency of the scale was computed using coefficient alpha and was equal to .61. (See Appendix B for a listing of all the items on the scale.)

Unilateral power and control scales. The "unilateral power scale" measures the extent to which an officer perceives herself or himself as taking control without attempting to enlist the partner's cooperation (Kipnis & Goodstadt, 1970). The scale includes five items that are rated from "all of the time" to "never" (Gold & Yanof, 1985).[9] For example, "How often do you see what your partner thinks before taking a stand?" Scores on these items are averaged to obtain a unilateral power score.

In addition, the "control over team activities scale" indicates the extent to which an officer perceives himself or herself as exercising control over the activities in the partnership. On this scale, the end points are labeled "none or not at all" and "extreme amount."[10]

On both these scales, a low rating indicates that the self is perceived as exercising little control; a high rating indicates that the self is perceived as exercising a great deal of control.

Other personal and job-related ratings. Officers' perceptions of themselves as intelligent (perceived intelligence) and whether their supervisors regard them favorably (perceived job success) were rated on seven-point scales. A low rating represents poor performance and a high rating represents good performance.

Additional scales measure officers' perceptions of their ability to work effectively with male coworkers and female coworkers (male and female coworkers scales). A low score indicates the self is perceived as ineffective; a high score indicates the self is seen as effective.[11]

Supervisor's Evaluations

The supervisor rated "team competence"—his evaluation of how well the partners work together as a team—on four items developed especially for this study: competent in their work together, effective in handling service-oriented calls, effective in handling enforcement situations, and effective in working with the public. The internal reliability of the scale was satisfactory (coefficient alpha = .85).

The supervisor also rated his assessment of the "individual performance" of each individual officer on two items: competent on the job and highly regarded by superiors. Again the internal reliability for the scale was satisfactory (coefficient alpha = .87). Finally, the supervisor rated the amount of leadership exercised by each officer on a single item.[12]

All items are rated from 1 to 7. For the team competence and individual performance scales, a low rating represents a poor performance evaluation by the supervisor, and a high rating represents a good performance evaluation. For the leadership scale, a low rating indicates that, according to the supervisor's assessment, the officer never acts as the leader; a high rating indicates that the officer always acts as the leader.

Demographic and Partnership Information

Each officer provided demographic information in addition to information about the partnership: sex category, age, education, race/ethnic group, number of years experience as a police officer, length of time the partners had worked together, tour or shift that was worked, and the partner's sex category.[13] The immediate supervisor also provided demographic and partnership information (with the exception of education).

The "relative work experience" of officers in the male–female team was categorized as follows: 1 = the man has more work experience (years as a police officer) than the woman; 2 = the man and woman have the same amount of work experience; 3 = the man has less work experience than the woman.

Structured Interviews

During each interview, officers were asked questions about the amount of influence they exercised over the decisions made in the partnership; they were asked to elaborate on their answers by giving examples from incidents that actually had taken place.[14] In addition, they were asked about the influence techniques they used with their partner, with civilians, and in making an arrest.

Officers described what they liked and did not like about working with their partner and how they felt about themselves in their work with their partner. If they previously had worked with a partner of the other sex, they were asked to describe these experiences. For example, if they were currently working with a female partner, they were asked about their previous experiences working with a male partner. In addition, they were asked to describe any differences they had observed between male and female officers in various aspects of police work— their relative effectiveness in various situations, the influence techniques they generally use, and the way they are treated by the police department. Finally, officers described their views of the typical and ideal police officers.

SUMMARY OF MEASURES

The police partners' questionnaire was filled out by members of police teams who participated in the large-scale empirical study. Each officer rated his or her perception of the self as well as the perception of the partner on the EPAQ, which is a widely used scale for measuring the gender-stereotyped personality traits. In addition, officers rated themselves on a number of other scales developed for this study. These included the Police Decision Scale, which measures each officer's influence relative to the partner, and the Self-Evaluation Scale, which is a "gender-neutral" measure of self-esteem.

On the supervisor's questionnaire, the supervisor rated the overall competence of each police team, the performance of each individual officer, and the leadership exercised by each officer.

Status and Personality: The Dominating, Instrumental, and Expressive Traits

> In police partnerships there always seems to be one dominant officer and one that's more passive. You're put together, and that's the way your relationship evolves.
>
> —*Male officer in an all-male police team*

Do women's and men's perceptions of their personality traits vary with their status? The status model of gender stereotyping maintains that they do. Or do men and women really have different personality attributes, as the gender-specific model contends? This chapter provides the crucial test of the status model of gender stereotyping by analyzing the way members of police partnerships perceive themselves on the expressive and instrumentally oriented personality traits.

According to the status model, officers' perceptions of their personality traits vary with their status. The critical test of the model involves individual status—the status of each officer vis-à-vis the partner. The status model predicts that the high-status officer in each partnership type will be perceived as having more instrumentally oriented (dominating and instrumental) traits and the low-status officer will be seen as having more expressive traits. In addition, the status model predicts that officers' perceptions of their personality traits will be affected by group status—the overall status of their partnership in relation to other kinds of partnerships.

By contrast, the gender-specific model simply assumes that both sexes will be perceived in traditionally stereotyped ways. All of the men will be characterized by instrumentally oriented traits, and all of the women will be characterized by expressive traits.

In this chapter, we also explore some intriguing findings involving all-female police teams that show how pressures from the immediate supervisor affect some of the officers' perceptions of their personalities. Finally, the chapter examines the "kernel of truth" issue—how people's observations can appear to support the gender-specific model of gender stereotyping, although this appearance is misleading.

DOMINATING AND EXPRESSIVE TRAITS

The dominating and expressive traits were analyzed separately using analyses of variance.[1] The purpose of these analyses was to test whether police officers' perceptions of themselves and their partners are related to individual status and group status. An overview of the findings is presented below; a more detailed description of the results can be found in Appendix C.

Individual Status

Perceptions of the self. The results provide strong support for the status model of gender stereotyping. As predicted, officers' perceptions of their own personality traits are consistent with their individual status (see Table 4.1). The high-status officer in each partnership perceives the self as having somewhat more instrumentally oriented, dominating traits than the low-status officer ($p < .10$). By contrast, the low-status officer perceives the self as having significantly more expressive traits ($p < .001$). These findings provide strong support for the status model of gender stereotyping; their implications for each of the partner types are discussed later.

In the male–female team, both officers perceive themselves in conventionally stereotyped ways, as we would expect, because the male officer has high status and the female officer has low status. The high-status male sees himself as having somewhat more of the dominating attributes believed to be characteristic of men, and the low-status female views herself as having more of the expressive attributes thought to be typical of women.

The critical results involve the same-sex partnerships, because here one of the officers' traits go directly counter to gender stereotypes, just as the status model predicts. In the all-male team, the lower-status, less-experienced male's perceptions deviate from gender stereotypes because he describes himself as having more of the expressive personality traits that people associate with women. In the all-female police team, the higher-status, more-experienced female's perceptions also deviate from gender stereotypes—she sees herself as having somewhat more of the dominating traits that are generally associated with men.

Perceptions of the partner. Results for the perceptions of the partner's personality traits are consistent with the findings that have already been described; they provide further support for the status model of gender stereotyping. The low-status officer is perceived as having significantly more expressive traits than the high-status officer ($p < .01$), as predicted (see Table 4.1 for means). This is consistent with the way officers perceive themselves on the expressive traits, indicating that individual status affects the way one sees oneself and it also affects the way one is perceived by others. (For the dominating traits, no difference between high- and low-status officers is found.)

Group Status

Perceptions of the self. Members of higher-status partnerships were expected to perceive themselves as having more dominating traits and fewer expressive traits than members of lower-status partnerships. Because group status is based on the proportion of male and female members in each partnership, the all-male partnership is highest, the male–female partnership is intermediate, and the all-female partnership is lowest in group status.

The predicted results for group status are found and provide additional support for the status model. Officers in the all-male partnership perceive themselves as having the most dominating traits and fewest expressive traits, officers in the male–female partnership see themselves as having intermediate levels of both traits, and officers in the all-female partnership

TABLE 4.1
Dominating and Expressive Personality Traits: Means for High- and Low-Status Officers

Person Being Perceived and Personality Traits	Status of Officer	
	High Status	*Low Status*
Perceptions of the Self		
Dominating	10.71	9.78
Expressive	22.55	24.16
Perceptions of the Partner		
Dominating	10.72	10.76
Expressive	21.30	22.71

view themselves as having the fewest dominating traits and most expressive traits in comparison with other partnerships.

The mean ratings for group status are presented in Table 4.2. Each mean represents the combined self-perceptions of both officers in each partnership, indicating that group status affects the perceptions of both officers. (The effects for group status are highly significant in the analyses of the dominating traits, $p < .005$, and the expressive traits, $p < .001$. In addition, linear trend analyses over the three partner types are significant for both traits, $ps < .05$.)

Perceptions of the partner. Contrary to prediction, when officers describe their *partner's* personality traits, the predicted results for group status are not found. The means for the three partnership types are significantly different from one another, but do not vary in the predicted direction.[2]

If we examine the means for the perceptions of the partner, which are presented in Table 4.2, we find that the means for the all-male and male–female teams appear to vary in the predicted direction. Only the means for the all-female team seem to be deviant—the partner is perceived as being higher on the dominating traits and lower on the expressive traits than had been predicted. In other words, members of all-female teams perceive one another as having traits that are more similar to higher-status police teams than had been expected.

These means are based on the combined partner perceptions of both partners, indicating that both members of all-female teams perceive the partner as manifesting more of the traits associated with higher-status police teams than predicted. These results are intriguing and lead to some interesting questions: Why do these discrepant findings occur only in all-female teams? Why do members of all-female teams perceive

TABLE 4.2
Dominating and Expressive Personality Traits: Means for Police Teams Varying in Group Status

Person Being Perceived and Personality Traits	Police Team		
	All-Male	Male–Female	All-Female
Perceptions of the Self			
Dominating	11.16	9.85	8.99
Expressive	22.30	24.00	24.41
Perceptions of the Partner			
Dominating	11.88	9.80	10.54
Expressive	20.91	22.94	22.59

Note. The all-male partnership is high, the male–female partnership is intermediate, and the all-female partnership is low on group status.

themselves as having attributes that are consistent with their low group status, while at the same time perceiving the *partner* as having attributes associated with a higher group status? These questions will be explored later in the chapter.

INSTRUMENTAL TRAITS

Contrary to prediction, the socially desirable instrumental traits do not vary as a function of status. We find that all police officers perceive themselves and their partners as high on the instrumental traits—higher even than the norm for college males (see Appendix C).[3] This indicates that police officers, as a group, see themselves as having the assertive, decisive qualities that are reflected in the instrumental traits, regardless of their status. These results are consistent with previous research that has shown that police officers need to be extremely self-assertive in order to enforce the law (Manning, 1997; Mills & Bohannon, 1980; Storms, Penn, & Tenzell, 1990).

But the findings appear to be in conflict with previous studies that have found the instrumental traits to be associated with status and power (Conway, Pizzamiglio, & Mount, 1996; Gerber, 1988, 1991; Smoreda, 1995). As we find in this study, the dominating traits are related to status, but the instrumental traits are not. The apparent conflict may be because of the way in which "instrumentality" was measured in previous studies.[4] In these earlier studies, the "instrumental" scale contained highly dominant personality attributes in addition to self-directive, goal-oriented instrumental attributes. Thus, the connections between status and instrumentality found in previous research may have resulted from the highly dominant traits that were included in the "instrumental" scales. Future research will need to explore this issue further, but the present study highlights the importance of using both a dominating scale and a self-directive instrumental scale in studying the connections between instrumentality and status.

SUPERVISOR'S EVALUATIONS AND THE ALL-FEMALE TEAMS

The results for group status, described previously, raise some intriguing questions about the all-female police teams. We find that members of all-female teams perceive themselves as having traits that reflect their low group status in comparison to other types of police teams. However, they both perceive one another as being more like the members of higher-status police teams—higher on the dominating traits and lower on the expressive traits than their group status would seemingly allow.

To explain these unexpected findings, we have to focus on the situation in which members of all-female teams find themselves. Because such teams are still rare within the police department, they are likely to come under close scrutiny from their immediate supervisor.[5] The supervisor may urge them to act more like the all-male teams—to be more dominating and less expressive—especially in enforcement situations. As a result, members of all-female teams may try to "prove" themselves by acting aggressively at times, for example, when they make an arrest.

These kinds of pressures are described by a woman officer who worked in an all-female police team. When she was interviewed for this study, she reported that she and her partner wanted to prove they could do their job as effectively as an all-male team:

> 'Cause you're two women working together and you're doing this job, you feel you have to prove yourself. You get to a "gun run," for example, before everyone else because you don't want people to think that women aren't capable of doing this job.

But in "proving" themselves with these highly aggressive behaviors, the women in all-female teams can find themselves in a quandary. On the one hand, they are expected to behave in the less dominating, more expressive manner that is consistent with their low group status; on the other hand, they are expected to enforce the law by acting in a dominant, high-status way. For example, later in the interview, the woman officer describes the conflict she experiences between maintaining her image of herself as a "sweet," "feminine" person while still meeting the requirements of her job: "You may be a very sweet person. . . . And you want to be yourself because you're female, you're feminine. But you're the law. Maybe there's a kind of tension because that's not exactly you—you have to play that role."

Members of all-female teams may attempt to resolve this conflict by acting in a high-status way in a limited number of enforcement situations, while behaving in a low-status, more accommodating way in most other contexts (Fiske & Taylor, 1991). This hypothesis is based on social cognition research, which has found situational pressures can bias the way others are perceived, but not the perception of the self (Jones & Nisbett, 1972). Even when we know that others are acting atypically because of situational pressures, this still affects our perception of them (Jones & Harris, 1967). By contrast, one's image of oneself is not so easily modified. Even though we sometimes act in atypical ways, we observe our own behaviors over a wide range of situations.

Consequently, we are not likely to modify our image of self in response to particular situational pressures.

Based on this reasoning, it was hypothesized that the supervisor would give higher competence ratings to all-female teams that responded to his pressure by acting at times in a more dominating, less expressive way. Teams that failed to respond to the supervisor's urging would be rated less competent.[6]

That is precisely what the results show. The correlations between the supervisor's ratings of the all-female team's competence and the perceptions of the *partner* on the dominating and expressive traits are strikingly high (see Table 4.3). The supervisor gives higher competence ratings to all-female teams who describe the partner as being more dominating and less expressive.

Also, as hypothesized, pressures from the supervisor have no effect on the way the *self* is perceived in all-female teams. The supervisor's ratings of the all-female team's competence are not correlated with the perceptions of the self, which means that team members see themselves as having the less dominating, more expressive characteristics consistent with their low group status.[7]

By contrast, in the all-male and male–female teams, pressures from the supervisor do not affect any of the perceptions—of self or of partner—as had been hypothesized. This is indicated by the finding that the supervisor's ratings of team competence are not significantly correlated with any of the trait ratings in these teams.[8]

The analyses described here are exploratory, but the findings are consistent with a hypothesis involving the "actor–observer" effect—that external pressure from the supervisor biases the perceptions of the partner (but not the self) in all-female teams (Jones & Nisbett, 1972). Further, the results have important implications for status characteristics theory, which was originally developed to explain how status affects the *behaviors* of dyad members. When the theory is extended to

TABLE 4.3
Correlations Between Supervisor's Evaluation of Team Competence and Team Members' Perceptions of the Partner

| Personality Traits | Police Team | | |
	All-Male	Male–Female	All-Female
Dominating	−.11	−.14	.58***
Expressive	−.06	.22	−.42*

Note. These correlations use the combined perceptions of the partner by both team members. For the all-male, male–female, and all-female teams, *df*s are 48, 44, and 20, respectively.
*$p < .05$. ***$p < .005$.

deal with *social perception*, biases can sometimes affect dyad members' perceptions; the circumstances under which biases occur need to be incorporated as part of the theory.

IMPLICATIONS FOR THE STATUS MODEL

The status model of gender stereotyping was strongly supported by the data. Even though the dominating and expressive traits traditionally have been associated with gender, none of the findings reflect any personality differences that are related to sex category.[9] In other words, the results show none of the differences between female and male officers that the gender-specific model had predicted.

The findings for individual status are most critical.[10] They show that status has a major impact on the way police officers perceive their personality traits. Most importantly, the results show that status can be designated by sex category in male–female teams or by seniority in same-sex teams. However status is designated, the effect on personality is the same: The senior officer is characterized by somewhat more dominating personality traits, and the junior officer is characterized by more expressive traits.

This means that in same-sex police teams, one of the officers manifests personality attributes that go directly counter to gender stereotypes. For example, in all-male police teams, the low-status man manifests the expressiveness, accommodation, and interpersonal sensitivity typically associated with women. Interviews with low-status male police officers dramatically illustrate these findings. In the first interview, the junior male officer describes the empathic and sensitive way he handles a rape situation with a woman victim:

> When we get rape calls, I usually do the talking because I'm a little more patient than my [more senior male] partner. I know what she's going through. Even though my partner knows too, I have the tendency of calming her and making her feel more comfortable. . . . I always try to put myself in the victim's shoes. I say, "I'm a police officer, and I'm here to protect you. Nobody's going to hurt you anymore."

Another low-status male officer describes how he gently comforts a mother with a little son whose father had just died:

> The mother was there in her early thirties, and she was sobbing hysterically. At first, I didn't say anything to her because her son was there—her little son. But then I started talking to her and reassuring her that things were going to be all right. And I could tell she was easing up and felt a lot better. A comforting word does a lot.

These illustrations are particularly striking because they conflict with the "macho" image generally associated with the police. They highlight the important impact that individual status can have on an officer's behaviors and personality attributes. Not only do these male officers manifest attributes that go counter to the macho image of a police officer, they also go counter to the stereotypic personality attributes usually associated with men.

As just described, police officers' perceptions of their personality traits are affected by their individual status vis-à-vis the partner. In addition, they are affected by group status—the status ranking of their partnership as a whole. Both types of status affect officers' perceptions of their personality traits, and both are expressed through the dominating and expressive traits.

The construct of group status is new. It extends status characteristics theory and helps elucidate some perplexing findings from previous research on group behavior (Dion, 1985; Ridgeway, 1988). It explains why groups with varying proportions of male and female members differ in the kinds of behaviors they express. When there are more male participants in comparison to female participants, the group has higher status and *all* of the members engage in more dominating behaviors and fewer expressive behaviors. The present results indicate that the critical factor that determines the behaviors in these groups is overall group status, not the fact that the participants are either female or male.

Results from previous research with police officers are consistent with the findings for group status (Lunneborg, 1989; van Wormer, 1981). They show that all-male police teams, which have a higher status than male–female teams, are more confrontational and aggressive. By contrast, all-female teams, which have the lowest status within the police department, are the least confrontational and most cooperative.

The following interviews illustrate the impact that group status can have on police officers' behaviors. For example, a woman officer discusses the more confrontational approach taken by all-male teams as compared with the male–female team in which she works: "Some males prefer to work with a male partner. But there are men who prefer to work with a female partner because they feel situations do not escalate when they work with a female."

Another woman officer describes how two-man police teams can sometimes escalate a potentially violent situation: "You have some [male] cops that walk into a location like—'I'm ready'—and they make it worse. They are escalating the whole situation because they go in there like gangbusters."

By contrast, she goes on to describe how her presence with her male partner helps to de-escalate potentially troublesome situations:

> My [male] partner and I would go into family disputes and immediately
> he would pull over the husband and I would get the wife and we would
> just talk it through.... I'm a firm believer that you can de-escalate a
> situation by the way you speak.

The officers themselves generally attribute these observed differences
in behavior to dissimilarities between men and women. Instead, the
present results show that the overall differences in personality attributes (and behavior) that characterize different types of police teams
stem from their group status.

Most important, we see that group status affects the attributes of both
team members (Dion, 1985). As the examples illustrate, both of the
officers in all-male teams are more confrontational (more dominating
and less expressive) than the officers in male–female teams. By the same
token, members of male–female police teams would be more confrontational than members of all-female teams.

GENDER STEREOTYPES: A MISLEADING VIEW OF "REALITY"

We find that status accounts for all of the variations in the dominating
and expressive personality traits in the present study. Why, then, do
people believe that men and women have different personalities? With
gender stereotypes, as with other kinds of stereotypes, there is generally
a "kernel of truth" that can appear to validate people's preconceptions
(Allport, 1954; Swim, 1994). If one assumes that men and women have
different personalities, then one's observations can appear to support
that assumption.

Most studies simply compare groups of women and men on various
characteristics and look for overall sex differences. Suppose we had just
looked for sex differences in our sample of male and female police
officers. Would we have found them? The answer is: Yes. If we had
analyzed the data in the present study by simply comparing male and
female officers' personality traits, we would have obtained results that
appeared to support the gender-specific model of gender stereotyping.
But even though most of the results would have reached statistical
significance, they would have failed to represent what was happening
in the data. They would have given us an oversimplified and misleading view of "reality."

To demonstrate this, we can show that the female and male officers
in our sample differed in stereotypic ways by correlating sex of officer
with the dominating and expressive traits. We find, as we would expect,
that male officers are perceived as higher on the dominating traits and
women officers are seen as higher on the expressive traits—for the

perceptions of both the self and the partner (see Table 4.4). Thus, the findings appear to support the gender-specific model.

However, when we examine sex of officer in relation to the two status variables, individual status and group status, we obtain a quite different picture. To do this, we need to perform hierarchical multiple regression analyses on the self-perceptions and partner-perceptions of the dominating and expressive traits. Sex of officer is entered on the first step, and the two status variables are entered on the second step of each analysis. (An overview of the findings is presented below; a complete description of the analyses is in Appendix C.)

When we enter sex of officer on the first step of each analysis, the results are the same as for the correlations, just as we would expect—sex of officer is either significant or tends toward significance, indicating that male officers are perceived as more dominating and women officers are seen as more expressive (see Table 4.5).

The critical test involves the second step of each analysis, when individual status and group status are entered. The picture then changes so that *all* of the variability in the ratings of the dominating and expressive traits is accounted for by the two status variables, and none of the variability is related to sex of officer. What is especially striking is that in the analyses of the self-perceptions, the two status variables account for even more of the variance than does sex category.[11]

These findings show that if we ignore status, we can obtain results that appear to support people's stereotypes about gender. But these results are misleading. Once we include status in our analyses, we find that it accounts for all of the variability in men's and women's perceived personality traits.[12]

As we have demonstrated here, the status model provides a far more accurate representation of how people perceive their personality traits than the gender-specific model, which simply looks for overall differ-

TABLE 4.4
Correlations Between Sex of Officer and the Dominating and Expressive Traits

	Personality Traits	
Person Being Perceived	Dominating	Expressive
Self	−.18**	.29****
Partner	−.10[a]	.19**

Note: Sex of officer was coded, male = 1 and female = 2. A negative correlation means males were perceived as higher on the traits than females; a positive correlation means females were seen as higher than males. $df = 285$.
[a]$p < .10$. **$p < .01$. ****$p < .001$.

TABLE 4.5
Standardized Beta Weights from Hierarchical Regression Analyses of the Dominating and Expressive Traits: Sex of Officer Entered First

	Dominating Traits		Expressive Traits	
Variable	Step 1	Step 2	Step 1	Step 2
	Perceptions of the Self			
Sex of Officer	−.18**	.06	.29****	.14
Individual Status		−.13[a]		.16*
Group Status		−.25*		.12
Increase in R^2	.03	.02	.09	.02
F test on increment	9.60**	2.98*	27.08****	2.58[a]
	Perceptions of the Partner			
Sex of Officer	−.10[a]	−.03	.19**	.05
Individual Status		.03		.11
Group Status		−.10		.12
Increase in R^2	.01	.01	.03	.01
F test on increment	2.70[a]	<1.00	10.10**	1.14

Note. In step 1, $df = 1/285$ and in step 2, $df = 3/283$.
[a]$p < .10$. *$p < .05$. **$p < .01$. ****$p < .001$.

ences between women and men. More important, it helps us understand some of the underlying processes by which "personality" is created in ongoing interactions.

STATUS EFFECTS ON PERSONALITY

Many personality theorists hold that personality traits, including the "gender-stereotyped traits," are enduring characteristics that remain constant across different situations (see Epstein, 1988; Pervin, 1990). In other words, an individual's "personality" remains the same, regardless of the role that he or she plays. This is consistent with the traditional approach to studying "police personality" that assumes police officers have personality attributes that remain essentially unchanged in different situations (Balch, 1972; Carpenter & Raza, 1987).

The alternative view, which is supported here, is that personality traits emerge from a social context: The processes that occur in social interactions give rise to inferences about personality traits (Johnston, 1985; Mischel, 1990; Morgan & Schwalbe, 1990; Stryker, 1987). According to this alternate view, people's behaviors vary from one situation to another, as do the personality traits that are attributed to them. Consistent with this alternate view, we find that police officers' perceptions of their personality traits are determined by status—their individual status vis-à-vis the partner and the group status of their partnership as a whole. These results imply that when a police officer works in a different partnership and has different status, the perceptions of his or her personality attributes will change as well.

We close this chapter by going back to the question we initially posed: Do men's and women's personality attributes vary with their status? The results clearly demonstrate that they do; they provide strong support for the status model of gender stereotyping. The personality attributes that are affected by status are the dominating and expressive traits. The dominating traits are instrumentally oriented, directive characteristics traditionally associated with men; the expressive traits are accommodating characteristics traditionally linked with women. But contrary to conventional beliefs, we find that higher-status police officers *of either sex* tend to be characterized by more dominating traits in comparison to their partners. By contrast, lower-status officers *of either sex* are characterized by more expressive traits.

Coping with Low Status: The Verbal-Aggressive and Submissive Traits

Question: How does your female partner get you to do what she wants?
Answer: She would keep bugging me until I would give in.
                                    —*Male officer in a male–female police team*

My [male] partner knows me very well. But someone who has heard me talk would think, "Wow, what a bitch!"
                                    —*Female officer in a male–female police team*

The basic premise of the status model is that stereotypes about men's and women's personality traits result from the status processes that take place in interactions. We have focused, thus far, on the instrumental and expressive traits that have been the subject of most theoretical and empirical work. We now look at other gender-stereotyped personality attributes, the verbal-aggressive and submissive traits, and ask the question: How are these traits linked with status?

The verbal-aggressive traits involve an indirect way of exercising influence (Johnson, 1976) and include characteristics such as complaining and nagging (Spence, Helmreich, & Holahan, 1979). The submissive traits involve submissiveness and a lack of sense of self and include attributes such as servility and subordinating oneself to others.

The verbally aggressive and submissive traits share common properties: both are socially undesirable attributes, and both are believed to be more typical of women than men. Since women have lower status

than men in our society, these attributes may reflect processes in interactions that are associated with low status. They may serve a function
for low-status individuals, especially women, by enabling them to cope
more effectively with their inferior status position. In this chapter, we
will explore whether the verbal-aggressive and submissive traits enable
low-status police officers to gain in influence, thereby enhancing their
sense of adequacy.

THE LOW-STATUS INDIVIDUAL

Status characteristics theory has been concerned primarily with the
functioning of the dyad as a whole (Berger, Fisek, Norman, & Zelditch,
1977). The satisfactions or dissatisfactions of the individual members
are irrelevant to this goal. But if individuals become dissatisfied with
their roles, the functioning of the partnership could very well be disrupted—and might even break up. Individuals in low-status roles
would be particularly vulnerable to feelings of discontent because they
are perceived as being less competent than their senior partners. As a
result, they exercise little influence over the way tasks are performed
and are expected to defer to their senior partners.

Women police officers who work with male teammates might be
especially likely to become dissatisfied because they are restricted to
a low-status role regardless of how much experience they have. In
one of the interviews for this study, for example, the higher-status
male police officer describes how his female teammate becomes
increasingly dissatisfied over the course of their relationship. Eventually, she becomes so upset over her lack of influence that she ends
the relationship.

When they first began to work as partners, the male officer describes
how he played the "instructor role" with her: "I was more of a guiding
hand and would brief her as to what she didn't know." They worked
together for a year, and toward the end of the partnership, the male
officer reports that his partner began to resist his influence: "She had
very low self-esteem [and so] you couldn't really tell her too many
things—you couldn't tell her that there might be an error in judgment
without her taking it as an insult." When it became clear that the
partnership was about to break up, he says, "It stopped becoming a
partnership; in her eyes it became more like a dictatorship. And that
was the beginning of the end."

As we see from this illustration, if the low-status member of a partnership is unable to exercise any influence, the relationship can become
so frustrating that she leaves. Providing ways to minimize discontent
to maintain the partnership as an effectively functioning unit is espe-

cially important for individuals who are designated low status because they generally experience few rewards in comparison to high-status persons. Any compensations they receive come through their identification with overall group goals, not through any prestige accorded them as individuals (Berger et al., 1977). In addition, they often have little influence over the way tasks are performed. The dissatisfactions associated with their inferior status may leave them little motivation to continue as a member of the partnership unless some way of coping with the situation can be found.

Research on interacting groups has shown that there are ways low-status individuals can cope with their inferior status and gain some measure of influence (Ridgeway, 1982; Wagner & Berger, 1997). Such measures might be particularly effective when the individual has other statuses that have not been made relevant—for example, when the low-status woman in a male–female police partnership has more seniority than her male partner.

These coping behaviors enable low-status individuals to exercise influence while acknowledging their inferior position. They accord individuals more impact on the interaction than their low status might otherwise allow. For example, a low-status individual who complains and nags might be able to influence the partner, but only in an indirect way (Johnson, 1976). The act of complaining implicitly acknowledges that the senior partner has the right to make the final decision.

Low-status individuals can also gain influence by accompanying their assertive behaviors with "status disclaimers" (Wagner & Berger, 1997), which include apologetic, hesitant, or submissive behaviors (Carli, 1990). At the same time as low-status individuals attempt to exercise influence, they stress through these disclaimers that they are not really seeking to attain higher status. For example, a low-status individual might make a suggestion but qualify it with the statement, "I'm sure you've already thought of this" (Wagner & Berger, 1997).

Because sex category is such an all-pervasive status characteristic, we might expect that women as a group would manifest more verbally aggressive and submissive behaviors than men. Based on these behaviors, people would infer that women are characterized by more of the corresponding dispositions. In actuality, we find this to be so, because women are stereotyped as being more verbally aggressive and submissive than men.

However, the verbal-aggressive and submissive traits need not be limited to women. Such traits may be used by low-status individuals of either sex to circumvent an established status order (Wagner & Berger, 1997),[1] for example, by low-status officers in all-male and all-female police partnerships. They would be most valuable when sex category serves as a basis for assigning women to low-status positions in partnerships with men, because this practice restricts women in perpetuity to an inferior role.

THE MALE–FEMALE PARTNERSHIP

The primary findings for the verbal-aggressive and submissive traits involve the officers in male–female police teams.[2] An overview of the results is presented here; a more detailed description of the results is given in Appendix C.

Verbal-Aggressive Traits

In male–female partnerships, the low-status female officer is perceived as significantly more verbally aggressive than her high-status male partner (see Table 5.1). These findings are particularly striking because they are consistent for the analyses of the self-perceptions and the perceptions of the partner ($p < .001$ and $p < .01$). In other words, both officers agree that the woman is more verbally aggressive than the man. By contrast, officers in all-male and all-female partnerships do not show any consistent differences in verbal-aggression.[3]

We might speculate that the verbal-aggressive traits serve a special function in the male–female partnership—especially for the low-status woman who is characterized by relatively high levels of these traits. The male–female partnership differs in a crucial way from the same-sex partnerships: Sex category is used to designate status, instead of the seniority used in the other partnership types (Martin, 1990; Niederhoffer, 1967). When a man and woman work together, these two highly salient status characteristics, sex category and seniority, can sometimes be inconsistent—at times the female officer can have *more* seniority than

TABLE 5.1
Verbal-Aggressive Traits: Means for High- and Low-Status Officers in Different Police Teams

Person Being Perceived and Status of Officer	Police Team		
	All-Male	Male–Female	All-Female
Perceptions of the Self			
High Status	5.22	3.95	6.27
Low Status	5.05	5.93	5.19
Perceptions of the Partner			
High Status	4.28	3.87	6.03
Low Status	5.92	5.51	4.85

her male partner. But even when the female officer is more experienced than her partner, she still must enact a low-status role. In order to exercise any influence from her low-status position, she would have to use an indirect form of power, such as verbal aggression (Falbo & Peplau, 1980; Johnson, 1976), that would help her to gain more influence and enhance her own sense of competence.

By contrast, the man in the male–female partnership is assigned a high-status position by virtue of his sex category. Because his high-status position entitles him to use very direct forms of power, he should have little need for indirect forms such as verbal aggression (Falbo & Peplau, 1980; Johnson, 1976). If he were to be verbally aggressive, it probably would be unrelated to his seniority relative to his partner and would have little impact on his power and his perceived competence.

These hypotheses were explored by correlating the woman's and the man's self-perceptions on the verbal-aggressive traits with their relative work experience, as well as their scores on the Police Decision Scale (perceived influence) and job success scale. The results are described next.

Female officer's verbal aggression. When the female officer has more seniority than her male partner, she is perceived as being more verbally aggressive, just as we had hypothesized (see Table 5.2). Her verbal aggression gains her increased influence in making decisions—as seen by herself, as well as by her male partner. In addition,

TABLE 5.2
The Male–Female Partnership: Correlations of Officers' Verbal-Aggressive Traits with Other Variables

Variables	Female Officer's Verbal Aggression	Male Officer's Verbal Aggression
Relative Work Experience	.38***	.04
Police Decision Scale		
Verbally Aggressive Officer	−.26[a]	−.11
Partner	.27*	.00
Job Success Scale		
Verbally Aggressive Officer	.33*	−.06
Partner	.38***	−.25[b]

Note. The "verbally aggressive officer" is the officer whose verbal aggression is correlated with other variables including self and partner ratings on the Police Decision Scale and the job success scale. For all correlations, $gf = 52$.
[a]$p < .06$. *$p < .05$. ***$p < .005$. [b]$p < .10$.

she perceives herself as more successful in her job, and—what is particularly striking—her male partner perceives himself as more successful as well.[4]

We can understand these results in terms of the highly masculine-
typed context of the police department in which a woman who works
with a male partner is expected to remain in a low-status position,
regardless of how much work experience she has. The only way a
woman officer is able to exercise power from her low-status position
without challenging her male partner's leadership is by using verbal
aggression—in other words, by complaining and nagging. The
woman's verbal aggression is functional—for her male partner as well
as herself—because both of them gain an increased sense of competence
and effectiveness in their work.

These results are consistent with an earlier study of female and male
police executives who had attained the rank of sergeant or above (Price,
1974). Female executives scored higher than male executives on verbal
aggression. This suggests that verbal aggressiveness may be an effective
way for women in the police department to gain influence and have
their competence recognized.

Male officer's verbal aggression. In contrast to the female officer, the
male officer is perceived as relatively low on verbal aggression. We
might hypothesize that a low level of verbal aggression is functional for
him.

To explore this hypothesis, the male officer's verbal aggression was
correlated with a number of other variables, but none of these
correlations was statistically significant. These results show that the
male officer's verbal aggression is unrelated to his relative work
experience and has no effect on his perceived influence or his
perceived job success (see Table 5.2). However, one of the correlations
does tend toward significance ($p < .10$): When the male officer is
verbally aggressive, his female partner tends to see herself as less
successful in her job.[5]

This latter finding is intriguing and was explored further using the
supervisor's assessment of each officer's job performance. Results show
that the female officer's devaluation of her performance does not appear warranted. Even though she tends to rate herself as less successful
when her male partner is verbally aggressive, the supervisor does not
perceive her as being less competent in her work (the correlation between the male officer's verbal aggression and the supervisor's evaluations of the female partner's competence is not significant).[6]

Strikingly, however, the supervisor's evaluation of the *male* officers
competence is negatively correlated with his verbal aggression, which
is statistically significant ($p < .01$).[7] In other words, when the male

officer is verbally aggressive, he receives significantly *lower* evaluations of his job performance from his immediate supervisor—and vice versa.

We can speculate about the meaning of these results. For example, why does the female officer perceive herself as less competent when her male partner is verbally aggressive? Perhaps he directs his verbal aggressiveness toward her and complains about her work, causing her to devalue her own abilities. Instead of enabling the low-status woman to cope more effectively, the male officer's verbal aggression may undermine her sense of competence.

A further question is: Why does the supervisor evaluate the more verbally aggressive man as being less competent in his work? From the point of view of the supervisor, it may be inappropriate for the high-status man to use influence techniques that are associated with a low-status position. The supervisor may take this as an indication that the male officer is unable to exercise the authority necessary for him to perform his job effectively and, consequently, give him lower performance evaluations. Another possibility is that male police officers who manifest traits that conflict with their gender role are evaluated unfavorably by supervisors—and as we know, verbal aggression is associated with women, not men. These issues need to be explored in future research.

Submissive Traits

Officers in the male–female partnership differ on the other socially undesirable traits that are associated with women—the submissive traits. The female officer is perceived by her partner as being relatively high on the submissive traits; by contrast, the male officer is seen as relatively low ($p < .05$; see Table 5.3).

These findings are more limited than those for verbal aggression because they involve only the officers' perceptions of one another. But if we focus on the way the female officer is perceived by her partner, we find that she is perceived as being both verbally aggressive and submis-

TABLE 5.3
Perceptions of the Partner's Submissive Traits: Means for High- and Low-Status Officers in Different Police Teams

Status of Officer	Police Team		
	All-Male	*Male–Female*	*All-Female*
High Status	4.57	3.74	4.78
Low Status	4.82	4.89	3.82

Note: High- and low-status classifications refer to the officer who is being perceived.

sive.[8] By contrast, the male officer is perceived as low on both these characteristics. The results for the low-status woman are intriguing because they suggest that, at least from the perspective of her male partner, her attempts to exercise influence by being verbally aggressive are accompanied by submissive actions that acknowledge her subordinate position. This would be consistent with previous research that has found low-status individuals need to accompany their acts of assertion with behaviors that signal their low-status position to others in order to be effective (Carli, 1990; Meeker & Weitzel-O'Neill, 1977; Ridgeway, 1982).

Not surprisingly, women police officers do not rate themselves as being more submissive than did men. Women officers would not likely acknowledge that they are submissive or servile, because these traits are incompatible with the role of police officer (Blumberg & Niederhoffer, 1985). Another possibility is that women officers may express submissiveness through nonverbal behaviors, such as a deferential posture or tone of voice (Henley, 1977). If so, then the women officers themselves would be unaware of their own submissiveness, but it would be readily apparent to outside observers such as their male partners.

COPING WITH LOW STATUS

We began this chapter by asking how the verbal-aggressive and submissive traits might be linked with status processes. We explored whether these traits reflect ways in which low-status individuals, such as women, might gain some measure of influence and cope more effectively with their low-status position. We asked whether these traits were employed by all low-status individuals, men as well as women, within all partnership types.

The results from our sample of police partners show that verbal aggression and submissiveness are not characteristic of all low-status officers. They are not even characteristic of women in low-status positions, because the low-status woman in the all-female partnership is neither more verbally aggressive nor more submissive than her high-status female partner. Instead, only the low-status woman in the male–female partnership is perceived as having more verbally aggressive and submissive attributes than her male partner.

First, let us focus on the verbal-aggressive traits, because these results are most striking. The male–female partnership differs from the other two partnership types in an important way. Because policing is one of the most highly masculine-typed occupational fields, men are presumed to be more competent than women (Martin & Jurik, 1996). A woman who works with a male partner can never be openly acknowledged as the leader in the partnership. Accordingly, it is possible for two highly salient status characteristics—sex category and seniority—to be in conflict. For example, in a male–female partnership, a more-experienced woman who works with a man would be expected to play a low-status role, despite her greater seniority. However, in a same-sex partnership these status characteristics can never be in conflict—for example, a more-experienced woman who works with a female partner is expected to be in the superior status position.

The results from the study show that when there is a conflict between the status characteristics of sex category and seniority, the woman in the male–female partnership is more verbally aggressive. In other words, when the woman is more experienced in comparison to her male partner, she is characterized by more verbal-aggressive traits. In this way, she is able to increase her influence within the partnership and her own sense of competence in her job. Further, her male partner's feeling of competence is enhanced as well.

Verbal aggression, which includes the attributes of complaining and nagging, is an indirect method of exercising power because it implicitly acknowledges that the other person has the right to make the final decision (Johnson, 1976). Because of this, the low-status woman's use of verbal aggression does not challenge the leadership position of her high-status male partner. It is functional for the partnership as a whole because it enables the low-status woman to contribute to the effective functioning of the partnership—which is particularly important when she has special skills and knowledge as a result of her seniority. It is functional for the woman herself because it enables her to cope more effectively with her low-status position and minimize any frustrations she might feel. In addition, it is functional for her high-status male partner because it enhances his sense of competence in his work—perhaps because he is acknowledged as the leader but can also draw on the knowledge and resources of the woman officer to enhance his overall job performance.

These findings have important implications for status characteristics theory. They show that there are two ways of exercising influence—"direct" and "indirect" (Falbo & Peplau, 1980; Johnson, 1976). The direct form of power is exercised by high-status officers in all partnership types; it is expressed through the dominating traits that were the focus of the previous chapter. The indirect form of power is expressed through the verbal-aggressive traits and is used by low-status individuals, such as women, primarily when there is a conflict between two highly salient status characteristics—in this case, between sex category and seniority.

It is striking to note that when a high-status individual, such as the man in the male–female partnership, utilizes an indirect form of power, he is penalized—in this case, by receiving lowered performance evaluations from his immediate supervisor. Since the man is entitled to use direct forms of influence by virtue of his superior status position, the supervisor may see his use of verbal aggression as dysfunctional—as undermining his authority and the performance of the team as a whole.

Now let us turn to the submissive traits. In the present study, the function of the submissive traits is less clear. Only the low-status woman in the male–female partnership is perceived as high on submissive attributes—in contrast to her male partner, who is seen as low on these attributes. Further, this difference is apparent only when the officers rate one another, not when they rate themselves.

If we focus on the perceptions of the low-status woman by her male partner, we see that she is characterized as both verbally aggressive and submissive. This suggests that the low-status woman's submissive traits may function as status disclaimers—a way of reinforcing the woman's inferior status while at the same time allowing her to exercise influence through her verbal-aggressive traits (Wagner & Berger, 1997). The high-status male officer may feel reassured by his perception of his female partner as deferential because she will not challenge his position as leader.

AN ILLUSTRATION FROM POLICING

Throughout this chapter, we have discussed the theoretical issues and empirical findings with respect to the verbal-aggressive and submissive traits. We will now examine how police partners themselves describe their experience. In the following illustration, both members of the male–female police team were interviewed separately, but their responses are remarkably similar.

During his interview, the male officer states that he makes most of the decisions in the partnership. He goes on to describe how this takes place: "On a routine day on patrol, if we happened to see a suspicious vehicle, I would explain to my [female] partner the way I would want it done tactically—what we would do before making a car stop or before an arrest situation."

He does acknowledge that his female partner makes some of the decisions—and says spontaneously that she does so by being verbally aggressive: "Usually when she feels she's right, she's demanding." When asked how she exercises influence, his female partner responds by saying, "I just keep [laughs]—you could call it nagging."

What becomes clear throughout both interviews is that even though the female officer uses verbal aggression to exercise influence, she still defers to her male partner as the final authority. For example, at the same time that the male officer describes his partner as "demanding," he also says she accedes to him: "If she sees someone suspicious, she'll ask me if we should investigate further."

The female officer, who agrees that she "nags" her partner to exercise influence, also indicates that she is usually the one who gives in whenever there is a conflict: "If there's a disagreement and I know I'm wrong—being a stubborn person, I'll sit there and argue. But eventually if I figure that I'm wrong, I'll give in and go with whatever he says."

Both officers state in their interviews that they feel competent in their work together, which is again consistent with the empirical findings described previously. The female officer says, "I feel confident in what I'm doing [with my partner]." The male officer concurs, "I feel very confident working with her; otherwise, we wouldn't be partners as long as we've been."

As we see in these interviews, both officers acknowledge that the man is the leader in the partnership and exercises very direct forms of power. But they also agree that the woman officer is able to have an impact on decisions by using an indirect form of power, namely, verbal aggression. This enables her to gain influence and an increased sense of confidence.

FURTHER ISSUES

Previous research has found that low-status individuals can increase their power by accompanying their influence attempts with other behaviors that disclaim any effort to seek higher status (Carli, 1990; Ridgeway, 1982; Wagner & Berger, 1997). The present study shows that low-status individuals, such as women, can increase their influence in another way—by using verbal aggression, which is an indirect means of exercising power.

Low-status women in male–female police partnerships are perceived as more verbally aggressive than their partners, particularly when they have more seniority. Their verbal aggression enables them to increase their influence and cope more effectively with their low-status position. By contrast, low-status officers in the other partnership types are not consistently characterized by more verbal-aggression in comparison to their senior partners.[9]

These findings suggest that verbal aggression may be effective only when there is a conflict between an ascribed status characteristic, such as sex category, and another highly salient status characteristic, such as seniority. Such a conflict could never occur in same-sex police partnerships because here status generally is designated by seniority alone. But in the male–female partnership, a woman is restricted to a low-status role because of her sex category, yet can have greater seniority than her male partner. Future research might explore whether verbal aggression is also effective when an ascribed status characteristic, such as race, serves to designate status and conflicts with other salient status characteristics.

Police Officers Who Violate Gender Norms: The Bipolar Traits

I think the police department keeps the women inside more. They see you as a female—more of a secretary. It makes you feel incompetent. If you're a police officer, why are you inside answering the phones?

—*Female officer in a male–female police team*

When you first get out there [on the street], you have to make yourself a reputation as a cop.... You're pushing yourself a little more out there . . . and the sergeant thinks, "Whoa, this guy is great."
—*Male police officer, quoted in Mark Baker,* Cops: Their Lives in Their Own Words

Most people believe that the ideal woman and man have fundamentally different natures and operate in totally different spheres: The ideal woman is vulnerable and emotional and belongs in the inner, sheltered world of the home; the ideal man is self-sufficient and nonemotional and belongs in the outside public world (Deaux & LaFrance, 1998; Parsons & Bales, 1955).

These beliefs are reflected in the "bipolar traits"—characteristics in which one pole is socially desirable for women and the other pole is desirable for men (Spence, Helmreich, & Stapp, 1975). For example, the ideal woman is home-oriented, but the ideal man is concerned with the outside world. Similarly, the ideal woman cries very easily, but the ideal man never cries (see Table 6.1).

TABLE 6.1
Items on the Bipolar Scale

The Ideal Woman Pole	The Ideal Man Pole
Very home-oriented	Very worldly
Very strong need for security	Very little need for security
Highly needful of others' approval	Indifferent to others' approval
Feelings easily hurt	Feelings not easily hurt
Cries very easily	Never cries
Very excitable in a major crisis	Not at all excitable in a major crisis
Not at all aggressive	Very aggressive
Very submissive	Very dominant

Note. For each item, one pole is characteristic of the ideal woman and the other pole is characteristic of the ideal man.

We can observe the behaviors that are reflected in the bipolar traits during the course of social interaction. Imagine, for example, an incident in which a woman police officer sees a holdup taking place. She shouts at her female partner to cover her and runs over to intervene. After a brief scuffle with the perpetrator, she puts him under arrest.

If we observed this incident, we would likely conclude that the woman officer took charge of the crisis situation in an authoritative, nonemotional way—just as a man ideally would have done. Most likely, we would be left with the impression that the woman officer was somewhat "masculine" and therefore deviant in terms of the behaviors that are expected of females in our culture.

Our impression would likely change if the woman officer appeared visibly upset and somewhat tearful after her female partner came to her assistance and handcuffed the perpetrator. The woman officer's vulnerable, tearful behavior[1] would have reinforced the perception that she was truly "feminine"—like the ideal woman—and had an appropriately feminine-typed gender identity after all (cf. McElhinny, 1993).

This hypothetical incident highlights one of the assumptions observers make about other people and their behaviors. Observers generally assume that people who exhibit feminine-typed behaviors are basically feminine in their gender identity and that those who manifest masculine-typed behaviors are fundamentally masculine (Spence & Sawin, 1985). As with many other beliefs about gender, research has shown that this is not the case. An individual's overt behavior often has little, if anything, to do with that individual's underlying identity as a man or a woman (Spence & Sawin, 1985). But such assumptions persist in the face of contradictory evidence and continue to affect the way others are perceived.

At times, police officers who work as partners take on roles and behaviors associated with the "opposite" sex. Because of their status position vis-à-vis their partners, their behaviors violate gender-related norms. Under these circumstances, the bipolar traits and the behaviors they represent may have an important impact on the way the police officer is perceived by observers. By examining some of the research on social cognition and group behavior, we may be able to gain a better understanding of how these police officers would be perceived.

GENDER-DISTINCT ROLES AND BEHAVIORS

In the male–female police team, the man and woman are expected to enact roles and behaviors that are normative for their sex category. The high-status male officer is expected to be the leader and engage in the dominating behaviors that are stereotypic for men; the low-status female officer is expected to be the follower and exhibit the expressive behaviors considered typical of women.

Within same-sex police teams, however, the situation is quite different. Here, one of the officers often violates very basic beliefs about the roles and behaviors that are considered appropriate for each sex category—beliefs that "all men should be leaders and all women should be followers" and that "all men should be instrumental and all women should be expressive" (Deaux & LaFrance, 1998).

In the all-male team, the less-experienced man generally acts as the follower and engages in the expressive behaviors typically associated with women; in the all-female team, the more-experienced woman usually acts the leader and manifests the dominating behaviors associated with men.

These nonnormative, or "gender-distinct," roles and behaviors are necessary for the effective functioning of the partnership. However, we know from laboratory research that penalties are imposed on those who violate gender norms, especially ones related to power and status (Falbo, Hazen, & Linimon, 1982). Studies have shown that individuals who engage in gender-distinct behaviors are perceived by others as less competent, less likeable, and most important, as having a gender identity inconsistent with their sex category (Costrich, Feinstein, Kidder, & Maracek, 1975; Cowen & Koziej, 1979; Gerber, 1990). For example, a woman who engages in gender-distinct dominant behaviors is perceived as even less feminine than a dominant man (Cowen & Koziej, 1979).

In ongoing relationships such as those between police partners, individuals in gender-distinct roles would also likely suffer penalties. However, if these individuals had other attributes that were considered normative for their gender, they might avoid some of the unfavorable impressions associated with their roles. They might escape the penalties usually imposed on individuals who violate gender norms (Carbonell, 1984).[2]

These countermeasures would have to be ones that did not interfere with the individual's functioning within the partnership. In other words, they would have to involve characteristics other than the status-related dominating and expressive traits.

We know from research on task-oriented groups that people can avoid the penalties associated with gender-distinct behaviors by engaging in other actions that are normative for their gender (Wagner & Berger, 1997). For example, a woman who behaves in a dominant way violates the norms for female behavior and is often penalized. However, if she accompanies her dominant behaviors with other actions that are "feminine-typed," she is more influential and better liked (Carli, 1990; Ridgeway, 1982). In this way, she can engage in gender-distinct behaviors without the usual penalties.

However, the gender violations associated with the low-status man and the high-status woman are very serious. The roles and behaviors enacted by these individuals are directly opposite to what gender norms prescribe. Instead of acting as a leader and manifesting dominating behaviors, the low-status man assumes the role of follower with expressive characteristics. By the same token, the high-status woman does not enact the expected role of follower; instead, she takes charge and assumes the role of leader.

Serious gender violations such as these can lead to very severe penalties; other people may even question these individuals' basic identity as male or female (Gerber, 1990). Unless the low-status man clearly demonstrates that he meets other culturally defined criteria for "masculinity," observers can invalidate him as a man; unless the high-status woman convincingly shows that she meets other criteria for "true femininity," observers might invalidate her as a woman (Hunt, 1990).

The bipolar traits are the only gender-stereotyped traits that could be used as indices of an individual's underlying gender identity. They are the only traits on which the two sexes are seen as "opposite" one another and as having mutually exclusive characteristics: the qualities that are desirable for a woman are diametrically opposite to those that are desirable for a man (Spence et al., 1979). By contrast, for all of the other gender-stereotyped traits, the desirable and undesirable poles are the same for both sexes (Spence, Helmreich, & Holahan, 1979).[3]

If individuals in gender-distinct roles show that they possess ideal qualities associated with their sex category, observers would likely conclude that they must have an "appropriate" gender identity. For example, if the high-status woman in the all-female police team demonstrates that she has the attributes of the ideal woman, others would likely assume that she is "truly feminine" after all.

IMPLICATIONS FOR POLICING

The low-status man in the all-male police partnership is expected to engage in "feminine-typed" expressive behaviors. Even though his behaviors are necessary for the effective functioning of the dyad as a whole, other people might still perceive him as deviant. According to the present formulation, he can avoid the deviant label and the penalties that go with it by accompanying his expressive behaviors with other bipolar actions consistent with his gender.

If he does this, he can show that he is appropriately "masculine" and, in addition, that he meets the requirements for a good police officer (Bonifacio, 1991; Manning, 1997). He is able to do so because the qualities that comprise the masculine pole of the bipolar scale are essentially identical with those of the model police officer. A good police officer is someone who handles crises effectively, controls his emotions, and works effectively in the outside world—just like the "ideal man" (Manning, 1997).

For the high-status woman in the all-female police partnership, the issue is not so simple. Because of her high status, she is expected to engage in "masculine-typed" dominating behaviors. If she accompanies her dominating behaviors with other actions that are consistent with her gender, she may be able to avoid the penalties that would otherwise be imposed (Wagner & Berger, 1997). She would have to show that she is home-oriented (even though working as a police officer), cries easily, and gets upset when confronted with a crisis situation at work (Hunt, 1990).

By engaging in these other actions, she could demonstrate that she fulfills the culturally defined requirements for the ideal woman. However, this would create other problems for her because the qualities associated with the ideal woman are totally incompatible with those of a police officer. When a woman is on patrol, she works in the public sphere, not the inner, home-oriented sphere that is traditional for women. In addition, as a police officer, she needs to maintain control of her emotions and avoid any appearance of the vulnerability associated with the ideal woman.

The discrepancy between the ideal qualities associated with femininity and the actual demands of patrol work may set up a conflict that is impossible for her to resolve in any satisfactory way. The traits considered ideal for women are diametrically opposed to those that are necessary for a police officer. This means that the high-status woman who acts like an ideal female may be evaluated favorably by others, but she also may have difficulty functioning effectively in her work.

THE SUPERVISOR AS OBSERVER

For police officers, it is the supervisor whose opinions and evaluations are most critical. The immediate supervisor, who is generally male, is the agent of the police department as a whole. He transmits the norms and expectations of the police department to the officers who work on patrol (Manning, 1997).

The supervisor is also an observer. It is his responsibility to evaluate the performance of the individuals and teams under his supervision. Because the immediate supervisor oversees only a small number of police teams, he is in a position to observe behaviors by members of these teams in a wide variety of contexts—in the station house and in different work situations. Ideally, the supervisor would reward those behaviors (and traits) that contribute to effective performance. However, as an observer, the supervisor might be subject to the same biases that affect other observers.

Laboratory studies have shown that individuals who violate gender norms, particularly those related to power and status, are perceived in an extremely unfavorable light. Most important, they are perceived by others as less competent than those who are in compliance (Cowen & Koziej, 1979; Falbo et al., 1982). If the supervisor's perceptions are biased in the same way as are other observers', his evaluations would reflect the degree to which police officers deviate from gender norms instead of being a valid indicator of their performance.

The police officers who would be most vulnerable to this kind of bias would be those who enact roles that violate gender norms—the high-status woman in the all-female police team and the low-status man in the all-male team. These "gender-distinct" police officers generally manifest behaviors associated with the "opposite" sex so that the partnership can function effectively. However, if supervisors are affected by the same biases as are other observers, they would perceive these officers as lacking in competence—unless the officers manifest additional behaviors consistent with their sex category.

The behaviors that correspond to the bipolar traits would be most critical and would determine how supervisors evaluate these police officers' job performances. In addition, these bipolar behaviors would determine how officers describe their personality characteristics on the corresponding bipolar traits (Buss & Craik, 1984). For example, a low-status male police officer who handles crisis situations effectively would describe himself as "not at all excitable in a major crisis" on the bipolar personality traits. Because his behaviors and personality traits are "masculine-typed" and conform with gender norms, the supervisor would give favorable evaluations to his work performance.

To summarize the proposed process: Police officers in gender-distinct roles—the high-status women in the all-female team and the low-status man in the all-male team—behave in gender-distinct ways to promote the effective functioning of the partnership as a whole. If they manifest additional bipolar actions that conform with gender norms, observers such as their immediate supervisor would evaluate their job performances favorably. However, if their bipolar behaviors deviate from gender norms, their supervisor would evaluate them unfavorably.

Supervisors base their evaluations on the officers' overt behaviors. But because an individual's behaviors and personality traits generally correspond (Buss & Craik, 1984), we would expect that the self-ratings on the bipolar traits by "gender-distinct" police officers—the high-status woman and the low-status man—would be correlated with the supervisors' assessments of their job performance.

GENDER MARKERS

We will explore whether the bipolar traits and the behaviors they reflect serve as "gender markers." Gender markers are defined here as characteristics that observers can use in making inferences about an individual's gender identity. They become salient to observers when individuals engage in behaviors that violate gender norms.

The behaviors that correspond to the bipolar traits can serve as gender markers, for these behaviors would lead to inferences that an individual's gender identity is basically "feminine" or "masculine" (Goffman, 1976). Bipolar characteristics would be salient to outside observers whenever individuals in particular status positions enact roles and manifest behaviors (and traits) associated with the "opposite" sex. If they accompany their gender-distinct behaviors with other actions (and traits) that are uniquely desirable for their sex category, these individuals would be perceived by others as having an appropriate gender identity after all. They would avoid being viewed in an unfavorable light by observers. In other words, a low-status man who manifests the expressive behaviors required by his status—and at the same time demonstrates that he can control his emotions and handle crisis situations effectively, just like an ideal man—would be perceived as having an appropriately masculine-typed gender identity and would be evaluated favorably by observers.

But why would bipolar characteristics become salient to observers only when individuals engage in behaviors that conflict with gender norms, not when their behavior is consistent with these norms? To answer this question, we need to think about interactions from the point of view of an outside observer. When one observes other people interacting, an automatic monitoring process takes place in which individuals are categorized as either "female" or "male" (West & Zimmerman, 1987). The most outstanding factor, from the point of view of an observer, would be an individual's sex category—and the extent to which that individual's behavior corresponds with the norms for that sex category.

If an individual manifests behaviors that correspond with gender norms, observers would not be motivated to seek other cues about that individual's gender identity. They would assume that these gender-normative behaviors are an indication that the individual has an appropriately sex-typed gender identity (Deaux & Lewis, 1984; Spence & Sawin, 1985).[4] In a male–female police partnership, for example, both officers manifest behaviors that are consistent with their sex category: the high-status man engages in the dominating behaviors that are stereotypic for men and the low-status woman engages in the expressive behaviors that are stereotypic for women. Hence, observers would infer that both members of the partnership are appropriately sex-typed, and they would not seek out any additional behavioral information that might confirm or disconfirm this assumption.

By contrast, when an individual manifests dominating or expressive behaviors that are not normative for his or her sex category, observers would look for other behavioral cues that would either confirm or disconfirm their impression that the individual's gender identity violates gender norms. When a woman police officer manifests masculine-typed dominating behaviors, for example, observers would look for additional cues—such as whether she manifests feminine-typed emotionality—to determine whether or not she has an appropriately feminine-typed gender identity after all.

Although gender markers would be salient to outside observers, they would not be noticed by the participants themselves. To explain why, we need to look at interactions from the point of view of the participants. As status characteristics theory has described, the participants in an interaction are focused on performing their assigned tasks most effectively (Berger, Fisek, Norman, & Zelditch, 1977). In doing so, one individual enacts a high-status role and engages in dominating behaviors; the other individual enacts a low-status role and engages in expressive behaviors. As shown by a considerable body of research, the sex-typing of their behaviors is not salient to the participants in an interaction (Webster & Foschi, 1988). What is important to the participants is the extent to which their behaviors conform with the status of the role that is expected of them.

The present formulation focuses on the way outside observers evaluate the competence of members of work groups instead of the way members evaluate themselves, which has been a primary concern of status characteristics theory (Foschi, 1992, 1998). Sometimes women and men engage in gender-distinct behaviors to ensure that the dyad as a whole functions effectively. It is proposed here that the bipolar behaviors and the behaviors they reflect would affect the way individuals in gender-distinct roles are evaluated by outside observers. In the present study, we will focus on police officers in gender-distinct roles and examine whether their self-ratings on the bipolar traits are related to supervisors' evaluations of their job performances.

SUPERVISOR'S PERFORMANCE EVALUATIONS AND THE BIPOLAR TRAITS

The supervisor's performance evaluations—for the team as a whole and for the individual team members—were correlated with each officer's self-perceptions on the bipolar traits. Correlations were computed for police officers in gender-distinct roles—the high-status woman in the all-female team and the low-status man in the all-male team—as well as for officers in roles that were consistent with gender norms. The findings are described here (see Appendix C for a complete description of the results).

High-Status Woman in the All-Female Police Team

The high-status woman in the all-female team is in a stereotypically "masculine" position. Because of her high status, she generally assumes the role of leader and acts in a dominating way. To counter any negative impression associated with her gender-distinct role, she would have to describe herself as "feminine" on the bipolar traits.

As expected, when the high-status woman identifies herself as "feminine-typed" on the bipolar traits, the supervisor gives more favorable evaluations to the team as a whole. When she describes herself as "masculine-typed," the supervisor rates the team unfavorably (see Table 6.2). The most striking result involves overall team competence. This correlation is not only statistically significant, it is extremely high ($r = -.50$).

These results are quite astounding, especially when we look at the items that comprise the feminine-typed pole of the bipolar traits (see Table 6.1). When the high-status woman describes herself as crying easily, feeling hurt, and being excitable in a major crisis, the supervisor gives higher competence rating to her team. Conversely, when the high-status woman describes herself as having traits similar to an ideal man, the supervisor gives lower competence ratings to her team. In sum, when the high-status woman indicates that she is comfortable in the outside world of the street and able to handle major crisis situations effectively, her supervisor downgrades her team's performance rating.

The high-status woman's description of herself on the bipolar traits has a pervasive effect on all of the supervisor's performance ratings—including the ratings of her as an individual and the ratings of her female partner (see Table 6.2). Both officers receive more favorable ratings when the high-status woman describes herself as having the qualities of an ideal woman. And conversely, both individuals are rated less favorably when the high-status woman describes herself as having the attributes of the ideal man—attributes that are essentially identical to those of a good police officer. The high-status woman's self-ratings on the bipolar traits are therefore critical not only for the way she herself is evaluated by the supervisor, but also for the way her female partner is evaluated.

TABLE 6.2
Gender-Distinct Officers and Their Bipolar Traits: Correlations with the Supervisor's Evaluations

Supervisor's Evaluations	High-Status Woman in All-Female Team	Low-Status Man in All-Male Team
Team as a Whole		
Competence	−.50*	.32*
Handling Service-Oriented Calls	−.39[a]	.35**
Handling Enforcement Situations	−.21	.12
Working with the Public	−.13	.24*
Gender-Distinct Officer		
Competent on the Job	−.21	.31*
Highly Regarded by Superiors	−.25	.19
Gender-Normative Partner		
Competent on the Job	−.26	.07
Highly Regarded by Superiors	−.37[a]	.02

Note. The gender-distinct officer's bipolar traits are correlated with the supervisor's evaluations of the team, the gender-distinct officer, and the gender-normative partner. On the bipolar traits, a low score is "feminine" and a high score is "masculine." For the high-status woman, $df = 20$; for the low-status man, $df = 48$.
[a]$p < .10$. *$p < .05$. **$p < .01$.

As can be seen from Table 6.2, all of the correlations are consistently negative, as predicted, but only a few approach statistical significance. However, the ones that do either reach or approach significance are strikingly high. If it had been possible to obtain a larger sample of all-female teams, similar to the sample sizes for the other teams, more of these correlations may have been significant. (There were relatively few all-female teams in the police department as a whole, and every eligible all-female team throughout New York City was included in the sample.)

Low-Status Man in the All-Male Police Team

The low-status man in the all-male team is in a stereotypically "feminine" position. Because of his low-status position, he assumes the role of follower and acts in a highly expressive way. We would expect that he would need to describe himself as "masculine" on the bipolar traits to counter any negative impression associated with his nonnormative behavior. From the point of view of the supervisor as observer, this is precisely what is found.

The supervisor gives higher competence ratings to the team as a whole when the low-status man describes himself as being more like an ideal male. Conversely, the supervisor assigns lower competence ratings to the team when the officer describes himself as being similar to an ideal female (see Table 6.2).

The supervisor rates the low-status man, as an individual, in a similar way. When the low-status man describes himself as "masculine," the supervisor gives him higher performance ratings; when he describes himself as "feminine," the supervisor gives him lower ratings. But the traits associated with the ideal male are almost identical with those of a good police officer, so the low-status man who manifests highly masculine-typed traits is also able to show that he performs his job in an effective way. The low-status man who meets the standard for an effective police officer is therefore rewarded by receiving favorable evaluations from his immediate supervisor.

None of the correlations involving the supervisor's evaluations of the high-status male partner are significant. Presumably, the supervisor sees the partner as a person in his own right and bases the evaluation of him on his own individual performance.

Police Officers in Gender-Normative Roles

According to the present formulation, when police officers enact roles consistent with gender norms, observers would not need to validate their masculinity or femininity through the bipolar traits. As a result, the supervisor's evaluations of officers in gender-normative roles would be unrelated to their bipolar traits.

That is precisely what is found: None of the correlations between the supervisor's performance ratings and the bipolar traits is statistically significant for individuals in gender-normative roles (see Appendix C). These include the low-status woman in the all-female team, the high-status man in the all-male team, and both members of the male–female team.

As described in Chapter 4, officers in gender-normative roles manifest the dominating and expressive traits that conform with gender norms. Male officers see themselves as having the dominating traits associated with men, and female officers perceive themselves as having the expressive traits associated with women. Because personality traits serve to summarize a large number of behavioral acts (Buss & Craik, 1984), we can assume that these officers engage in numerous behaviors consistent with gender stereotypes. Under these circumstances, the supervisor, as observer, would take these dominating and expressive behaviors as an indication that these officers have an appropriately sex-typed gender identity and would not look for further cues involving bipolar characteristics. The present results are consistent with this hypothesis: The self-ratings on the bipolar traits by officers in gender-normative roles are unrelated to the supervisors' evaluations of their job performances.

Gender Markers and the Supervisor as Observer

These findings show that supervisors' evaluations of officers in gender-distinct roles are based on the degree to which these officers' bipolar personality attributes conform with gender norms.[5] The high-status woman in the all-female team is evaluated most favorably when she describes herself as feminine on the bipolar traits; the low-status man in the all-male team is evaluated most positively when he describes himself as masculine. By contrast, the supervisor's evaluations of individuals in roles consistent with gender norms are unrelated to their bipolar traits.

The results support the hypothesis that the bipolar traits (and the behaviors they reflect) serve as gender markers for individuals in gender-distinct roles. Individuals in roles associated with the "opposite" sex are penalized unless they also describe themselves as having attributes considered desirable for their sex category. If they fail to do so, their immediate supervisor perceives them in an unfavorable light and gives them and their team more negative job performance evaluations.

HOW OFFICERS EVALUATE THEMSELVES

A further issue involves the way officers in gender-distinct roles view themselves. Do they evaluate themselves in the same way as does the supervisor? In other words, does the high-status woman perceive herself more favorably when she has the characteristics of an ideal woman? Does the low-status man see himself more positively when he is like an ideal man?

To answer these questions, the officers' bipolar traits were correlated with self-esteem (Self-Evaluation Scale), perceived influence (Police Decision Scale), and their perceptions of their supervisors regard (job success scale).

The High-Status Woman

The high-status woman in the all-female team does not evaluate herself in the same way as does her supervisor. Instead, her self-evaluations are diametrically opposite to those of the supervisor: She sees herself as having a more desirable personality when she manifests traits associated with an ideal man—not an ideal woman. Further, she sees herself as more influential—and presumably more effective as a leader in the partnership—when her attributes are similar to those of an ideal man (see Table 6.3). These results have important implications for the high-status woman in the all-female team. The male-typed attributes that the high-status woman values and associates with an effective job performance are the very ones her supervisor rates as unsatisfactory for her.

This discrepancy—between the high-status woman's evaluations of herself and the evaluations made by her supervisor—would probably

TABLE 6.3

Gender-Distinct Officers and Their Bipolar Traits: Correlations with their Views of Themselves

Self-Ratings	High-Status Woman in All-Female Team	Low-Status Man in All-Male Team
Self-Esteem (Self-Evaluation Scale)	.40*	.19
Relative Influence (Police Decision Scale)	−.44*	−.10
Perceived Job Success (Highly Regarded by Superiors)	.41*	.16

Note. On the Police Decision Scale, a low score means the self is perceived as more influential; a high score means the partner is seen as more influential. For the high-status woman, $df = 25$; for the low-status man, $df = 58$.
*$p < .05$.

be the source of many problems. Most likely, it would create stress for the high-status woman and make it difficult, if not impossible, for the supervisor to oversee her work effectively.

The high-status woman's response to the perceived job success scale indicates that she is totally unaware that her supervisor's evaluations are so discrepant from her own. This scale measures the extent to which she thinks she is highly regarded by her superiors. The significant correlation between this scale and her bipolar traits indicates that she thinks her superiors are pleased with her performance when she is more like an ideal man—not like an ideal woman. Instead, as we have seen, the exact opposite is true.

The Low-Status Man

The self-evaluations by the low-status man in the all-male team do not show any of the bias that characterizes the evaluations by the supervisor. The low-status man's perceptions of himself are unrelated to his bipolar traits—as indicated by the finding that none of the correlations in Table 6.3 is significant. Evidently, his masculinity or femininity on the bipolar traits is not at all salient for him and has no effect on the way he views himself.

It is interesting to note that the low-status man is unaware of the way his supervisor evaluates his job performance. The correlation involving his perceived job success scale is not significant, indicating that he does not know that his supervisor sees him in a more favorable light when he manifests masculine-typed bipolar traits.

PERCEPTIONS BY THE SELF AND BY OUTSIDE OBSERVERS

The supervisor's evaluations of the high-status woman and the low-status man differ from the way these individuals evaluate themselves. The supervisor evaluates both of them more favorably when their self-perceptions on the bipolar traits conform with gender norms, but they themselves do not: The low-status man's self-evaluations are un-related to his bipolar traits, and the high-status woman's are in the exact opposite direction from the supervisor's.

The reason for this discrepancy may be that the supervisor, as outside observer, uses different information in arriving at his evaluation than an officer does in evaluating herself or himself. We know from research on attribution processes that the information that is available and salient to outside observers often differs from the information that is available and salient to oneself (Fiske & Taylor, 1991).

In the perception of others, gender is highly noticeable, but not in the perception of the self. For example, when we refer to others as objects of perception, we use the gendered terms, "him" or "her." By contrast, when we refer to the self as an object, we do so in a nongendered way—by using the term "me."

For the supervisor, as an outside observer, a person's gender would be highly salient and any deviations from gender-related norms would be highly salient as well. Consequently, deviance from these norms would be penalized and compliance would be rewarded. By contrast, gender would not be salient in the perception of the self, and so any deviance from gender norms would be irrelevant to one's self-evaluations (Spence & Sawin, 1985).

The notion that gender is not important in the perception of the self may explain why the high-status woman evaluates herself more favorably when her attributes are similar to those of the ideal male—and less favorably when her attributes are like those of the ideal female. If gender is not salient for the high-status woman (McElhinny, 1993; Spence & Sawin, 1985), then other issues would be pertinent for her. Because the high-status woman is more experienced than her female partner, she is expected to be the leader in the partnership. As a result, she may feel that it is especially important for her to show she is an effective police officer.

The traits associated with the ideal male are almost interchangeable with those of a model police officer (Manning, 1997). Thus, when asked to rate herself on the bipolar scale, the high-status woman may not see the alternatives as being between either an ideal female or an ideal male. Instead, for her, the choice may be between being an ideal female or a model police officer (McElhinny, 1993).

Under these circumstances, she would evaluate herself more favorably when she perceives herself closer to the "good cop" pole of the bipolar scale. Furthermore, she would expect that her supervisor, like herself, would want her to be a good police officer as well.

THE POLICE SUPERVISOR AND THE MAINTENANCE OF GENDER NORMS

Previous research has described the role of departmental policies and informal practices in maintaining gendered distinctions within police organizations (Lunneborg, 1989; Martin, 1990; Martin & Jurik, 1996). The emphasis has been on the way gendered distinctions serve to disadvantage women police officers. These include gendered assignment patterns in which women are assigned to the station "house" and to quieter beats more than men, as well as performance evaluations that undervalue women police officers (Martin & Jurik, 1996).

The findings described in this chapter highlight the central role of the police supervisor in maintaining gendered distinctions by rewarding behaviors consistent with gender norms—not just for women officers, but also for men. In the interviews conducted as part of this study, police officers repeatedly referred to the supervisor's role in enforcing gender stereotypes as well.

The overwhelming response to the question about whether the police department treats male and female officers differently was "Yes!" The theme that came up repeatedly during the interviews was that supervisors are protective toward women officers and assign them to work in the station "house" more than men. This is consistent with the stereotype included in the bipolar traits that women should be home-oriented but men should be oriented toward the outside world. Many women officers express their resentment over this, and many men are resentful as well. During one of the interviews, for example, a woman officer expresses her bitterness over the differential assignments given to women: "The police department treats us differently. They'll assign us to do inside work a lot more than a male—like a switchboard operator, operator assistant, or assistant desk officer. I think they're unfair."

But many male officers also resent what they perceive as unfair privileges given to women officers over men. In another interview, a male officer expresses his dissatisfaction over the preferential treatment given to women by keeping them inside and "home-oriented," while men are required to perform onerous tasks in the outside world: "Female officers are kept inside; they become chauffeurs for the supervisors. They're treated nicer if it's raining; they won't have to see a foot post where the male would have to be, regardless of whether it's raining or if it's 30 degrees below zero."

Sometimes women officers rebel and refuse to be treated differently from the way men are treated. In the following incident, which took place when she was a rookie, a woman officer describes how she refused to cooperate with the sergeant's attempt to be protective of her:

> I was assigned to drive a sergeant, and we received a call for a man with a gun. When we arrived at the location, there was a man on the corner that fit the description that had been given. The sergeant turned to me and said, "Stay in the car so you don't get hurt."—I doubt he would have said that to a man. I didn't say anything to the sergeant; I just got out of the car and backed him up as any officer would do.

Another theme that was mentioned in a number of interviews has to do with women's presumed emotionality. Other research had shown how, through their actions, superior officers can falsely perpetuate stereotypes about women's excessive sensibility (McElhinny, 1993). In the interviews conducted for this study, several male officers mentioned that even though women officers are stereotyped as being more emotional than men, they themselves had never seen a woman officer break down and cry. One male officer says he has never seen a female officer get upset, but he himself sometimes has difficulty controlling his own feelings: "I personally have not observed it [female officers showing their emotions by crying]. But I can see where it could happen because there have been times when I've been choked up, but I keep it in because I have to try to maintain a professional image."

In this interview excerpt, we see the flip side of the stereotype about emotions that stipulates that male police officers are not permitted to exhibit any feelings. The mandate that men suppress their feelings can be a source of considerable stress for them (Bonifacio, 1991; Jourard, 1974).

The results presented in this chapter have demonstrated that the police supervisor, as the agent of the police department, plays a key role in enforcing gender norms. What becomes evident throughout the interviews is that, by enforcing these norms, the supervisor creates difficulties for both sexes. The supervisor fosters resentments between male and female police officers, further widening the gap between them and making it more difficult for them to work together.

IMPLICATIONS FOR STATUS CHARACTERISTICS THEORY

This chapter brings together research on social cognition, which involves the biases that affect the perception of others, and status characteristics theory. The findings show how the cognitive biases affecting individuals in gender-distinct roles, which have been demonstrated in laboratory research (Fiske & Taylor, 1991), operate in an everyday work situation. They also highlight an important issue for status characteristics theory—how biases affect observers' evaluations of individuals who enact gender-distinct roles.

The theory distinguishes between "double standards" and "biased evaluations" (Foschi, 1992, 1998). According to the theory, low-status individuals, such as women, are often evaluated by a stricter standard than high-status individuals, such as men, when an objective evaluation of their performances shows them to be equal. By contrast, biased evaluations can occur when there are no objective means of evaluation and the status characteristics of the actor are used instead. The results in this chapter illustrate a particular type of bias that can affect the evaluation of others. Police supervisors use different criteria in evaluating male and female police officers who enact roles that violate gender norms—criteria that are reflected in the bipolar personality traits.

The findings also are relevant to another issue in status characteristics theory: why sex category is used so often to designate status—within police partnerships and in many other situations as well. When this occurs, the man is high status and the woman is low. As a result, both sexes are able to display gender-normative attributes, thereby avoiding the penalties associated with gender-deviant roles.

Self-Esteem: The Impact of Status and Personality Traits

I don't bring anything home with me because it's not worth it. Unfortunately, a lot of cops bring their work home—that's why a lot of marriages break up. Or they might drink or even commit suicide.
—Junior officer in an all-male police team

A typical police officer has the same problems as everyone else in any other work environment. The only difference is we can't go to anyone; we have to deal with it ourselves. We have no one to talk to.
—Senior officer in an all-male police team

People often assume that status is associated with self-esteem; they assume high status leads to good self-esteem and low status leads to poor self-esteem. Because men have greater status than women in our society, people believe they must have better self-esteem. Yet research does not support this assumption. Numerous studies show that men and women are similar in their levels of self-esteem (Kristen, Hyde, Showers, & Buswell, 1999; Maccoby & Jacklin, 1974; Major, Barr, Zubek, & Babey, 1999),[1] suggesting that status is *not* the primary determinant of self-esteem; other factors are more important.[2]

This issue is of critical importance for policing. A considerable body of research has documented the problems of many police officers in maintaining a positive view of themselves (Bonifacio, 1991; Niederhoffer, 1967). These difficulties are manifested in the alcoholism, marital problems, and even suicide that are endemic to the job of policing

(Terry, 1985). In some cases, as officers gain more experience and become more competent in their work, they suffer *decreased* self-esteem (Adlam, 1982; Doerner, 1985). Again, these results suggest that status is not the central factor in maintaining a positive view of the self.

Some theories in psychology and sociology have highlighted the role that traits play in the evaluation of the self (James, 1890; Mead, 1934; Wyer & Srull, 1989). People who perceive themselves as having positive traits are thought to evaluate themselves more favorably than those who see themselves as having negative traits. According to these theories, we can speculate that status plays a role in self-evaluations, but only an indirect role. The critical factor would involve the social desirability of the traits associated with status. If high-status persons perceive themselves as having positive traits, they would evaluate themselves favorably; but if they see themselves as having negative traits, they would evaluate themselves unfavorably.

We will explore this issue further in our sample of police partners by examining how status and other variables relate to self-esteem. In doing so, we may be able to determine some of the factors that contribute to low self-esteem and thereby identify officers who are at risk for personal and interpersonal difficulties. The questions we will pose are: Which officers suffer from lowered self-esteem? What determines self-esteem—is it status or the personality traits associated with status?

SELF-ESTEEM

Self-esteem is defined as the evaluative component of the self—the degree to which one prizes, values, approves, or likes oneself (Blascovich & Tomaka, 1991). It involves a global evaluation of the self that is based on a variety of factors, including a sense of competency and mastery in the performance of tasks as well as the capacity to be supportive and helpful towards other people (Rosenberg, 1986).

Self-esteem plays a central role in many theories of personality (Allport, 1961; Erikson, 1959; James, 1890; Rosenberg, 1979). According to these theories, the motive to maintain a positive view of oneself overrides all other motivations. A threat to one's self-image can arise from negative life events, the negative judgments of others, or one's own behavior (Spencer Josephs, & Steele, 1993). Whenever a threat to the self occurs, one reinterprets one's experience in order to restore a positive image of the self. For example, if a citizen expresses anger at a police officer for giving her a parking ticket, the officer might say (as did one of the officers we interviewed for the study), "I don't make the law; I just enforce the law." This statement enables the officer to maintain a positive self-image by implicitly telling himself (and the angry citizen),

"I'm a good police officer who is doing my job effectively. You should be angry at the law, not me, because it's not my fault you received a parking ticket."

There is general agreement that people use a variety of mechanisms to help them maintain a sense of moral and adaptive adequacy (Spencer et al., 1993). However, some theorists have raised questions about the primacy of the self-esteem motive (Baumeister, 1998; Swann, 1990). Baumeister (1998) argues that people's basic motive is to maintain interpersonal bonds and that concern with self-esteem is simply a way of achieving these ends. According to this view, the drive to maintain social bonds is one of the main and most powerful motives for human conduct.

The latter argument is consistent with status characteristics theory, which holds that people who work together on a task are focused primarily on performing the task effectively and that they establish the kinds of interpersonal bonds that will enable them to do so. The maintenance of self-esteem is irrelevant to this goal. To be sure, the high-status member of the task group perceives the self as more competent at the assigned task than does the low-status member (Webster & Sobieszek, 1974a, 1974b). But an individual's sense of task-related competence is very specific and refers only to the particular task that is performed in a given situation; it is not equivalent to the global self-assessment involved in "self-esteem."

Otherwise, it would be impossible to comprehend why people would voluntarily accept a low-status role in a task group. If a low-status position always resulted in low self-esteem, one would have to explain why people would agree to enact such a role. One would have to posit that they were motivated by masochism or by some other motive that seeks to maintain a negative view of the self.[3] Alternatively, they might prefer to avoid the responsibility that is associated with a leadership position, perhaps because they feel they are not legitimately entitled to do so.

However, if we think of global self-esteem as based on a variety of sources, which include interpersonal sensitivity as well as overall task competence, we can understand how individuals could comply with status expectations and at the same time maintain a positive view of self. Whereas the high-status member of a task group might derive self-esteem from the ability to perform the assigned tasks effectively, the low-status member of the group might derive self-esteem from the ability to be interpersonally sensitive and concerned about other people.

According to personality trait theory, people's *behaviors* are not critical in determining self-esteem; instead, it is the *personality traits* that correspond to these behaviors that affect self-esteem. In a long-term, intensive relationship, such as the one between police partners, certain behaviors are repeated numerous times in many different situations. As a result, these behaviors would become summarized as personality traits that officers ascribe to themselves (Buss & Craik, 1983). These personality traits would then determine the officers' global self-esteem. Officers who perceive themselves as having positive personality attributes would have high self-esteem, but those who see themselves as having negative attributes would have low self-esteem.

We found, in a previous chapter, that high- and low-status police officers are characterized by differing amounts of the dominating and expressive personality traits. The dominating traits are considered to be socially *undesirable*, whereas the expressive traits are thought to be socially *desirable*. One of the questions we will explore here is: Since the dominating and expressive traits vary in social desirability, do they also have an impact on the officers' self-esteem?

POLICE OFFICERS' SELF-ESTEEM

Many of the personal and interpersonal problems experienced by police officers, such as depression, alcoholism, marital difficulties, and suicide, have been linked with low self-esteem (Abramson, Metalsky, & Alloy, 1989; Baumeister, 1990; Beck, 1975). It is therefore surprising to find that empirical studies of police officers rarely have looked at global self-esteem. The few studies that have done so have determined that police officers who suffer from low self-esteem experience greater stress and more physical and mental health symptoms than officers with high self-esteem, as we would expect (Lester, 1986; Rosse, Boss, Johnson, & Crown, 1991).

The question that has gone unanswered, however, is: What causes a police officer to devalue himself or herself? One factor might involve the personality changes often associated with the role of police officer. As police officers gain in experience, they feel an increased self-confidence and pride in their work (Arcuri, 1976), but, as a number of investigators have noted, they are frequently unhappy with the kind of person they become (Adlam, 1982; Bonifacio, 1991; Doerner, 1985). This suggests that as police officers become more experienced, their global self-esteem may actually show a decrease. Such observations are limited because they are based on autobiographical accounts by police officers or an impressionistic analysis of interview data; they have not been substantiated through the use of well-validated empirical measures of global self-esteem. Nevertheless, these anecdotal accounts are extremely interesting because they are consistent with personality trait theory, namely, that changes in an individual's personality traits can lead to changes in self-esteem.

STATUS, PERSONALITY TRAITS, AND SELF-ESTEEM

The following analyses explore the interconnections among status, personality traits, and self-esteem in our sample of police partners. Self-esteem was measured by the Self-Evaluation Scale, a "gender-neutral" scale developed especially for this study (see Appendix B). In contrast to many other self-esteem measures that are biased in favor of "masculine-typed" personality traits (Nicholls, Licht, & Pearl, 1982), the Self-Evaluation Scale is designed to give equal weight to "masculine-typed" and "feminine-typed" characteristics.

The findings are summarized here; for a complete description of the analyses, see Appendix C.

Status and Self-Esteem

The first issue we will address is: Does status affect police officers' self-esteem? Most people assume that high status enhances self-esteem, so the present analysis was designed to test this assumption. Police officers' scores on the Self-Evaluation Scale were analyzed using an analysis of variance.[4]

Contrary to popular belief, we find that increased status does not lead to greater self-esteem, because the high-status man in the all-male police team evaluates himself *least* favorably in comparison with all other officers (see Table 7.1). Not only is his self-esteem lower than his partner's ($p < .01$), it is lower than almost everyone else's (with one exception, all $ps < .01$).[5]

These results are very striking because the senior man in the all-male police team has the *highest* possible status in comparison to everyone else. Not only does he have more status than his less-experienced partner (individual status), he also is in the partnership with the greatest status, the all-male partnership (group status). The present findings indicate that status is related to self-esteem, but not in the way people generally assume. In contrast to conventional wisdom, we find the highest possible status is associated with the lowest self-esteem.

TABLE 7.1
Self-Esteem: Means for High- and Low-Status Officers in Different Police Teams

	Police Team		
Status of Officer	All-Male	Male-Female	All-Female
High Status	5.19	5.49	5.55
Low Status	5.53	5.48	5.35

We might understand these results in terms of the personality traits that are associated with status. Previous analyses had shown that higher status is associated with *increased* levels of the socially undesirable dominating traits and *decreased* levels of the socially desirable expressive traits (see Chapter 4). This is true for the partnership as a whole (group status) and for the ranking of each officer vis-à-vis the partner (individual status). In other words, with increased status, police officers attribute more undesirable traits and fewer desirable traits to themselves. Because the very highest-status police officer—the senior man in the all-male partnership—perceives himself as having the least-desirable personality traits in comparison to his partner and everyone else, his feelings of self-worth might have been affected adversely.

By contrast, all of the other officers have relatively high self-esteem (none of the means for the other officers differ significantly from one another; see Table 7.1 and Appendix C). Because all of these lower-status officers have at least some positive traits on which to draw, this could help them maintain a sense of personal adequacy. Most likely, they are able to use a variety of mechanisms, described in previous research (Blaine & Crocker, 1993), to maintain a positive view of themselves.

Personality Traits Determine Self-Esteem

Our next analyses are designed to answer the following questions: Why does the senior man in the all-male partnership have such poor self-esteem? Is it because he has so many socially undesirable personality traits in comparison to his partner and everyone else?

To test whether the senior man's perception of himself as having relatively few desirable personality traits might account for his low self-esteem, hierarchical multiple regression analyses were performed (see Appendix C). The first analysis compared the senior man with his partner; the second analysis compared the senior man with all other officers. In both of these analyses, the dominating and expressive traits account for a highly significant portion of the variability in the self-esteem score when they are entered into the equation on the first step, as we had hypothesized (see Table 7.2). The officers' status does not account for any additional variability in self-esteem when it is entered on the second step; nor do the interaction terms account for any additional variability when they are entered on the third step.

These results indicate that the senior man develops an unfavorable view of himself because he has more undesirable personality traits as compared with his partner and everyone else—he has more of the negative dominating attributes and fewer of the positive expressive attributes than the other officers. According to these findings, the only

TABLE 7.2
Multiple Regression Analyses for Self-Esteem: Senior Man in the All-Male Police Team in Comparison to His Partner and All Other Officers

Step	Variable	Senior Man in All-Male Team Versus His Partner			Senior Man in All-Male Team Versus All Other Officers		
		R	R^2 Change	Beta	R	R^2 Change	Beta
1.	Dominating Traits (A)	.54	.29****	−.39***	.55	.30****	−.41****
	Expressive Traits (B)			.23***			.21****
2.	Status of Officer(s) (C)	.56	.02		.55	.00	
3.	A X C, B X C	.57	.02		.56	−.01	

Note. For the senior man versus his partner, $N = 120$, versus all other officers, $N = 282$.
***$p < .005$. ****$p < .001$.

reason status was related to self-esteem in the previous analysis was that the senior man has so many socially undesirable personality traits in comparison to all other officers.

These findings indicate that status plays a role in self-evaluations, but only an indirect role. The critical factor involves the desirability of the traits that are associated with status. In policing, increased status is associated with more negative personality attributes and fewer positive attributes. As a result, the officer with the highest possible status, the senior man in the all-male police team, develops an unfavorable view of himself.[6]

PERVASIVE EFFECTS OF LOW SELF-ESTEEM: THE "DUMB COP" STEREOTYPE

One might expect officers who suffer from low self-esteem to be most vulnerable to negative aspects of the stereotypes about police officers. The "dumb cop" is a long-standing stereotype that may have had some basis in reality at one time (Thurstone, 1922) but has not been true of New York City police officers for many years (Fenster & Locke, 1973; Fenster, Wiedemann, & Locke, 1978).[7]

As part of the study, police officers had been asked to rate their own intelligence. Unexpectedly, we find that the senior man in the all-male partnership rates himself as having lower intelligence than his partner—and also than most of the other officers (see Table 7.3; three of the

TABLE 7.3
Self-Perceptions on Intelligence and the Ability to Work with Female Coworkers: Means for High- and Low-Status Officers in Different Police Teams

Status of Officer	Police Team		
	All-Male	Male–Female	All-Female
	Intelligence		
High Status	5.13	5.74	5.44
Low Status	5.70	5.67	5.26
	Female Coworkers		
High Status	4.72	5.96	6.15
Low Status	5.55	5.82	5.63

five comparisons with other officers reach significance, one comparison is in the predicted direction—see Appendix C).

But here there is a check on the validity of the senior man's perceptions. We had obtained information about the highest educational level attained by the officers in our sample. To be sure, educational level is not perfectly correlated with intelligence, but if the senior man is less intelligent than the other officers, we would expect that he would have less education.

An analysis of variance was performed to determine whether the senior man had less education than the other police officers (see Appendix C). None of the effects in the analysis of variance is significant, indicating that the senior man does not have a lower level of education; his poor self-rating on intelligence has to be explained by some other factor. Perhaps, as we had speculated previously, the senior man has such low self-esteem that he is vulnerable to the negative stereotypes about police officers—in particular, the stereotype that "cops are dumb."

Further exploratory multiple regression analyses were designed to test this hypothesis using the perceived intelligence score as the dependent variable (see Appendix C). In one analysis, the senior man in the all-male police team was compared with his partner and, in another analysis, he was compared with all other officers including his partner.

When status of officer is entered into the equation on the first step of both analyses, it accounts for a significant proportion of the variance in the perceived intelligence score, as we would expect (see Table 7.4). These results simply confirm our previous findings, namely, that the senior man perceives himself as less intelligent in comparison to his partner and all other officers. When the dominating and expressive traits are brought into the equation on the second step of both analyses,

TABLE 7.4
Standardized Beta Weights from Multiple Regression Analyses of the Perceived Intelligence Scale: Senior Man in the All-Male Police Team in Comparison to His Partner and All Other Officers

Variable	Senior Man in All-Male Team Versus His Partner			Senior Man in All-Male Team Versus All Other Officers		
	Step 1	Step 2	Step 3	Step 1	Step 2	Step 3
Status of Officer	.25**	.21*	.11	.18***	.13*	.10
Dominating Traits		−.14	.12		−.13	.06
Expressive Traits		.12	−.02		.10	.01
Self-Evaluation Score			.67****			.46****
Increase in R^2	.06	.05	.31	.03	.04	.15
F test on increment	7.92**	3.05*	61.35****	8.96***	5.50***	52.67****

Note. For the senior man versus his partner: In Step 1, $df = 1/118$, in Step 2, $df = 3/116$, and in Step 3, $df = 4/115$; in the final equation, $R = .65$, $p < .001$. For the senior man versus all other officers: In Step 1, $df = 1/280$, in Step 2, $df = 3/278$, and in Step 3, $df = 4/277$; in the final equation, $R = .47$, $p < .001$.
*$p < .05$. **$p < .01$. ***$p < .005$. ****$p < .001$.

they account for an additional proportion of the variance. However, a large part of the variability in the perceived intelligence score still needs to be explained.

The critical test of the hypothesis occurs when the self-evaluation score is brought into the equation on the third step of both analyses. We find that it accounts for all of the variability in the perceived intelligence score (see Table 7.4). The beta weights for the other variables are no longer related to perceived intelligence; only the self-evaluation score (self-esteem) is related to perceived intelligence in a highly significant way.

These findings support the hypothesis that the senior man's low self-esteem has such a pervasive effect on his self-image that it leads him to devalue his own intellectual ability. They suggest that the senior man in the all-male partnership not only suffers from a negative self-view but is also vulnerable to other aspects of the negative stereotypes about police officers.

PROBLEMS WITH WOMEN OFFICERS

A good deal of research has shown that individuals with low self-esteem tend to derogate other people, especially members of minorities or out-groups (Spencer, Josephs, & Steele, 1993). Because women still comprise a small minority within the police department, police officers who suffer from low self-esteem might also have difficulties working with women. Again, an unexpected finding shows that the senior man in the all-male police team describes himself as having more trouble working with women than do the other officers (see Table 7.3 and Appendix C; comparisons between the senior male and the other officers are highly significant, $ps < .001$ or $.01$).

This is a very intriguing finding that needs to be substantiated by further research, but we might speculate that the senior male's poor self-esteem leads him to derogate women officers, resulting in his own self-perceived problems in working with women.

These problems are specific to women because the senior male does not perceive himself as having any difficulties in working with men (an analysis of variance shows that he perceives himself as just as effective in working with male coworkers as do the other officers; see Appendix C). This lends support to the hypothesis that the senior man has difficulty working with women coworkers because they comprise a small minority within the police department; he does not have problems working with men who comprise the overwhelming majority of police officers.

IMPLICATIONS FOR POLICING

Adverse Effects of Status

The present findings highlight the potentially adverse effects of status within policing. Increased status is associated with more of the negatively valued dominating traits and fewer of the positively valued expressive traits. As a result, the highest-status police officer, the senior man in the all-male team, finds himself with more unfavorable personality attributes than everyone else. He is not happy with the kind of person he has become and suffers from feelings of low self-worth.

These results highlight the quandary in which senior male police officers find themselves. If they behave in ways that are consistent with status expectations, they do not feel good about themselves. Instead, they are plagued with feelings of self-doubt. On the other hand, if they fail to meet status expectations, they may feel better about themselves as persons—but not as police officers. In addition, they also face the likely disapprobation of other officers and their supervisors.

An autobiographical article by a police officer vividly describes the dilemma that confronts police officers (Doerner, 1985). Officers who try to be "good cops" by meeting the demands associated with a high-status role are often perplexed by what happens to them—they do everything right, yet they feel bad about themselves. Even their personal lives can become disrupted.

The present findings make it possible to target officers who are at risk for suffering from low self-esteem and help them with preventive interventions. This is crucial because we have seen how pervasive the adverse effects associated with a very high-status role can be. Senior men in all-male police partnerships, who are most at risk for feelings of low self-worth, may have doubts about their own intellectual abilities and difficulties working with women as coworkers as well.

The problems with low self-esteem experienced by the senior members of all-male police teams are illustrated in the following interview with a senior male police officer. During the interview, it becomes clear that the senior officer suffers from pervasive feelings of low self-worth. He feels cynical, mistrustful, and isolated from other people, including his fellow officers. He describes most police officers as being "very cynical," and he goes on to say, "Police officers look at everybody as if they're doing something wrong; they're up to no good."

He does not believe the public likes police officers: "I think the public says that we're not trustworthy. They think we're deceitful; we're looking out to deceive everybody." Regarding the way police officers relate to other officers, he says, "I don't think that any one of us trusts any one of us." In addition, he resents female officers because he feels they are given preferential treatment by the police department: "I feel very frustrated; I see it every day and it annoys the s–t out of me."

The senior man's attitudes are in marked contrast to those of his less-experienced partner, who is friendly and trusting during his interview. The partner has a far more positive view of the typical police officer, describing him as "understanding, compassionate, and aggressive when he has to be." He portrays the senior officer very positively as having "street experience, a sense of humor, and compassion toward people." He does indicate that the senior officer sometimes does things that cause friction with his supervisors: "He voices his opinion too often at the wrong place and wrong time; he gets a little agitated." But despite these problems, he feels very good working with his partner. The junior officer has positive feelings toward other officers as well: "In the precinct where I work, everybody is considered more or less a family. Overall, everybody treats each other with respect and concern—like I said, it's a big family."

These interviews highlight some of the difficulties experienced by senior men in all-male police teams. The senior officer has a very poor self-image and feels cynical and mistrustful toward other people, including other police officers. He feels frustrated and angry toward women officers because of the preferential treatment he thinks they receive from the police department.

By contrast, his junior partner has a positive image of himself and of police officers in general. He feels trusting of others and part of a cohesive group within his police precinct. Although he acknowledges that the senior officer has some problems in being too opinionated with supervisors, overall he sees the senior officer's personality in a positive light.[8]

Female and Male Police Officers

Contrary to what we might have expected, none of the women police officers in our sample is low in global self-esteem. Most probably, the warmth, compassion, and empathy that have been found to characterize women officers in other research (Lunneborg, 1989), as well as in the present study, enable them to maintain a positive view of themselves. We found in a previous chapter that the women officers' expressiveness is due to the lower-status roles they play within police partnerships rather than any sex-linked characteristics (see Chapter 4). However, their greater expressiveness and lesser dominance in comparison to male officers probably serve to protect the women officers' global self-esteem.

Other research has shown that male police officers often experience more personal problems than do female police officers—they suffer from more perceived stress, emotional exhaustion, and dissatisfaction with their work (Norvell, Hills, & Murrin, 1993). The present findings suggest that these overall differences between male and female officers may result from differences in their global self-esteem.

It is important to differentiate between global self-esteem and specific task-related self-confidence when looking at sex differences, because women officers are found to experience less self-confidence in their work than do men (Davis, 1984; Lunneborg, 1989). As we would expect, women officers see themselves as being less effective in the specific tasks required of police officers—most probably because of their lower status within policing.

Thus, the present findings, along with other research, indicate that male and female officers are at risk for very different problems. Because of their high status, many of the male officers can suffer from serious problems in their global self-esteem. By contrast, female officers, who have lower status, can have difficulty seeing themselves as competent in performing the specific tasks required of police officers.

THEORETICAL IMPLICATIONS

Status Characteristics Theory and Self-Esteem

Status characteristics theory has focused on the way members of task-oriented groups evaluate their competence in performing specific tasks (Webster & Sobieszek, 1974a, 1974b); it has not addressed the issue of global self-esteem. By extending the theory to include personality traits as well as behavior, we are able to draw on personality trait theory and make predictions about self-esteem.

It is important for the theory to differentiate between specific task competence and global self-esteem because they are associated with status in very different ways. Status is related directly to task competence: high-status individuals are perceived as more competent in performing assigned tasks and are given more "prestige" in the group as a result (Webster & Sobieszek, 1974a). By contrast, based on the results from our police sample, global self-esteem is related to status only indirectly; the critical factor involves the personality traits associated with status.

By extending status characteristics theory to include global self-esteem, we are able to gain further understanding of some perplexing issues. For example, we are able to understand why individuals would voluntarily accept a low-status role within a task group. Even though such individuals see themselves as relatively ineffective in performing the required tasks, they still are able to maintain a positive view of themselves. In one of the interviews we conducted with police officers as part of this study, for example, the junior officer in an all-male police team says he defers to his partner because his partner is more experienced and knows much more about police work. But he goes on to say that he feels good about himself despite the fact that his partner is more knowledgeable about policing: "I feel very self-confident; I feel great about myself."

Thus, when we extend the theory to include global self-esteem, we are able to understand why increased status can sometimes lead to high self-esteem and sometimes not; it depends on the personality traits that are associated with status. Under some circumstances, such as policing, increased status is associated with less-favorable personality traits and leads to low self-esteem (Bales & Slater, 1955). But under other circumstances, perhaps when increased status is expressed through the socially desirable instrumental attributes instead of the undesirable dominating attributes, status might be associated with a more positive view of the self. By focusing on the *process* by which personality traits relate to status, we are able to make predictions across a wide range of situations. We are able to determine whether a superior status is likely to produce a favorable or unfavorable view of the self.

A Model for Integrating Status and Self-Esteem

We can integrate status characteristics theory with self-evaluation theory by amplifying on the model proposed by Wyer and Srull (1989). To do so, we need to expand the model to include a factor that is wholly external to the individual—the individual's status in an important work relationship. According to the formulation developed here, status affects the behaviors of members of police partnerships, which in turn become summarized as personality traits (Buss & Craik, 1983). These personality traits then affect an individual's evaluation of himself or herself, that is, the individual's global self-esteem.

This evaluative assessment of the self functions independently of the traits that originally determined it, which means that it can affect a person's evaluations of other personal characteristics (Wyer & Srull, 1989). The results with respect to perceived intelligence in the present study are consistent with this formulation. We find that the senior man in the all-male police team perceives himself as having lower intelligence than all of the other officers. When we explore this finding further, we discover that the senior man's perception of himself as having low intelligence is most strongly related to his low self-esteem, not to his dominating and expressive traits. These results are consistent with the postulate that the evaluative assessment of the self functions independently and can affect an individual's evaluations of the self in other areas.

Which Is Primary—Status or Self-Esteem?

Many personality theories postulate that people are motivated primarily to maintain a positive view of the self and that this overrides all other motivations. If so, we would expect the senior man in the all-male police team to find some way of maintaining a positive view of himself even if it meant failing to live up to the expectations associated with his superior status position. However, this is not the case; instead, the senior man perceives himself as having the high levels of dominating traits and low levels of expressive traits that are associated with his superior status role.

What this indicates is that status considerations override the senior man's motive to maintain a positive view of himself. Despite the fact that his status is associated with very unfavorable personal attributes, the senior man presumably still behaves in a way that is consistent with his status and attributes the corresponding personality traits to himself. This supports the view that the motive to maintain a positive view of the self is not always primary (Bales & Slater, 1955; Baumeister, 1998). The traits (and behaviors) associated with the senior man's high-status position facilitate the effective performance of the partnership as a whole. So the needs of the partnership take precedence over the senior man's wish, as an individual, to enhance his self-esteem.

In contrast to the senior male officer, we find that all of the other officers are able to maintain a relatively high level of self-esteem. Because they all enact lower-status roles in police partnerships, they all perceive themselves as having at least some favorable personality attributes and are able to maintain a positive level of self-esteem.

Gender Issues and Self-Esteem

We began this chapter by asking why women and men have similar levels of self-esteem when women have lower status than men in our society. To address this issue, we had to learn more about the processes that take place in interactions—how status and the traits associated with status affect the evaluation of the self.

Based on our findings, we can speculate that women and men evaluate themselves in similar ways because they attribute traits to themselves that are equal in favorability. Research on the gender-stereotyped personality traits generally has focused on the instrumental and expressive traits, both of which are socially desirable. If higher-status men perceive themselves as being more instrumental and lower-status women perceive themselves as being more expressive, then both sexes would see themselves as possessing valuable personality attributes. Consequently, we would expect them to have similar levels of self-esteem—as, in fact, they do.

When we study the relative contributions of the instrumental and expressive traits to self-esteem, it is important to use a "gender-neutral" self-esteem scale such as the Self-Evaluation Scale developed for this study (cf., Nicholls et al., 1982).[9] Because the instrumental and expressive personality traits are both considered to be valuable attributes, they both would be expected to enhance self-esteem.

The Patterning of Traits Within Individual Personality

Sometimes you have to show authority. You can't just say, "Excuse me, sir, I really hate to trouble you, but please if you would be so kind as to step out of the car." You say, "Get out of the car and put your hands where I can see them right now."
—*Male officer in an all-male police team*

A long-standing issue in personality theory involves the way traits are patterned within individual personality—how the elements or traits that constitute the basic building blocks of personality are organized into higher-order types or dimensions (Allport, 1961; Pervin, 1990). Originally, it was assumed that the instrumental and expressive traits were organized into a "masculine–feminine" dimension (Lewin, 1984a, 1984b). Individuals who were at the "masculine" pole of this dimension were thought to be high on the instrumental traits and low on the expressive traits; those at the "feminine" pole were thought to manifest the opposite pattern.

Contrary to this assumption, research showed that personality is not organized in terms of a masculine–feminine dimension (Bem, 1974; Spence, Helmreich, & Stapp, 1974, 1975). The instrumental and expressive traits are essentially uncorrelated within individual personality. Individuals who rate themselves as being extremely instrumental, for example, are neither more nor less apt to rate themselves as being expressive.

Most important, however, research found other kinds of inter-correlations between the so-called gender-stereotyped personality traits: the dominating and expressive traits are correlated negatively, as are the instrumental and expressive traits (Helmreich, Spence, & Wilhelm, 1981; Spence, Helmreich, & Holahan, 1979). This means that an individual who is highly dominating, for example, would manifest few expressive attributes. By the same token, someone who is extremely instrumental would manifest little or no submissiveness.

The dimensions that comprise personality are reflected in the observed intercorrelations of traits (Buss & Craik, 1983; Eysenck, 1990). Hence, based on the argument made by trait theorists (Eysenck, 1990; Pervin, 1990), these intercorrelations between traits would reflect dimensions within individual personality. The status model of personality highlights the role that status and power play within individual personality, particularly with respect to the so-called gender-stereotyped traits. Consequently, the status model might help us conceptualize the meaning of these dimensions.

According to various theories, two dimensions of individual personality are related to status: (a) the power dimension, which involves a concern with having power and influence over others, and (b) the efficacy dimension, which involves a sense that one is personally effective and capable of accomplishing one's goals (Ellyson & Dovidio, 1985; Gecas, 1982; Henley, 1977).

The power dimension would reflect a self-centered focus on power versus a concern with the wishes and needs of others (Ellyson & Dovidio, 1985; Henley, 1977). It would be based on the balance between the dominating and expressive traits. Individuals who are at the dominating pole of this dimension would exercise their own will regardless of the wishes of others; individuals who are at the expressive pole would be most concerned with others and their needs.

The efficacy dimension would reflect the sense that one is effective and capable of bringing about one's intended results versus the feeling that one is ineffectual and in need of others to give direction (Bandura, 1977, 1982). It would be based on the balance between the instrumental and submissive traits. Individuals at the instrumental pole would see themselves as highly effective in performing work-related tasks, and individuals at the submissive pole would see themselves as relatively ineffectual and as dependent on others for direction.

The meaning of these dimensions in terms of actual personality functioning is illustrated by the quote from a police officer at the beginning of the chapter. This quote reflects the officer's concern with the power dimension in individual personality. The officer describes his alternatives after making a "car stop"—either he can act in a dominating way and order the civilian to obey his commands or he can be expressive, that is, very polite and concerned about the civilian's feelings. The officer decides to exercise his authority by ordering the civilian out of the car. But what is interesting in terms of the present discussion is that the officer sees his other alternative as being overly "nice" and concerned about the needs and feelings of the civilian being arrested. In other words, the officer sees his alternatives in terms of the power dimension within personality—as being dominant and powerful versus being expressive and empathic, thereby giving the civilian increased power.

The officer's overall position on the power dimension would depend on his behaviors across many different situations; these behaviors would become summarized into personality traits. If his dominating traits far outnumber his expressive traits, he would have a strong desire to influence others. But if his expressive traits predominate, he would have little need to exercise influence.

The power dimension, which is expressed through the balance between the dominating and expressive personality traits, would be part of a more general pattern that characterizes women police officers as well as men. By the same token, the efficacy dimension, which is reflected in the balance between the instrumental and submissive traits, would also characterize members of both sexes.

Previous research has used male and female college students to examine the pattern of intercorrelations between the "gender-stereotyped" personality traits (Helmreich et al., 1981; Spence et al., 1977). The present chapter will explore whether the negative correlations found previously—between the dominating and expressive traits and between the instrumental and submissive traits—are also found in our police sample. If these patterns of intercorrelations between traits reflect general dimensions within individual personality, they should characterize high- and low-status officers within each of the partnership types.

DIMENSIONS WITHIN INDIVIDUAL PERSONALITY

Personality theorists have highlighted the importance of various dimensions within human personality (Leary, 1957; Parsons & Bales, 1955; Pervin, 1990; Wiggins, 1982). According to personality theorists, such dimensions reflect universal polarities in human experience. They are higher-order constructs that are composed of opposing pairs of personality traits. Over the course of development, an individual's position on a particular dimension can change (Greenberg & Mitchell, 1983). But once adult personality is formed, these personality dimensions are viewed as essentially stable. Although change is possible (often requiring intensive psychotherapy), in general, an individual's position on a particular dimension is seen as being relatively constant from one situation to another.

The dimensions within personality are based on experiences with other people in the environment. These experiences give rise to enduring psychological structures or patterns that reflect these experiences. The way in which important interpersonal relationships can become part of the self is highlighted in psychoanalytic object relations theory (Greenberg & Mitchell, 1983). As one plays a particular role in relation to another person, the images of the self and the interaction partner become internalized and part of one's personality. But even more important, the personality traits that are associated with these complementary images become internalized as well, so that the interconnected personality traits form a dimension within individual personality (Kernberg, 1976; Kohut, 1977).

The Power Dimension

Power refers both to a personality characteristic and to relationships within a group (Ellyson & Dovidio, 1985; Henley, 1977). As a personality characteristic, power refers to individual differences in the desire and predisposition to attempt to influence others. As an interpersonal characteristic, it describes the patterns of influence among members of a group.

There are many different types of power, but the type of power that is exercised within police partnerships would be called "legitimate power" (French & Raven, 1968). It is based on norms that specify that one officer has the right to influence another. The high-status officer has a legitimate right to influence the low-status officer, who has an obligation to accept that influence. The senior officer's legitimate right to exercise influence would be expressed through the dominating personality traits, and the junior officer's obligation to accept that influence would be expressed through the expressive traits—just as we found previously in the results from this study (see Chapter 4).

Because power differences *between* the officers in police partnerships are reflected in dominating and expressive attributes, we would expect that the dominating-expressive dimension *within* individual personality would also be related to power. Individuals who are at the dominating pole of this dimension would have a strong desire to influence others; those at the expressive pole would have little desire to exercise influence.

Psychoanalytic object relations theory can be used to explain how the traits that are manifested between the partners become internalized as structures within individual personality (Greenberg & Mitchell, 1983).

The roles associated with superior and inferior status positions are expressed through the dominating and expressive personality traits. By participating in one of these roles, officers form internal representations of the traits manifested by the self and the interaction partner. Because the dominating and expressive traits reflect the relative interpersonal power of both officers, these traits would become internalized as a personality dimension that also reflects power. Dominance would be at one pole of this dimension, and expressiveness would be at the opposite pole. An individual's *own* need for power would then be reflected in the balance between the dominating and expressive traits. Individuals with a high need for power would be at the dominating pole of this dimension, and those with little desire for power would be at the expressive pole.

People vary in their need for power, regardless of the status position they hold. Hence, we would expect variations in personality among the group of high-status officers, as well as among the group of low-status officers. Within each of these groups, some officers would have a greater desire to exert power and others would have a lesser need to exercise influence. For example, senior officers in police partnerships have the legitimate right to exert power and make most of the decisions. However, senior officers can vary in their need to exercise control—with some being more directive and others more easygoing (Hollander, 1985). These variations in leadership style would be reflected in the relative strength of the dominating and expressive traits. On the dominating–expressive dimension of personality, the more directive leader would be closer to the dominating pole and the more easygoing leader would be closer to the expressive pole.

The differing leadership styles of senior officers are illustrated in the following interviews with police officers. A very directive senior officer in an all-male police team describes how he exercises power and influences his partner to do what he wants. He states, "I would just do it and he would have to follow me. If he doesn't want to do it—fine; then I will just do it and he will follow." In contrast, a less-directive senior officer is depicted by his partner as "a very easygoing guy; very laid back." This senior officer's less directive style of exercising influence is described in the following way: "He'll have a conversation with you and he'll either convince you to do it his way or he'll explain the way it has to be done because it's the law." Despite his easygoing style, this senior officer still retains the legitimate right to exercise power because his less-experienced partner goes on to say: "I would always go with his seniority and his experience and follow that decision. If he wanted it to be done, I would always agree with his seniority because he had the experience."

Personality theorists have described dimensions within personality that bear some similarities to the dominating–expressive dimension proposed here. David Bakan (1966) emphasizes the importance of the agency-communion dimension within individual personality. Agency is similar to domination because it is manifested in the urge to master as well as in self-expansion, self-assertion, and self-protection; communion is similar to expressiveness because it is manifested in cooperation and a sense of being at one with other organisms.[1] Although Bakan posits that women are more often at the communal pole and men are at the agentic pole, he acknowledges that this is a universal dimension within human personality, and variations can occur among the members of both sexes.

Within psychoanalysis, Kohut (1977) postulates that one of the basic components of the self involves a dimension in which self-assertive, grandiose attributes are linked with empathic, nurturing attributes. This dimension is formed during childhood but can be modified later in adulthood as a result of new experiences in important relationships. The developing child's self-assertive, grandiose, and exhibitionistic impulses are promoted by the nurturing and empathic responses the child receives from the parents. These experiences then become internalized as psychic structures in which the self-assertive, grandiose image of the self is linked with another internalized image that is nurturing and empathic (Greenberg & Mitchell, 1983; Kohut, 1977). The images of self and parent then form abstract structures that are represented as interconnected personal attributes; in other words, grandiose self-assertion and empathy form a dimension within personality. Both of these personal attributes are necessary for a healthy and cohesive self, but individuals can vary along this dimension in the relative strength of their grandiose, self-assertive tendencies and their empathic tendencies.

In contrast to the present formulation involving the dominating and *expressive* traits, some personality theorists have postulated that one of the basic dimensions within personality involves the dominating and *submissive* traits (Leary, 1957; Wiggins, 1982). But evidence does not support this postulate. Dominating and submissive characteristics have been found to be essentially uncorrelated—for people's perceptions of their personality traits and for people's reports of their behaviors (Buss & Craik, 1983; Spence et al., 1979).

This is an issue we will explore in the present study with police partners: Are the dominating traits negatively correlated with the expressive traits, as proposed here? Or are they negatively correlated with the submissive traits, as postulated by some other theorists?

The Efficacy Dimension

Perceived self-efficacy refers to people's sense of their own ability to regulate events in their lives (Bandura, 1977, 1982). It is concerned with judgments of how well one can execute the actions required to deal with prospective situations. People undertake and perform actions that they judge themselves capable of managing but they avoid activities that they believe exceed their coping capabilities.

People vary in their perceived self-efficacy. Those with a high degree of self-efficacy have a strong belief in their ability to cope with and master new and stressful situations; those with little sense of self-efficacy suffer from dysfunctional fears and are not able to do what they dread (Bandura, 1977). By implication, then, perceived self-efficacy forms a dimension within individual personality in which a sense of agency or instrumentality would be at one pole and fearfulness and self-doubt would be at the other pole.

The traits comprising this dimension would be similar to the socially desirable instrumental traits and the submissive traits. The instrumental traits reflect a sense of competence and effectiveness as well as the ability to persist at tasks in the face of obstacles or aversive experiences, all of which are included in the complex cognitive, social, and behavioral skills that reflect a high degree of personal efficacy. The submissive traits, by contrast, reflect an inability to cope effectively with the environment, a lack of effectiveness, and a willingness to submit to others' judgments.

This formulation goes beyond self-efficacy theory because it proposes that perceived self-efficacy is a higher-order construct that is reflected in opposing pairs of personality traits. The complex set of skills and self-perceptions that comprise a sense of personal efficacy would relate to these opposing traits.

Support for this conceptualization comes from psychoanalytic personality theorists. Erich Fromm (1941, 1951) describes a conflict he considers to be universal within human experience—the conflict between being an independent, autonomous individual and being dependent on and submissive to an external authority. According to Fromm, the process of individuation begins in childhood. Along with a growing sense of autonomy there is an increasing awareness of one's essential aloneness. To avoid the feeling of alienation, one attempts to submerge oneself in the world outside by giving up the integrity of the self and submitting to external authorities. This conflict is acted out in childhood between the child and the parent but then becomes internalized as a conflict or "dimension" within individual personality, with autonomy or instrumentality at one pole and submissiveness at the other pole.

Erik Erikson (1959) postulates that the conflict between autonomy and self-doubt is universal within human life. Again, this conflict is rooted in early childhood and involves the child's growing sense of his or her separateness and autonomy. At issue is the child's struggle to gain self-control rather than being controlled by the parents. As before, this interpersonal conflict becomes internalized as a dimension within personality.

The notion that a sense of autonomy or personal efficacy is rooted in childhood is consistent with self-efficacy theory, which holds that a sense of personal efficacy is dependent, to a large part, on actual mastery experiences. Experiences of success heighten perceived self-efficacy; repeated failures lower it, especially if these failures occur early in one's life (Bandura, 1982).[2]

Although variations exist among individual police officers, we would expect that, as a group, police officers would be high in perceived self-efficacy (Kenney & McNamara, 1999; Manning, 1997). As part of their job, police officers frequently need to confront stressful situations; thus, in order to perform their job effectively, they would need to have a strong sense of personal efficacy. In this light, it is interesting to note that all police officers in the present study are extremely high on the instrumental traits and extremely low on the submissive traits, as we would expect (see Appendix C). This is true of all officers, regardless of their status. As a group, police officers describe themselves as being even more instrumental and less submissive than do college males.[3]

Within this group of highly efficacious police officers, however, we would expect variations in the balance between the instrumental and the submissive traits. Some officers would be closer to the more instrumental pole of this dimension, and other officers would be closer to the more submissive pole. This is illustrated in the following interview with a woman police officer. Despite her relatively short stature (she is five feet, four inches tall), she describes herself as having a strong sense of personal efficacy: "I'm a firm believer that you can de-escalate a [potentially violent] situation by the way you speak, not necessarily if you're big and they're scared. A lot of times it's not your size but what you say. If you have no brains on this job, you can really escalate the situation into something worse." She then goes on to describe how she and her male partner were able to handle situations involving family disputes between husband and wife ef-fectively—among the most dangerous situations that confront police officers in their work.

Later in the interview, she recounts an incident in which she played a major role with her partner in handcuffing a big, burly man who was undergoing a psychotic episode, complete with hallucinations:

> We had this guy who was huge; he was in the middle of the street having flashbacks and figuring a helicopter was coming down on him. He started wielding this stick around and the two of us pushed him into a car. I held his head down by his hair; I was able to hold him down so he wouldn't

bite. My partner called for backup and other civilians came over to help, so we were able to put the 'cuffs on. I don't even remember if they fit; we just held him until they brought something else. Then, finally, backup came.

When asked by the interviewer whether she had felt afraid during this episode, she responds, "I'm not going to say I wasn't scared, but you become very brave—it's just something that takes over you."

From the description she gives of her male partner, he is also high on personal efficacy but at times seems to enjoy submitting to her coaxing. For example, he did not like to do paperwork, so she would say, "'Come on, it would take 10 minutes to do the report, and I'll help you.' Then he would say, 'Fine, I'll do it myself.'"

We see from this illustration how variations in personal efficacy can be reflected in the balance between the instrumental and submissive traits. Clearly, both the female police officer and her male partner are high in personal efficacy. But the female officer appears to be closer to the instrumental pole of the instrumental–submissive dimension of personality than her male partner, who appears to have somewhat more submissive traits.

INDIVIDUAL POLICE OFFICERS AND THE PATTERNING OF THEIR PERSONALITY TRAITS

The theoretical formulation developed here proposes that individual personality is organized into two dimensions that are related to status: the power dimension and the efficacy dimension. These dimensions would be reflected in the patterning of traits among individual police officers, and so we would expect to find negative correlations between the dominating and expressive traits as well as between the instrumental and submissive traits (see Buss & Craik, 1983). The following analyses test whether these patterns are found in our sample of police officers by examining the intercorrelations between all of the "gender-stereotyped" personality traits included in the EPAQ (Spence, Helmreich, & Stapp, 1975; Spence et al., 1979).[4] Traits that are negatively correlated with one another would form the end points of a higher-order dimension of personality (Buss & Craik, 1983).

The gender-stereotyped personality traits originally were selected on the basis of their social desirability or undesirability. As a result, correlations between attributes that are similar in social desirability are likely to be spuriously high—for example, the dominating and verbally aggressive traits might be correlated positively only because both traits are considered to be unfavorable. Further, if we were to correlate desirable and undesirable personality traits, we might find spuriously high negative correlations simply because these traits differ in social desirability.

To control for the effects of social desirability, the Self-Evaluation Scale, which measures perceptions of the overall desirability of one's personality, was used as a covariate.[5] Partial correlations between pairings of personality traits were computed separately for high- and low-status officers within each of the three partnership types—all-male, male–female, and all-female police partnerships.

Dominating and Expressive Traits

All-male and male–female partnerships. The hypothesis that the dominating and expressive traits would be negatively correlated is supported by the findings for the all-male and male–female partnerships (see Tables 8.1 and 8.2). In these partnerships, negative partial correlations between dominating and expressive traits are found for police officers with high status as well as low. All of the partial correlations are highly significant ($ps < .001$ and $.01$), except for one that tends toward significance ($p < .10$).[6]

In a previous chapter, we found that the dominating and expressive traits were related to differences in status *between* police officers. The present findings show that, in addition, these traits vary inversely *within* individual personality, suggesting that individual differences in

TABLE 8.1
All-Male Police Team: Partial Correlations Between the Personality Traits of High- and Low-Status Officers

Personality Traits	Personality Traits			
	Expressive	Instrumental	Submissive	Verbal-Aggressive
High-Status Officer				
Dominating	−.24[a]	−.03	.07	.46**
Expressive		.31*	−.08	.10
Instrumental			−.37**	−.11
Submissive				.29*
Low-Status Officer				
Dominating	−.39**	.03	−.13	−.39**
Expressive		.05	.12	−.17
Instrumental			−.22[a]	−.13
Submissive				.12

Note. $df = 57$.
[a]$p < .10$. *$p < .05$. **$p < .01$.

TABLE 8.2
Male–Female Police Team: Partial Correlations Between the Personality Traits of High- and Low-Status Officers

Personality Traits	Personality Traits			
	Expressive	Instrumental	Submissive	Verbal-Aggressive
	High-Status Officer			
Dominating	−.50****	.37**	−.16	.16
Expressive		−.08	.23[a]	.19
Instrumental			−.33*	.12
Submissive				.00
	Low-Status Officer			
Dominating	−.34**	.23[a]	−.19	.28*
Expressive		−.02	.27*	.08
Instrumental			−.29*	.02
Submissive				.05

Note. $df = 54$.
[a]$p < .10$. *$p < .05$. **$p < .01$. ****$p < .001$.

the balance between the dominating and expressive traits are also related to status.

The inverse relation between dominating and expressive traits is found for high- and low-status officers in all-male and male-female police teams. Within each of these subgroups, officers who are most dominating and directive in their personal attributes are also the least expressive and accommodating, and vice versa.

We can think of these findings in terms of the hypothesized power dimension in individual personality. Within each group of senior officers in all-male and male-female teams, some officers would be more motivated to seek power, and others would be less motivated to do so. In the same way, the groups of junior officers in these teams would also show variations in their tendency to seek power.

All-female partnership. In the all-female police team, the partial correlation for the low-status officer is in the predicted direction, indicating that the dominating and expressive traits are correlated negatively (see Table 8.3). This partial correlation does not reach statistical significance ($p < .20$)—perhaps because the sample size for the all-female team is small in comparison to the other police teams, and a larger sample would have been necessary for statistical significance.

Strikingly, the partial correlation for the high-status officer is *positive* —a finding that is directly opposite to the hypothesis. Because this

TABLE 8.3
All-Female Police Team: Partial Correlations Between the Personality Traits of High- and Low-Status Officers

	Personality Traits			
Personality Traits	Expressive	Instrumental	Submissive	Verbal-Aggressive
		High-Status Officer		
Dominating	.14	.03	.02	.23
Expressive		−.12	.25	.19
Instrumental			−.27	−.19
Submissive				.25
		Low-Status Officer		
Dominating	−.30	.09	.60****	.64****
Expressive		.14	.05	−.24
Instrumental			−.04	.42*
Submissive				.05

Note. df = 24.
*p < .05. ****p < .001.

correlation does not approach statistical significance, caution needs to be exercised in interpreting its meaning. However, it appears that some senior women tend to be *both* expressive and dominating, while others tend to be low on both these traits.

Instrumental and Submissive Traits

All-male and male–female partnerships. The hypothesis that the instrumental and submissive traits would be negatively correlated is supported in all-male and male–female police partnerships (see Tables 8.1 and 8.2). In these partnerships, negative partial correlations between the instrumental and expressive traits are found for both high- and low-status officers. All of the correlations are significant ($ps < .01$ and .05), except for one that tends toward significance ($p < .10$).[7]

These findings indicate that officers who are the most highly assertive and autonomous are also the least submissive in their personal attributes, and vice versa. We know that police officers as a group score extremely high on the instrumental traits and extremely low on the submissive traits in comparison with college student samples.[8] If we interpret these results in terms of the efficacy dimension within individual personality that we have proposed, it would mean that police officers in all-male and male–female teams would have a high degree of self-efficacy. In addition, individual variations would occur with some officers experiencing themselves as having more personal efficacy than others.

All-female partnership. For the high-status woman in the all-female team, the partial correlation between the instrumental and submissive traits is in the predicted direction but fails to reach statistical significance ($p < .20$). Again, this failure might have resulted from the smaller sample size in all-female teams in comparison to the other police teams. With this qualification, the negative correlation found here is consistent with the prediction that the senior woman's instrumental and submissive traits would form a dimension within her personality (see Table 8.3).

By contrast, the correlation for the low-status woman fails to conform to the hypothesis. This correlation is close to zero, indicating that the instrumental and submissive traits are totally unrelated. Contrary to prediction, the junior woman's instrumental and submissive traits do not form any sort of dimension within her personality.

Negative Traits in the All-Female Partnership

Low-status woman's self-perceptions. Findings for the all-female partnership differ from the other partnership types. Few of the predicted correlations between personality traits are found and none of these reach statistical significance.

The low-status woman in the all-female partnership is most deviant in the patterning of her personality traits (see Table 8.3). Her dominating and submissive traits are correlated positively, and this partial correlation is strikingly high, $r = .60$, $p < .001$. In addition, we find high positive partial correlations between her dominating and verbal-aggressive traits, $r = .64$, $p < .001$, as well as between her submissive and verbal-aggressive traits, $r = .42$, $p < .05$.

This group of correlations indicates that the junior woman in the all-female team is either high or low on *all three* of the socially undesirable personality traits.[9] Most surprising is the positive correlation between the dominating and submissive traits, indicating that when the junior woman describes herself as being extremely dominating, she also describes herself as being extremely submissive, and vice versa.

These results may be explained by previous research on group interactions that has found that, in order to be effective, low-status individuals often need to accompany their acts of domination with behaviors that signal their inferior position to others (Carli, 1990; Ridgeway, 1982). Such submissive actions enable low-status individuals to exert influence over other group members. Hence, the junior woman may find it necessary to manifest submissive attributes along with her dominating attributes in order to exercise influence effectively.

But what kind of influence does she exert? Women who see themselves as occupying a weaker or subordinate position often use unilateral strategies of exercising power (Falbo & Peplau, 1980). Because they anticipate noncompliance by their partner, they take control without attempting to enlist the partner's cooperation. In contrast, people who perceive themselves as having greater status than their partner are more willing to use bilateral strategies of exercising influence because they anticipate that their partner will be compliant.

To examine whether the junior woman's constellation of negative traits reflects a unilateral strategy of exercising influence, each of these traits was correlated with the unilateral power scale. We see in Table 8.4 that all three correlations are positive, and all are very high ($ps < .01$ and .05), indicating that the junior woman's dominance, submissiveness, and verbal aggressiveness are all associated with her increased unilateral power. To explore this issue further, the junior woman's negative personality traits were then correlated with a scale that indicated how much control she perceived herself as exercising over the activities in her partnership. Again, we find that all three correlations are positive and extremely high ($ps < .001$ and .01).

These results raise some perplexing questions. One can understand easily how domineering and verbally aggressive attributes would be related to unilateral forms of power, which, by definition, ignore the needs and wishes of the partner. It is harder to comprehend why

TABLE 8.4
Low-Status Woman in All-Female Police Team: Correlations of Her Undesirable Personality Traits with Other Ratings

	Personality Traits		
Scale	Dominating	Submissive	Verbal-Aggressive
Self-Ratings by Low-Status Women			
Unilateral Power Scale	.53**	.43*	.51**
Control over Team Activities	.64****	.55**	.62****
Supervisor's Ratings of Low-Status Women			
Leadership	.50*	.35[a]	.27
Team Competence	.30[a]	.30[a]	.31[a]

Note. For self-ratings by the low-status woman, $df = 25$; for supervisor's ratings, $df = 20$.
[a]$p < .10$. *$p < .05$. **$p < .01$. ****$p < .001$.

submissiveness would also be related to the use of unilateral strategies of influence. Perhaps submissive attributes serve to discount and disguise the self-centered nature of the power that is being exercised (Ridgeway, 1982). If the low-status woman appears to be submissive, her partner might be distracted and not fully aware of the extent of the control that is being implemented (Johnson, 1976; Raven & Kruglanski, 1970). In addition, submissive attributes may serve as a form of pseudo-connectedness with the partner. At the same time that the junior woman in the all-female team is self-centered in her use of domineering and verbal-aggressive methods of exercising control, she also presents herself in other actions as being connected to her partner and even deferential.

Role of the supervisor. This is not the first time we have found deviant patterns in the all-female partnership as compared with the other partnership types. In previous chapters, we found that the supervisor played a role in encouraging deviant patterns by members of all-female teams (see Chapters 4 and 6). Perhaps here as well, the supervisor plays a role by rewarding less-conventional patterns of behaviors and traits, thereby encouraging the junior woman in the all-female police team to engage in both power-seeking and submissive behaviors and traits.

To explore this issue further, the junior woman's negative traits were correlated with the supervisor's rating of her leadership within the partnership and the supervisor's evaluation of overall team competence. We find that the supervisor's rating of the junior woman's leadership ability and overall team competence are positively correlated with all three of her negative traits (see Table 8.4).[10] These results indicate that when the junior woman describes herself as being domineering, verbally aggressive, and submissive, the supervisor evaluates her leadership ability more favorably and gives higher competence evaluations to her team.

In a previous chapter, we found that supervisors encourage deviant patterns in *senior* women from all-female police teams by rewarding them with more positive evaluations when they depict themselves as having stereotypic feminine-typed attributes, such as crying easily and having difficulty handing crisis situations (see Chapter 6). Based on the results found here, supervisors apparently promote deviant patterns in the *junior* women in these teams as well by encouraging their expression of negative personality characteristics. When junior women in all-female police teams manifest the seemingly contradictory characteristics of dominance and submission, supervisors evaluate their leadership abilities and their teams' job performances more favorably.

The present results are based on exploratory analyses of the data. However, they are consistent with findings from previous research and with other findings in this study that show that pressures from the immediate supervisor can promote unconventional patterns of traits (and also, presumably, behaviors) in members of all-female police teams (see Chapter 4).

Sex-Typing in the Male–Female Partnership

People often assume that all of the "feminine" gender-stereotyped personality scales would be related to one another, as would the "masculine" scales (cf., Spence et al., 1979). They believe that individuals who are strong in instrumentality would also be strong in domination because both are masculine-typed personality traits. Similarly, it is presumed that individuals who are high in expressiveness would also be high in submissiveness, both of which are feminine-typed traits. However, research does not support this assumption. The masculine-typed scales have very low correlations with one another, as do the feminine-typed scales (Helmreich et al., 1981; Spence et al., 1979).

Given this context, it is particularly interesting to note that masculine-typed and feminine-typed scales are significantly related to one another in the present data—but only for the male-female police partnership. When a man and woman work together as partners, the masculine-typed instrumental and dominating traits are correlated with one another for both sexes ($ps < .01$ and $.10$; see Table 8.2). Similarly, the feminine-typed expressive and submissive traits are also correlated for both sexes ($ps < .05$ and $.10$).

The male–female partnership is the only police team in which the partial correlations involving sex-typed traits approach significance; this does not occur in either of the same-sex teams. These patterns are found for both the man and the woman in the male–female partnership and involve both sets of traits—the masculine-typed as well as the feminine-typed traits. This suggests that when a man and a woman work together as partners, gender is highly salient, and their perceptions of their own personality traits reflect the use of gender-typed schemas. For example, when the man and the woman perceive themselves as being strong in instrumentality, both of them also see themselves as being strong in domination. In same-sex teams, by contrast, gender would not be salient; consequently, their personality traits would not reflect any gender-related schemas.[11]

These findings highlight the complex, multi-determined patterns that are reflected in the organization of individuals' personality traits. They suggest that instead of always reflecting universal dimensions within personality, the patterning of an individual's personality traits can be affected by situational influences—in this case, by working with a member of the "opposite" sex.

THE ORGANIZATION OF TRAITS WITHIN PERSONALITY

The question we posed at the beginning of this chapter was: How are the so-called gender-stereotyped personality traits organized within personality? Do we find the same kinds of intercorrelations in our police sample as have been found in previous research with college students—so that the dominating and expressive traits are correlated negatively, as are the instrumental and submissive traits? If so, this would lend support to the hypothesis that these interrelated pairs of traits reflect frequently occurring dimensions within individual personality.

Strong support for the hypothesis is provided by the all-male and male–female police teams. The organization of personality traits for all of the officers in these teams is consistent with the proposition that the dominating and expressive traits form a dimension within individual personality, as do the instrumental and submissive traits.

But this raises a further question: Why would these particular pairs of traits be linked together as dimensions within personality? Various theorists have proposed an answer to this question, namely, that the social structure is represented within individual personality (Leary, 1957; Morgan & Schwalbe, 1990; Parsons & Bales, 1955). People's experiences interacting with others in relationships give rise to cognitive structures that reflect these experiences (Baldwin, 1992; Berscheid, 1994). Most task-oriented relationships are structured in terms of power, so people's experiences in these relationships would give rise to the internal organization of personality along a power dimension. Similarly, the development of a sense of self-efficacy is a basic experience in human life that would lead to the organization of personality traits in terms of this continuum.

Of particular interest are the dominating and expressive traits that are related to status and power differences *between* the officers in police teams. The inverse relation between the dominating and expressive traits *within* personality parallels the interpersonal differences between officers that are found. It lends support to the idea, proposed here, that the dominating–expressive dimension within personality reflects an individual's tendency to seek power and status.

Regardless of the role that is played, whether it be one of superior or inferior status, individuals vary in their motivation to seek power. These differences would be reflected in the balance between an individual's dominating and expressive personality traits and would be manifested in stylistic differences as the officers enact their designated roles. For example, low-status officers as a group would be more accommodating than their partners, but some would appear to be more directive and others would seem to be more easygoing.

With respect to the other proposed dimension, the efficacy dimension, which involves the instrumental and submissive traits, we find that these traits are inversely related within personality as we had predicted. We would expect to find parallel differences *between* people as well but do not find any differences between high- and low-status police officers. However, when we compare police officers as a group with college student samples, we find that police officers as a group are higher on the instrumental traits and lower on the submissive traits than are college students. This suggests that the instrumental and submissive traits do, in fact, reflect differences between people.

The proposition that the instrumental–submissive dimension of personality reflects a feeling of personal efficacy—the sense that one can effectively cope with new and stressful experiences—is consistent with the expectation that police officers as a group need to be high in self-efficacy in order to perform their job effectively. Future research needs to explore further whether this dimension does indeed reflect a sense of personal efficacy.

Most intriguing are the results for the all-female police teams, which raise some interesting theoretical and empirical issues. They suggest that the power and efficacy personality dimensions proposed here are not universal; instead, the organization of personality traits can be changed by situational pressures and demands.

In the all-female teams, only weak support is found for the dominating–expressive and instrumental-submissive dimensions of personality. None of the hypothesized correlations between traits reaches statistical significance, and one is opposite to the predicted direction. Instead, low-status women in all-female police teams describe themselves as being either high or low on *all three* of the socially undesirable personality traits. Most surprising is the positive correlation between the dominating and submissive traits, which indicates that low-status women who are extremely domineering are also extremely submissive, and vice versa. This counterintuitive organization of traits can be understood from the perspective of previous research, which has found that women who attempt to exercise power from a low-status position are successful only when they accompany their influence attempts with other actions, such as submissiveness, that signal their inferior position to others.

Further exploration indicates that the low-status woman's constellation of undesirable traits reflects her use of a unilateral form of power. Because she anticipates noncompliance from her senior partner, she utilizes a type of power that ignores the needs and wishes of her partner. Apparently, supervisors play a role in encouraging low-status women to employ this form of power because they reward low-status women who manifest domineering, verbal-aggressive, and submissive personality characteristics by attributing more leadership ability to them and giving more favorable competence evaluations to their teams.

Most important, the deviant patterns we observe in all-female teams highlight the situational nature of the dimensions within individual personality. Currently, many theorists emphasize the reciprocal interactions between persons and environments (see Cervone, 1991). Not only do people influence their environment, but the environment can also have an impact on individual personality. As a result, people can change over time as new experiences become internalized and change the shape of cognitive representations (Cervone, 1991; Markus & Cross, 1987). This contrasts with the more traditional view, which assumes a basic structure of personality that is relatively unchanged in different situations (Leary, 1957; Parsons & Bales, 1955; Wiggins, 1982). Certainly, some personality characteristics appear to remain constant across different situations—and even across different cultures (McCrae & Costa, 1994, 1997). However, in the present study we find that attributes that are related to status—the so-called gender-stereotyped personality traits—reflect changing environmental circumstances. In this case, low-status women in all-female police teams appear to be strongly affected by the supervisor who encourages unconventional patterns of personality attributes and, presumably, unconventional patterns of behavior as well.

The present field study, along with previous research (Buss & Craik, 1983; Spence et al., 1979), calls for a different way of conceptualizing the patterning of personality attributes. The status model of personality organization, with its emphasis on the interconnections between interpersonal experiences and the internal structure of personality, can provide the new conceptualization that is needed. Contrary to popular belief, personality traits that are conceptually or semantically opposite one another are not correlated. No support is found for a "masculine–feminine" dimension of personality involving the instrumental and expressive traits, nor for a "dominant–submissive" dimension of personality involving the dominating and submissive traits.[12] Instead, the patterning of personality traits appears to reflect the experiences that people have in their ongoing relationships.

Status, Gender, and Personality: Toward an Integrated Theory

People assume that females would be better with kids—we know what to do. And they think it's instinct, but it's not. I'm sure there are women out there who wouldn't know where to begin with taking care of a child.
—*Female officer in a male–female police team*

It's a matter of experience. If the male officer is more experienced than the female, they'll probably do their job better. Or if the female officer has more experience than the man, many times they'll do the job just as well, if not better.
—*Male officer in an all-male police team*

The question we posed at the beginning of this book was: Why do women and men appear to have different personality traits? The answer is provided by data throughout the book: because men have higher status than women. Men typically hold positions of greater status in our society, so "male-typed" traits are associated with increased status; women generally hold positions of lesser status, so "female-typed" traits are associated with decreased status.

The status model, which was supported here, challenges the fundamental premise of the gender-specific model of gender stereotyping—namely, that gender is the primary determinant of an individual's perceived personality attributes. As the results from the police study clearly show, the major determinant involves status. Under certain circumstances an individual's sex category can become salient and can be used to designate status—as it does when a man and woman work together as police partners—but this is simply one part of the more general status processes that serve to organize interactions.

The status model challenges another assumption, implicit in the gender-specific model of gender stereotyping—that "personality" is essentially fixed in adulthood and does not vary substantially from one situation to another (Spence, Deaux, & Helmreich, 1985). By contrast, the status model draws on more recent conceptualizations of personality and postulates that one's perceived personality traits can vary from one situation to another (Cervone & Shoda, 1999; Markus & Cross, 1990). One holds differing status positions as one interacts with different people; consequently, one's behavior and perceived personality traits will vary as well.

The goal of this chapter is to integrate the various findings throughout the book into an overall theoretical framework that extends status characteristics theory to include social cognition (cf. Berger & Zelditch, 1993; Wagner, 1984). In doing so, we will develop concepts to describe how the status processes in interactions affect the personality traits attributed to the self and to the interaction partner.

As we integrate the study of the gender-stereotyped personality traits into the broader framework of social interaction and social cognition, we are able to incorporate a variety of other findings involving gender as well. In doing so, we are able to gain a better understanding of some perplexing issues involving gender and the processes that give rise to gender stereotyping. In addition, we are able to address more general issues in personality as they relate to status—issues involving self-esteem and the organization of traits within individual personality.

Finally, we will address a critical issue regarding gender: If the so-called gender-stereotyped traits relate primarily to status, what, if anything, do they have to do with gender? To answer this question we need to look at the differing perspectives of the participants in an interaction and outside observers. To the participants themselves, status is most salient, but from the point of view of an outside observer, the most salient aspect of an interaction involves gender. Consequently, for the outside observer, expectations involving gender swamp and obscure the more subtle status processes that occur in interactions, so that people are evaluated according to whether their behaviors and personality traits conform with gender norms.

SOCIAL INTERACTION AND SOCIAL COGNITION

According to the status model, the gender-stereotyped personality traits reflect the status processes that organize ongoing interactions.

Our understanding of these dispositions and the ways in which they function provides a link between social interaction and social cognition.

Social cognition traditionally has been studied by social psychologists and has been limited to issues of the mind as it functions within the individual (Fiske & Taylor, 1991; Morgan & Schwalbe, 1990). Little attention has been paid to how membership in particular social categories shapes the self (Banaji & Prentice, 1994). The latter topic has been of long-standing interest to sociologists concerned with how the organization of social life impinges on the content and functioning of human minds—how ongoing experience modifies the content of the self (Morgan & Schwalbe, 1990).

Our goal is to understand how the status processes in interactions shape the images of the self and of others. We are interested in discovering not just how people organize and represent information about themselves and others, which has been a central task of social cognition research, but how this organization is shaped by forces within the social structure (Berscheid, 1994; Gerber, 1973; Gerber & Kaswan, 1971; Kelley, 1983).

Our concern is with how the self and the other are represented in terms of traits—how the status processes in interactions shape and structure the images of the self and the other. Personality traits comprise the end point of a process that starts with characteristics that participants bring to an interaction and use to designate their relative status—characteristics such as work experience and sex category. After comparing themselves on these characteristics, the participants evolve a status order within the interaction that leads to differences in their behaviors. Based on observations of their own and their partner's behaviors, the participants then make inferences about their respective personality traits.

Most of the research involving status has been concerned with the link between the status characteristics that participants bring to an interaction and their subsequent behaviors (Webster & Foschi, 1988). By contrast, in the police study, we have focused on the link between status and people's perceptions of their personality traits. We find that status affects participants' perceived personality attributes, just as it does their behavior. Even though the gender-stereotyped personality traits have strong gender-linked associations, these associations do not determine how police officers attribute personality traits to themselves.

STATUS AND PERSONALITY TRAITS

Recent developments in social cognition have been concerned with understanding how people's cognitions relate to interactions; they have been concerned with tracing how the mental representations relevant to interactions are formed (Berscheid, 1994; Gerber, 1993). By studying members of police partnerships, we are able to examine the cognitions formed in actual ongoing relationships as these cognitions relate to status.

The images of self and the other resulting from the status processes that occur in interactions are represented by means of personality traits (Markus & Cross, 1990; Wiley & Alexander, 1987). These images are like snapshots that give a picture of reality at a single point in time. Like pictures, frozen in time, they show us the effects of various forces within the social structure on the personality traits that are attributed to the self and the other.

To conceptualize the various forces that affect personality attributions, we turn to the concept of "schema." Schemas are the building blocks of social cognition and consist of knowledge about the people and situations that comprise the social world; they are mental knowledge structures in which social information is represented (Fiske & Taylor, 1991). "Interpersonal schemas" refer to cognitive structures that represent regularities in the pattern of interpersonal relatedness (Baldwin, 1999; Planalp, 1987). They consist of a self schema, an other schema, and an interpersonal script. In this "self-with-other unit," both the self and the other are represented, in large part, by personality traits (Ogilvie & Ashmore, 1991). We are concerned here with the interpersonal schemas associated with status that represent recurring patterns of interpersonal relatedness.

Status Schemas

A "status schema" is defined here as a type of interpersonal schema in which the critical links between self and other are the expectations associated with one another's status. It includes the interpersonal script, which represents the typical interaction patterns associated with these expectations, and the personality traits associated with each individual. In an all-male police partnership, for example, the senior officer would be expected to be more competent than his partner and would have the higher status. His interpersonal script specifies that he engage in more dominating behaviors and fewer expressive behaviors than his less-experienced teammate. Associated with the high-status officer's interpersonal script would be a self schema of "officer with dominant traits" and an other schema of "officer with expressive traits."

Social cognition theory has assumed that people have multiple self schemas, and the particular subset that is activated in working memory at any given time defines the "working self-concept" of the moment (Markus & Kunda, 1986). We are concerned here with the subset of status schemas that is activated at a particular point in time and simultaneously affects the images of self and interaction partner. Based on the results from the police study, two types of status schemas are activated simultaneously: the "individual status schema," which refers to the status of each individual vis-à-vis the partner, and the "group status schema," which refers to the status of each partnership in relation to other partnerships within the larger organizational structure.

Each of these status schemas is expressed through the dominating and expressive traits. In the individual status schema, the individual with higher status has more dominating traits and fewer expressive traits than the individual with lower status. In the group status schema, partnerships with higher status are characterized as having more dominating traits and fewer expressive traits than partnerships with lower status.

As we found in the police study, both types of status schemas are activated at a given point in time and affect perceptions. Most important, each schema—the individual status schema and the group status schema—has *separate* and *independent* effects on the personality traits that are attributed to oneself—and to the interaction partner. If we again take as our illustration a high-status male police officer in an all-male team, two schemas affect his perceptions of himself on the dominating personality traits: One schema involves his status vis-à-vis his partner (individual status), and the other schema involves his own team's status in relation to other police teams (group status). At the same time that he sees himself as having higher status than his partner, he also sees himself as a member of an all-male police team, which has the highest possible status in comparison with the other police teams. Both of these schemas simultaneously affect his perceptions of himself on the dominating personality traits—he has more dominating traits in comparison to his partner and also is in the partnership characterized by more dominating traits than any of the other partnerships. The effects of each of these schemas on the dominating traits are additive. As a result, the high-status male police officer perceives himself as having more dominant traits than any of the other officers who work in police teams.

Influence Schemas

In addition to the dominating and expressive personality traits connected directly with status, other gender-stereotyped personality traits are also linked with status but in a less direct way. These gender-stereotyped traits, such as the verbal-aggressive traits, have received little attention in theory and research. But as we found in the police study, they can serve important functions within interactions (cf. Wagner & Berger, 1997).

An "influence schema" is defined here as a type of interpersonal schema (Baldwin, 1999; Planalp, 1987) that is linked only indirectly with status and involves the less-researched gender-stereotyped personality traits, such as the verbal-aggressive or submissive traits. It is based on interaction patterns that occur under certain limited circumstances; these interaction patterns serve a function for the relationship as a whole and/or for the individual participants. Influence schemas are formed during the course of social interaction as the participants observe one another's behaviors and draw inferences about the personality traits that are associated with the self and other.

In the male–female police partnership, the officers develop influence schemas of "verbal-aggressive woman" and "non–verbal-aggressive man." These are based on interaction patterns established because they are functional for the individual officers—particularly the low-status woman officer—and for the partnership as a whole.

The male–female partnership is unique in comparison with the other kinds of police partnerships because two highly salient status characteristics—sex category and seniority—can sometimes be in conflict. This means that even though the woman may have greater seniority than her male partner, she is restricted to a low-status role on the basis of her sex category. By contrast, in the all-male and all-female partnerships it would be impossible for these two status characteristics to conflict because here the partners are in the same sex category, so their relative status is designated by seniority.

Despite her inferior status position, the woman in the male–female police partnership is able to gain influence indirectly, by being verbally aggressive. In doing so, she is able to exercise more power without challenging the leadership position of her high-status male partner. Furthermore, the woman's verbal aggression enables her to experience a sense of competence on the job and serves to augment her male partner's feelings of competence as well. In addition to serving a function for the low-status woman, verbal aggression is also functional for the partnership as a whole; it provides a way for the low-status woman's experience and skills to be utilized in the decisions made within the partnership. This is of critical importance when the woman has more seniority than her male partner.

By contrast, various pressures on the high-status man discourage his use of verbal aggression. In the male–female partnership, the man is expected to take charge and is entitled to use very direct forms of power. When he attempts to use an indirect form of power such as verbal aggression, he fails to gain any increased influence and is sanctioned by his supervisor, who evaluates him unfavorably.

Because verbal aggression is functional for the low-status woman, particularly when she has more seniority than her partner, the participants evolve an interaction pattern in which the woman complains and nags more than the man. Based on the interaction patterns that are established, the participants form influence schemas of a "verbal-aggressive woman" and "non–verbal-aggressive man."

Future research can determine whether verbal aggression is functional when there is a conflict between other kinds of ascribed status characteristics and highly salient task-relevant status characteristics. For example: Would verbal aggression also be effective when race is used to designate status and there is a conflict with another salient status characteristic, such as seniority?

Another area to explore in future studies involves the submissive personality traits. Previous research has found that low-status individuals who accompany their assertive acts with submissive behaviors are able to be more effective (Carli, 1990; Meeker & Weitzel-O'Neill, 1977; Ridgeway, 1982). By signaling their low-status position to others, submissive behaviors appear to act as status disclaimers and allow the low-status person to be assertive without being penalized. In the present study, the low-status woman who worked with a male partner was perceived by her partner as both verbally aggressive and submissive. These results suggest that the low-status woman's submissive traits may have functioned as status disclaimers; they may have reinforced the woman's inferior status while permitting her to exercise influence through her verbal-aggressive traits.

Biases That Can Affect Schemas

Most of the time personality traits act as summaries of the behaviors that take place during interactions and, thereby, correspond directly to these behaviors. But sometimes biases can affect social cognition, leading to a mismatch between behaviors and traits (Fiske & Taylor, 1991). One type of bias, called the "actor–observer effect," is likely to occur when outside pressures are exerted on the participants in an interaction (Jones & Harris, 1967; Jones & Nisbett, 1972). Such pressures bias the way others are perceived but not the perception of the self. This type of bias may explain why status schemas occasionally do not correspond with predictions from the theory.

In the present study, some of the findings involving the group status of all-female police teams deviate from the theory. In their group status schemas, both members of all-female police teams perceive the partner as being more dominating and less expressive than had been predicted.[1] By contrast, results for the perception of the self correspond with the theoretical predictions. Further analyses show that supervisors give higher competence ratings to all-female teams that perceive the partner as being highly dominant and nonexpressive. It is possible that all-female teams behave more aggressively in certain situations, thus affecting their perception of the partner, and the supervisor then rewards them for their aggressive actions. But these results are also consistent with the hypothesis that external pressures from the supervisor lead to more aggressive actions under certain circumstances, thus biasing the perception of the partner—but not the self—in all-female police teams.

Most likely, members of all-female teams are torn between acting in the low-status way that is expected of their team and acting more aggressively, as is expected of police officers. They may resolve this conflict by behaving in a low-status, nonassertive way most of the time and acting aggressively in only a limited number of enforcement situations. This is an intriguing issue to be explored in future research. Most important, however, as we develop a theory that brings together social interaction and social cognition, we need to specify the conditions under which various biases can occur.

PATTERNING OF PERSONALITY TRAITS WITHIN PERSONALITY

Various theorists have proposed that the social structure is represented within individual personality (Leary, 1957; Morgan & Schwalbe, 1990; Parsons & Bales, 1955): As people interact in relationships with others, this gives rise to cognitive structures that reflect these experiences (Baldwin, 1992; Berscheid, 1994). Because most work-oriented relationships are structured in terms of status, this universal experience would give rise to the internal organization of personality along dimensions that relate to power and status. Thus, the schemas that organize the personality traits *between* people would be paralleled by the way personality traits are organized *within* individual personality.

According to this formulation, personality traits are the elements that make up the basic building blocks of personality. These elements or traits are organized into higher-order types or dimensions (Allport, 1961; Pervin, 1990). We can observe these dimensions in the patterning of the intercorrelations of personality traits—traits that are inversely related to one another would form the end points of a higher-order dimension of personality (Buss & Craik, 1983; Eysenck, 1990). The police study, as well as other research (Spence, Helmreich, & Holahan, 1979), has found the dominating and expressive traits to be correlated negatively, as are the instrumental and submissive traits, suggesting that these interrelated traits form two dimensions within individual personality.

As proposed here, the dominating and expressive personality traits would form a dimension that relates to power. Status and power differences between different types of police partnerships, as well as between the officers in each police team, are reflected in the dominating and expressive traits, so we would expect that these personality traits would form a power dimension *within* individual personality. Individuals who are at the dominating pole of this dimension would have a strong desire to influence others, and those at the expressive pole would have little desire to exercise control. Future research needs to test more specifically whether the dominating-expressive dimension in individual personality does indeed relate to power.

It is intriguing to note that the very definitions of power suggest an interconnection between the social structure and individual personality, for power refers both to interpersonal relationships and to a personality characteristic: As an interpersonal concept, power refers to the patterns of influence among members of a group; as a personality characteristic, it designates individual differences in the desire to influence others (Ellyson & Dovidio, 1985; Henley, 1977). The link between social interaction and personality implied in these definitions is highlighted by Deaux (1985, p. 72) who writes, "Concepts of power may in fact provide an important bridge between the more macro-level concerns of sociologists and the more micro-analysis of psychologists."

It also is intriguing to discover that as we go from a more macro level of analysis to a more micro-analysis, we see repeating, fractal-like patterns (Briggs, 1992) involving the dominating and expressive traits: At the organizational level, these traits reflect the relative status of different types of police partnerships; at the dyadic level, they involve the relative status of the partners; and at the individual level, they reflect a dimension within personality.

Another dimension within individual personality is formed by the instrumental and expressive traits; as proposed here, this dimension would relate to self-efficacy—people's sense of their own ability to regulate events in their lives (Bandura, 1977, 1982). Individuals at the instrumental pole of this dimension would see themselves as highly effective in performing work-related tasks, but those at the submissive pole would see themselves as relatively ineffectual and would be dependent on others for direction.

Police officers as a group would be expected to be high in self-efficacy; they would feel effective, capable of having an impact on their environment, and able to cope with and master new and stressful situations. Consistent with this presumption is the finding that police officers as a group score extremely high on the instrumental traits and low on the submissive traits as compared with college student samples.[2] Even within our sample of police officers, however, we would expect individual variations in self-efficacy, with some officers experiencing themselves as high in self-efficacy and others experiencing themselves as low. Findings in the police study support this proposition: In almost all of the police samples, the instrumental and expressive traits are inversely correlated. But again, the proposition that the instrumental–submissive dimension of personality is associated with self-efficacy needs to be tested further in subsequent research.

As proposed here, both of the dimensions within individual personality relate to status: the power dimension is related directly to status because it involves a concern with having power and influence over others; the efficacy dimension refers to a sense of personal effectance and competence, which in previous research also has been associated with status (Berger, Wagner, & Zelditch, 1985; Gecas, 1982; Webster & Foschi, 1988).

External Pressures Can Change Cognitive Representations

Personality theorists frequently have assumed that a basic structure of personality exists that is relatively unchanged across different environmental conditions. But some of the results for all-female police teams suggest that pressures from other people in the environment can become internalized and can change the shape of cognitive representations; they can change the way personality traits are organized within personality.

Results from the all-male and male–female police teams provide strong support for the proposition that personality traits are organized into two dimensions—the dominating–expressive dimension and the instrumental–submissive dimension. However, only weak support for these dimensions is found in all-female teams, suggesting that the power and efficacy personality dimensions proposed here are not universal; they can be changed by situational pressures and demands.

The low-status woman in the all-female police team perceives herself as being either high or low on *all three* of the socially undesirable personality traits—the dominating, the verbally aggressive, and the submissive traits. This constellation of negative attributes is associated with a unilateral strategy of exercising power in which the low-status woman sees herself as taking control without attempting to enlist her partner's cooperation. Most unexpected is the positive correlation between the dominating and submissive traits, which shows women who are extremely dominating are also extremely submissive, and vice versa. Also surprising is the positive correlation between the low-status woman's submissive traits and her use of a unilateral form of power—one would not expect submissiveness to be associated with taking control unilaterally with little regard for the wishes of the partner.

Previous research has shown that women are able to exercise power from a low-status position only when they accompany their influence attempts with other behaviors, such as submissiveness, that acknowledge to others their inferior status (Ridgeway, 1982). In this case, the low-status woman's submissive attributes also may have served to discount and disguise her self-centered, unilateral strategy of exercising power.

Strikingly, it is the supervisor who encourages the low-status woman to manifest the seemingly contradictory traits of dominance, verbal aggression, and submissiveness by attributing more leadership ability to her and by giving more favorable competence ratings to her team. These results suggest that the deviant patterning of personality traits that characterizes low-status women in all-female police teams is functional for them and emerges in response to external pressures from the work supervisor. In doing so, the supervisor fosters and promotes the low-status woman's use of a unilateral form of power.

A Different Way of Conceptualizing the Patterning of Traits

Conventional wisdom holds that personality traits that are conceptually or semantically opposite to one another form dimensions within individual personality. However, this assumption has not been supported empirically for the gender-stereotyped personality traits, either here or in previous research (S. L. Bem, 1974; Buss & Craik, 1983; Spence, Helmreich, & Stapp, 1975).

Commonly, it has been assumed that the gender-stereotyped traits would be organized into a "masculine–feminine" dimension, with the masculine-typed instrumental traits at one pole and the feminine-typed expressive traits at the other pole. But other studies, including the present one, have shown this *not* to be the case; the instrumental and expressive traits are essentially uncorrelated with one another (S. L. Bem, 1974; Spence et al., 1975).

Another common assumption has been that a basic dimension of personality involves power and that the dominating and submissive traits form a power-related continuum within individual personality. The present formulation does not quarrel with the postulate that personality traits can be organized into a power dimension. However, results from college student and other samples (Buss & Craik, 1983, 1984; Spence et al., 1979), in addition to the police samples that were studied here, indicate that the dominating traits form a continuum with the expressive personality traits—not with the submissive traits.

If, as we have postulated, the structures within personality parallel the interpersonal interactions that take place within the larger social structure, it would make logical sense for the dominating traits to be linked with the expressive traits, not the submissive traits. Within task-oriented relationships, such as the ones between police partners, it is most adaptive for dominating characteristics in one partner to be associated with expressive or accommodating characteristics in the other partner. One would want the less-powerful members of police partnerships to be accommodating and supportive toward the partner and capable of self-assertion whenever necessary; one would *not* want them to be submissive and self-effacing.

Sometimes, deviant patterns of personality traits can be found in limited samples, particularly in response to pressures from the environment.[3] However, in most task-oriented groups, such as police partnerships, we would expect that personality traits would be organized along the power and efficacy dimensions described here. The status model of personality organization, which emphasizes the link between interpersonal experiences and the internal structure of personality, provides the new conceptualization that is needed for understanding the patterning of traits within individual personality.

A DYNAMIC VIEW OF SELF—AND OTHER

The concept of "self" used here is a highly complex mental structure (Gergen, 1991; Robins, Norem, & Cheek, 1999; Scheibe, 1995). It is constantly responding and adjusting to the social environment by incorporating expectations involving status and expectations from other people. It is a dynamic concept of self that evolves out of a relational context (Berscheid, 1994; Markus & Cross, 1990). By the same token, one's images of others are also dynamic and evolve in response to forces in the social environment.

The personality traits that comprise the images of one's self and one's interaction partner result from multiple overlapping factors. The status schemas that organize these personality traits go beyond the notion of an interpersonal self that is affected simply by the expectations of other people. Instead, larger, overarching expectations involving status organize the personality traits attributed to *both* the self and the interaction partner so that the images of self and other are interlinked and interdependent. In addition to the status and influence schemas that organize the personality traits attributed to both interaction partners, other schemas organize the within-person dimensions of personality. All of these schemas simultaneously affect the way personality traits are attributed to the self.

In contrast to the dynamic concept of the self described here, much of the inquiry in personality psychology has been guided by the view that human nature consists of a set of dispositional tendencies that are essentially unchanging across the life cycle (McCrae & Costa, 1996, 1997). The belief that personality consists primarily of static trait structures has tended to deflect attention from the dynamic social and psychological processes through which people's personality characteristics develop (Cervone & Shoda, 1999).

This static view of personality is reflected in the metaphors for the units of the self—and others—which continue to be entity- or product-like rather than process- or relation-like (Markus & Cross, 1990). For example, within police personality research, researchers have often used the label "authoritarian" to refer to the typical police personality, as if these were qualities of individuals that remain constant over time, instead of personality attributes that may emerge as a result of forces within police organizations (Adlam, 1982; McNamara, 1999). Similarly, in work on gender, it has frequently been assumed that women are expressive and men are instrumental, thereby obscuring the situational forces that create these apparent differences in personality (Spence et al., 1985).

A further problem with much theorizing in psychology has been the use of an "individual" model that focuses on the individual actor without adequately acknowledging the impact of the social environment on personality (Howard, 1990). By contrast, the status model, proposed here, moves away from the individual models that have been prevalent and postulates that the individual is *not* primary. Instead, many of the characteristics we often think of as individual, such as personality traits, are determined situationally and result from social processes (Morgan & Schwalbe, 1990; Stryker, 1987).

As Markus and Cross (1990, p. 601) recommend, we need to develop different units to represent the "open and flexible" nature of the interpersonal self and to represent the self in ongoing relations with others as it responds to forces in the social environment. The concept of multiple status schemas, in particular, with its emphasis on over-arching patterns of organization that include the images of both the self and the interaction partner, is a step in that direction; these status schemas affect the images of *both* persons' selves as they emerge in ongoing interactions.

The Evaluation of the Self

Self-evaluation is an important component of the self. Typically, self-esteem has been viewed as a relatively stable mental structure that shows continuity over time and across situations, but more current efforts are concerned with determining how various factors in the social world contribute to self-evaluation processes (Robins et al., 1999). According to this more current view, self-evaluations are being constructed constantly during the course of social interactions; they are part of a constantly changing and malleable system.

Global self-esteem differs from the competence evaluations made by members of task-oriented groups that have been of concern to status characteristics theory (Webster & Sobieszek, 1974a, 1974b). Whereas evaluations of competence relate directly to status, with high-status individuals perceived as being more effective in performing group-related tasks, global self-esteem relates to status only indirectly. According to the results found here, status affects the personality traits that members of police partnerships attribute to themselves; the favorability or unfavorability of these traits then determines an individual's global self-esteem.

Because status is only indirectly connected to self-esteem, we can understand why increased status would sometimes lead to positive self-evaluations and sometimes not. The critical factor involves the traits associated with status. When high-status individuals possess favorable personality traits, they have high self-esteem; but when they possess unfavorable personality traits, they have low self-esteem. In the police study, increased status is associated with more of the undesirable dominating traits and fewer of the desirable expressive traits; as a result, the very highest status police officers suffer from the poorest self-esteem.

The indirect link between status and self-esteem also enables us to understand more fully a perplexing issue in status characteristics theory —why individuals would accept voluntarily a low-status role within a group when so often it has been assumed that this role is associated with poor self-esteem. However, according to the results from the police study, this is not the case. Individuals in low-status roles can evaluate themselves positively; it depends on the desirability of the traits that are associated with their inferior-status role. By focusing on the processes by which personality traits relate to status, we are able to determine whether decreased status is likely to produce a favorable or unfavorable view of the self.

In contrast to the position taken by many self-evaluation theorists (Allport, 1961; James, 1890; Rosenberg, 1979), the findings from the police study demonstrate that the motive to maintain a positive view of the self is not always primary: People do not always seek to maintain a positive view of the self. In the police study, the determining factor is the desire to comply with status expectations regardless of the impact on self-esteem. This provides support for the argument that the motive to maintain social bonds and meet social expectations—in this case, expectations involving status—can override the motive to maximize one's self-esteem (Baumeister, 1998; Meeker & Weitzel-O'Neill, 1977; Swann, 1990).

GENDER IS SALIENT—BUT ONLY TO OUTSIDE OBSERVERS

The most remarkable finding in this study, even though predicted by the theory, is that from the point of view of the participants in an interaction, the so-called gender-stereotyped personality traits do not relate to gender. Instead, these traits relate directly to status. The fact that the dominating traits are associated with men and the expressive traits are associated with women is irrelevant to the participants themselves.

But from the perspective of an outside observer, gender is extremely salient. It is such a powerful stimulus that expectations involving gender overwhelm and obscure the other aspects of interactions. Even to an outside observer such as a police supervisor, who might be expected to encourage police partners to comply with status expectations in order to enhance their job performance, gender is still the most salient aspect of the interaction. It is so overwhelmingly important to the supervisor, as outside observer, that his evaluation of certain police team members is dependent on whether or not their personality traits comply with gender norms (cf. Foschi, 1992, 1998).

This phenomenon is not unique to policing; many studies have demonstrated that outside observers evaluate the competence and likeability of women and men according to whether or not their behaviors correspond with gender norms (Costrich, Feinstein, Kidder, & Maracek, 1975; Cowen & Koziej, 1979).

We can understand this phenomenon by noting that expectations involving gender are not simply descriptive; they are prescriptive as well (Deaux & LaFrance, 1998; West & Zimmerman, 1987). Men and women are not just believed to possess different personality traits; in addition, they are *supposed* to manifest personality traits consistent with their sex category. Outside observers are particularly sensitive to the prescriptive nature of gender stereotypes because for them sex category is highly salient. As a result, observers constantly monitor the behaviors of others to judge whether or not their behaviors are consistent with gender norms.

As a first step, the outside observer engages in an automatic monitoring process in which individuals are categorized as either "female" or "male" (West & Zimmerman, 1987). After this categorization is made, the observer then looks for behavioral cues to confirm that the individual is in compliance with gender norms. It is assumed that individuals possess an "essential nature" or gender identity—a nature that can be discerned through the behaviors or "signs" expressed by them (Goffman, 1976, p. 75). It is also assumed that men and women will manifest behaviors that correspond to a sex-consistent gender identity; when they do so, observers are not motivated to look for other cues to validate their gender identity.

Thus, when individuals enact roles *consistent* with their sex category because of their status position, observers use the instrumentally oriented dominating characteristics and the expressive characteristics to confirm that the individual is in compliance with gender norms. In a male–female police partnership, for example, the high-status man manifests the dominant behaviors prescribed for males and the low-status woman exhibits the expressive behaviors prescribed for females. Observers would then assume that both officers have appropriately sex-typed gender identities and would not seek out other cues as to their essential natures.

But when a woman or a man engages in behaviors that go *counter* to gender norms, observers actively seek out clues to that individual's essential nature. When a person's dominating and expressive characteristics deviate from gender norms, gender becomes highly salient to observers, and they look for other "gender markers" or cues in order to confirm—or disconfirm—whether the individual has an appropriate gender identity. Thus, from the point of view of an observer, individuals are able to engage in gender-distinct behaviors without being penalized *as long as they also manifest other behaviors considered appropriate for their sex category*. When they fail to do so, observers penalize them by evaluating them as less competent, as less likeable, and as having an inappropriate gender identity (Costrich et al., 1975; Cowen & Koziej, 1979; Gerber, 1990).

The bipolar personality traits, which reflect idealized characteristics associated with femininity and masculinity, serve as gender markers. As the present research with police partners indicates, the supervisor as outside observer uses the behaviors reflected in these traits to determine whether or not individuals manifesting gender-distinct characteristics possess an appropriately sex-typed gender identity.

The high-status woman in the all-female partnership and the low-status man in the all-male partnership are expected to engage in gender-distinct behaviors. Upon observing their behaviors, the immediate supervisor, as outside observer, would seek out other behavioral cues or gender markers to confirm that the officer is in compliance with gender norms. From the point of view of the supervisor, the need to find confirmations (or disconfirmations) of the officers' "essential" gender identity overrides all other considerations—including the motivation to supervise the officers under his command effectively and reward behaviors that facilitate good job performance.

Because of her high status, the more-experienced woman in the all-female police partnership is expected to assume a leadership role and manifest gender-distinct behaviors, which include being more dominant and less expressive in comparison to her female partner. Unless she also describes herself as having feminine-typed bipolar characteristics, such as crying easily and having difficulty handling crisis situations, the supervisor downgrades her job performance ratings and the competence evaluations of her team.

The masculine-typed bipolar characteristics that the supervisor penalizes are essentially interchangeable with those of a good police officer. Most probably, without being aware of what he is doing, the supervisor therefore promotes behaviors that are totally incompatible with good police work. From the supervisor's perspective as outside observer, gender becomes so salient that it swamps all other considerations, including the promotion of effective police work by the high-status female officers under his supervision.

The low-status man in the all-male police partnership is also in a gender-distinct role. Because of his low status, he manifests more feminine-typed characteristics—he is more expressive and less dominant—in comparison to his partner. But here the supervisor's biased evaluations work to the low-status man's advantage. When the low-status man describes himself as having masculine-typed bipolar characteristics, the supervisor awards more favorable job performance evaluations to him and to his team. The masculine-typed bipolar characteristics, which include keeping one's emotions under control and handling crisis situations effectively, are essentially interchangeable with those of an ideal police officer, so the low-status man benefits from the supervisor's biased evaluations because they reward characteristics that enhance his work.

The gender-linked biases that affect outside observers have been demonstrated in laboratory studies of social cognition (Costrich et al., 1975; Cowen & Koziej, 1979; Foschi, 1998). The way in which normative gender-associated behaviors can mitigate the potentially damaging effects of people's nonnormative gender-related behaviors has been demonstrated in laboratory settings as well (Ridgeway, 1982; Wagner & Berger, 1997). But these biases are most striking when they are manifested by police supervisors in an actual work situation and when the behaviors that are rewarded go directly counter to ones that make for good, effective job performances.

Most important, the present research demonstrates the crucial role the bipolar personality traits play in mitigating the potentially damaging effects of people's gender-deviant behaviors on evaluations of their competence by outside observers in actual work situations. The research with police partners shows that even though the bipolar personality traits appear to be related primarily to gender, because they reflect idealized characteristics associated with femininity and masculinity, they are actually related to status processes. The bipolar traits reflect the way status interacts with gender norms to affect the evaluations made by outside observers.

TOWARD AN INTEGRATED THEORY

Implications for Gender Stereotyping

By using the status model as our conceptual framework, it becomes possible to develop a unified theory involving the gender-stereotyped personality traits and social interaction. In doing so, we are able to integrate a variety of findings involving gender and personality into an overarching theory (cf., Berger & Zelditch, 1993; Wagner, 1984).

The status model extends recent theoretical work on gender in which status is viewed as one component—often an important component—of gender stereotyping (Collins, 1990; Connell, 1987; Eagly, 1987; Lorber, 1994). It goes beyond this work by positing that status is the *primary* determinant of the so-called gender-stereotyped personality traits. The status model describes how sex, as well as many other variables, such as job seniority or education, can all be used similarly to designate status. As a result, they can all have similar effects on people's behavior and apparent personality traits.

Further, the status model extends previous work on gender and personality by encompassing all of the gender-stereotyped personality traits, not just the instrumental and expressive attributes that have been the concern of most theoretical and empirical work (Spence et al., 1985). It includes gender-stereotyped personality attributes, such as the verbal-aggressive and submissive traits, that have received relatively little attention in research, and shows how all of the gender-stereotyped attributes, including the less-researched attributes,[4] relate to the status processes that take place in interactions. These include interactions between members of the same sex as well as between women and men.

The research with police partners extends the empirical work on gender and personality in an additional way—by showing that status can account for the personality traits attributed to *actual people*. Previous studies have shown that status differences between the sexes can account for people's *stereotypes* about men's and women's personality traits (Conway, Pizzamiglio, & Mount, 1996; Gerber, 1988, 1991; Smoreda, 1995). The present findings demonstrate that status also accounts for the way actual people perceive themselves and their interaction partners on these personality traits.

The status-related personality traits. As we have seen throughout the book, each of the so-called gender-stereotyped attributes is associated with the status processes that take place in task-oriented interactions. Because each of these personality attributes is linked in some way with status processes, it is proposed that they be renamed the "status-related personality traits."

Some status-related traits, such as the dominating and expressive attributes, are directly linked to status. In police partnerships, these attributes reflect differences in status between the partners, as well as between different types of partnerships. Other status-related traits, such as the verbal-aggressive and submissive attributes, are only indirectly associated with status. Within police partnerships, they make it possible for women in low-status positions to gain in power and influence: The verbal-aggressive attributes provide a way for low-status women officers who work with male partners to acquire influence without challenging the leadership position of their partner. The submissive attributes, in combination with other overtly dominant personality attributes, enable junior women in all-female police teams to attain greater control.[5]

The instrumental traits have been related to status in a number of previous studies (Conway et al., 1996; Gerber, 1988, 1991, 1993; Smoreda, 1995) but were not associated with status differences in the present study. Police officers as a group perceive themselves as being high on these traits, regardless of their status. But this may be typical of law-enforcement occupations, such as policing, in which everyone needs to manifest highly assertive, instrumental characteristics in order to be effective. Studies with other populations, such as college students, may very well show that the instrumental traits do indeed relate to status. Even though instrumental attributes are not associated with status differences *between* police officers in the present study, they are included in the status-related efficacy dimension *within* individual personality.

The bipolar traits are most intriguing from the point of view of status theory because, on the surface, they appear to be associated with gender—they reflect idealized characteristics associated with femininity and masculinity. But in the police study, we found that the bipolar attributes, and presumably the behaviors they reflect, are also associated with status processes; they serve a special function for outside observers, such as police supervisors. Whenever police officers are required by their status to manifest personality characteristics that go contrary to gender norms, the bipolar attributes serve to counter the negative impressions associated with their gender-deviant characteristics.

Gender issues from a status perspective. Sex category is one of the first distinguishing categories that infants can discern and is used throughout the life span as a primary strategy for categorizing the world and one's observations of other people (Constantinople, 1979). The assumption that sex category or gender is primary has also pervaded many of our implicit theories of personality, for it often has been assumed that gender is a major organizing factor in personality (Epstein, 1988; Hare-Mustin & Maracek, 1990; Lewin, 1984a, 1984b).

During the past thirty years, as empirical research on gender and gender stereotypes has burgeoned, we have found, often to our surprise and initial disbelief, that gender does *not* play a central role in personality. The discovery that many of our assumptions about gender and personality have been wrong has opened the way for us to gain a deeper understanding of some perplexing issues in personality. As we explore these issues further, we are able to gain a better understanding of the processes that affect personality (Cervone & Shoda, 1999; Hare-Mustin & Marecek, 1994).

Most fundamental has been the assumption that women and men have different personality traits. As shown throughout the book, all of these presumed differences in personality can be accounted for by status.[6] But assumptions about gender have pervaded other aspects of our theorizing as well. Earlier research had found that, contrary to people's assumptions, the instrumental and expressive traits do *not* form a masculine–feminine dimension within individual personality; these traits essentially are uncorrelated with one another (S. L. Bem, 1974; Spence et al., 1975). Instead, the status-related personality traits are generally formed into two dimensions within personality: a dominating–expressive dimension, which as we have proposed is related to power, and an instrumental–submissive dimension, which is hypothesized here to relate to self-efficacy—a sense of one's ability to bring about one's intended effects.

Another issue involves self-esteem. Often, it has been assumed that status is associated directly with self-esteem. Because women generally have lower status than men, investigators have looked for substantial self-esteem differences between the sexes. But instead, they have discovered women and men to be very similar in their self-evaluations (Kristen, Hyde, Showers, & Buswell, 1999; Maccoby & Jacklin, 1974; Major, Barr, Zubek, & Babey, 1999). Studies find that sometimes men score higher in self-esteem, and sometimes women (Maccoby & Jacklin, 1974; Major et al., 1999). These perplexing findings lead us to question the assumption that status is linked directly with self-esteem; further, they underscore the importance of understanding the processes that affect self-evaluations.

In the police study we found that, contrary to conventional beliefs, status bears only an indirect relation to self-esteem; the critical factor involves the personality traits that are associated with status. When status is linked with high levels of undesirable traits, as in our sample of police officers, high status can lead to diminished self-esteem. But in other populations, when status is linked with more desirable personality traits, higher status would be associated with increased self-esteem.

Based on our expanded understanding of the processes that affect self-evaluations, we can return to the question of sex differences and self-esteem. Typically, women and men are perceived as having both favorable and unfavorable personality attributes (Spence et al., 1979). As a result, we would expect them both to have similar levels of self-esteem. When men and women show differing levels of self-esteem in certain samples, we would expect differences in the social desirability of the personality traits each sex attributes to the self.

In our theories about gender, we also need to differentiate between the perspective of individuals who participate in interactions and the perspective of outside observers. As we found in the police study, the participants are focused on status and on the behaviors and personality traits that are expected of their status. But for outside observers, gender is most salient—whether or not the individuals' personal attributes correspond with gender norms.

These differing perspectives can help us integrate seemingly disparate findings involving outside observers and participants. Because gender is so salient for outside observers, they often disapprove of individuals who engage in gender-distinct actions; but the participants themselves would perceive their actions as valuable and legitimate (Denmark, 1980).

By differentiating between these two perspectives we can begin to understand some of the ongoing pressures that are exerted on individuals in an attempt to bring their behaviors and traits into compliance with gender norms. We can also understand why men and women would choose willingly to engage in behaviors and manifest traits that appear to others to be in conflict with gender norms; for the individuals themselves such a conflict would be irrelevant and, without the interventions of outside observers, would likely go unnoticed.

Implications for Social Cognition and Social Interaction

As we build a bridge between social interaction and social cognition, the status-related personality traits are most critical because, according to the status model, these traits reflect the behaviors that emerge in task-oriented interactions. By examining people's perceptions of themselves on these traits and comparing them with their observable behaviors, we can begin to delineate more precisely the links between social interaction and social cognition in future research studies. We can also lay out more specifically the interconnections with other internal processes, such as self-evaluation.

Current theorizing in psychology and sociology has been concerned with the images of self and other that are formed during interpersonal relationships (Berscheid, 1994; Markus & Cross, 1990; Wiley & Alexander, 1987). According to Markus and Cross (1990), the most evident roadblock to greater specification of these images is the lack of theories and models that meaningfully incorporate the roles of self and other. The status model, with its emphasis on overarching schemas that emerge from the status processes in interactions, holds promise for being able to specify more precisely the way the self and the interaction partner are perceived. These schemas indicate that the self does not necessarily hold a central position in one's cognitions about relationships. Instead, status schemas summarize overall interactional patterns and determine the personality attributions that are made to both the self and the interaction partner in the context of ongoing relationships.

Implications for Policing

If a woman is a cop—a real cop—then she's going to be the same as
a real male cop who's going to be the same as she is.
                                        —*Male officer in an all-male police team*

One of the critical questions in policing is whether men and women
police officers have different personality traits. Many people believe
that if they do, women police officers never will be able to function as
effectively as men; they never will be able to manifest the highly
assertive personality characteristics that are necessary for the job of
police officer.

In this study of police partners, we find that women officers can
appear to have different personality attributes, but only because they
have lower status in relation to men. The personality traits that are
affected by status are the dominating and expressive traits; these traits
reflect the status of different types of police teams as well as the status
of the individual officers within each team. Higher status is associated
with dominating attributes and lower status with expressive attributes.

Remarkably, however, police officers as a group, both female and
male, are characterized by very high levels of the instrumental traits—
attributes that often have been viewed as the defining characteristics
for men (Spence, Deaux, & Helmreich, 1985).[1] These findings indicate
that police officers are seen as decisive and assertive—most probably
because police officers need to possess these qualities in order to enforce
the law (Manning, 1997; Storms, Penn, & Tenzell, 1990).

An alternate interpretation would be that the high level of instrumental traits that characterizes police officers reflects the masculine-typed nature of the field of policing. To be sure, policing is a masculine-typed occupational field with a greater proportion of men in comparison to women. But these traits reflect behaviors that are required of all individuals who occupy the role of police officer, regardless of their sex.[2]

The status approach to studying the personality attributes of police officers, which is supported here, is very different from the approach that traditionally has been used. Generally, it has been assumed that a modal personality typifies all police officers and distinguishes them from other occupational groups (Burbeck & Furnham, 1985; Skolnick, 1994). By contrast, the status approach postulates that police officers are subject to the same kinds of processes that operate in other work groups. These processes affect police officers' behaviors, which in turn affect their perceptions of their personality attributes.

The relationship between police officers who work together as partners rarely has been studied empirically. This is an important area of research because many police officers work as partners, particularly in large urban areas (Department of Justice, 1992). By utilizing the status model as our conceptual framework, we are able to draw on basic psychological and sociological principles to understand better the processes that operate in police partnerships. In the present chapter, we will review how these processes affect the personalities of male and female officers who work in police partnerships and discuss their implications for policing.

By focusing on status and the situational factors that affect police officers' personality traits, we are able to integrate other areas of research into the study of "police personality." These include the impact of supervisors' evaluations on individual officers and the study of police officers' self-esteem. Most important, we are able to see how situational factors in different types of police partnerships can put certain police officers at risk for low self-esteem and other kinds of stress.

STATUS EFFECTS ON MALE AND FEMALE OFFICERS' PERSONALITY TRAITS

Despite the fact that research has shown that women officers perform their job as competently as men, many people still believe that men make better police officers. Men are thought to have more of the dominant personality traits that are believed to be necessary for effective police work. By contrast, women—even women police officers—are thought to have more accommodating traits (Lunneborg, 1989; Martin, 1990).

Contrary to popular belief, the present study has demonstrated that police officers' perceptions of themselves on the dominating and expressive personality traits are determined by status, not sex category. For example, when women are in high-status roles, they are characterized by more dominance in comparison to their partners, and when men are in low-status roles, they are characterized by more expressiveness. The question we need to ask ourselves is: What maintains the belief that women police officers have different personality traits than men? Usually there is a "kernel of truth" that appears to validate people's stereotypes (Allport, 1954); hence, people's observations must in some way appear to substantiate the belief that female and male police officers have different personalities.[3]

We know from the police study that the members of police partnerships themselves are focused on status. They want to perform their assigned tasks most effectively; in order to do so, the officers who are believed to be more competent are perceived as having higher status. The reason male and female police officers can appear to have different personalities is because sex-related variables are used, at times, to designate status. When a man and a woman work as partners, their relative status is determined by their sex category; in addition, the overall status of different types of police teams is designated by the proportion of women and men who work in these teams.

Because sex plays a role in the way status is assigned—both to the officers in male–female police teams and to different types of teams— male officers as a group generally hold higher-status positions than female officers.[4] As a result, a majority of men appear to have dominating attributes and a majority of women appear to have expressive attributes (Gerber, 1996).[5] On the basis of their observations, people then conclude that male and female police officers have different personality traits—a conclusion that simply confirms people's preconceptions about sex differences in personality. But this is a misreading and misinterpretation of reality. The observation that female officers, as a group, appear to be more expressive and less dominating than male officers is a consequence of their lower status, not their sex category.

If one were to maintain that greater dominance and lessened expressiveness is necessary for women to function more effectively as police officers—a debatable point (Jurik & Martin, 2000)—then the key issue would involve women's status within policing. If women were given equal status, then we would expect they would be perceived as having the same personality attributes as men (Denmark, 1977; Gerber, 1988; Hare-Mustin & Marecek, 1994).

In that case, the proportion of males and females would no longer be used to designate the status of different police teams; all-female and male–female teams would be equal in status to the all-male teams. Further, sex category would no longer be used to designate status in male–female police teams. When a woman officer worked with a man as partner, status would be determined on the basis of seniority, as it is in the all-male and all-female teams (see Webster & Hysom, 1998).

A strong case can be made for the relevance of experience to performance as a member of a police team. To be sure, some tasks within policing do require physical strength, but these comprise only a small part of the functions performed by police officers (Egan, 1991; Goldstein, 1990; Martin & Jurik, 1996; see also Yoder, 1989). It can be argued that the judgment and wisdom that come with experience supercede the ability to perform the limited number of acts that require physical strength.

IMPACT OF STATUS IN DIFFERENT POLICE TEAMS

Not only do status processes affect the personality traits that characterize officers who work in police teams, but they can impact other aspects of their functioning as well. By taking a closer look at the way in which status affects different types of police teams, we can understand better some of the pressures that operate on the individual officers in these teams.

Male–Female Police Teams

In male–female police partnerships, status is determined by the officers' sex category. A woman who works with a man is restricted to a low-status position within the partnership, regardless of how much seniority she has (Lunneborg, 1989; Martin & Jurik, 1996). The only way women in such partnerships can gain influence is by using an indirect form of power, namely, verbal aggression. This is particularly important when a woman has greater seniority than her male partner. As the results from the study clearly show, women with more seniority are more likely to be verbally aggressive. By using this indirect form of power, women are able to exercise influence from their low-status position without challenging the leadership position of their male partners. In doing so, they feel more successful in their work, and their male partners feel more successful as well.[6]

Thus, by using verbal-aggression, women are able to circumvent the established status order and cope more effectively with their low-status position. They gain more influence over the decisions made in the partnership, thereby minimizing some of the frustrations they might feel as a result of being restricted to a low-status role. This makes it possible for the woman's experience and knowledge to be utilized in the decisions made in the partnership, thereby enhancing her and her male partner's feelings of competence (Hollander, 1992; Hollander & Offermann, 1990).

However, for men in male–female teams, verbal aggression fails to serve a useful function. It fails to gain them any increased influence and is unrelated to their sense of competence.[7] Further, when men are verbally aggressive, they are penalized by their supervisors, who evaluate them as being less effective in their work. Because men already hold a high-status position by virtue of their sex category and are entitled to use very direct forms of power, supervisors may feel they have no need to use an indirect form of power such as verbal aggression and that when they do so, they undermine their own authority. Another reason supervisors impose sanctions on verbally aggressive men may be that nagging and complaining traditionally have been associated with women and are inconsistent with the expected masculine role.

These findings are important because they indicate that, in male–female police partnerships, the woman's verbal aggression is functional for her, for her male partner, and for the partnership as a whole. They implicitly acknowledge that the women in such teams are restricted to a low-status role and need to have some means of exercising greater influence, particularly when they have more experience than their male partners.

But such an exercise of power requires a complicated balancing act for the women as well as for the men. On the one hand, women are expected to manifest the expressive personality attributes associated with their lower-status position. But on the other hand, they are expected to exercise more influence—albeit indirectly, by using verbal aggression. For the men in these partnerships, it may be problematic as well. They are expected to manifest the dominant personality attributes associated with their higher status, yet at the same time they are expected to relinquish some of their power and allow their female partner to participate in making more of the decisions. Would it not be simpler to acknowledge openly that more senior women who work with male partners are entitled to assume the high-status position within the partnership and are entitled to be more directive? To be sure, this would violate the cultural expectation that the man should act as the leader whenever he works with a woman. But if police administrations were to encourage officers to use seniority to designate status in male–female teams—as is done in the all-male and all-female police teams—it might help relieve some of the pressures on both officers (see Webster & Hysom, 1998).

Such status designations could be encouraged as part of the initial training of police officers. Guidelines could be established by which police officers with more seniority, whether female or male, would be expected to exercise greater leadership in all types of police partnerships—including those in which a woman and man work together. This expectation would simply be an extension of the regulation that higher-ranking police personnel, female as well as male, have the right to exercise leadership over those of lower ranks.

Thus far, we have discussed the use of sex to designate the relative status of the individual officers in male–female police teams. But the status of a team as a whole is also dependent on a sex-related variable, namely, the proportion of male and female officers who make up each team. Because of this, male–female police teams are intermediate in status between the all-male and all-female police teams. This means that a male officer who works with a woman as partner, instead of with a man, suffers a *decrease* in his team status—a factor that may explain partially men's reluctance to work with women.[8]

Because overall team status affects personality, men who work with female partners are perceived as less dominating and more expressive than those who work in all-male police teams. This finding is consistent with observational accounts of police officers showing that men who work with women are less aggressive and less likely to precipitate violent confrontations with civilians than men who work with other men (Adler & Denmark, 1995; Kennedy & Homant, 1983; van Wormer, 1981).

Thus, the decreased aggressiveness of men who work with female partners can have beneficial effects for police organizations and for the communities they serve. The problem is that the decreased aggressiveness of male–female police teams, as compared with all-male teams, is based on their lower status.[9] It must be frustrating for men who work in male–female teams to find that they have lower status and are perceived as less competent than those who work in all-male teams. This may explain why male police officers are often reluctant to work with women officers (Martin & Jurik, 1996). As shown by the initial survey of all police teams throughout New York City, fewer male–female teams existed than would be expected if partnerships were formed simply on the basis of chance.[10]

One way of dealing with the problem is for police organizations to find ways of equalizing the status of male–female police teams in relation to all-male teams without increasing their overall aggressiveness. To equalize the status of different police teams, overall team status would need to be redefined so that it no longer was based on the proportion of men and women; instead, it would be based on another variable like seniority. Consequently, male–female and all-male police teams that were comprised of officers with equal seniority would be perceived as equally competent.

Another issue involves the behaviors and personality traits associated with overall team status. The problem now is that officers in the highest-status (all-male) police teams can sometimes be overly aggressive. One way of reducing excessive aggressiveness in high-status police teams, regardless of the way in which status is designated, would be to change the norms that govern police organizations so that the interpersonal skills reflected in the expressive traits are valued, as are the enforcement skills reflected in the dominant and instrumental traits (Herbert, 1997; Hollander & Offermann, 1990). During their initial training, police officers could be encouraged to be flexible in their behavior; their instruction could emphasize how many situations, such as domestic disputes, require police officers to show patience and compassion in addition to assertiveness and strength (Herbert, 1997). If officers in high-status police teams were encouraged, at times, to be more expressive and less dominant, their potential for overaggressiveness would be reduced, and they would be able to fulfill more effectively all aspects of the police officer's role.

All-Male Police Teams

In the overwhelming majority of police teams, two men work together as partners, but research rarely has focused specifically on the problems associated with these teams. Thus, it is of critical importance to find, as we did in this police study, that the highest-status police officer in our sample has the poorest self-esteem. The more experienced man in the all-male police team has higher status than his partner and, in addition, he is in the team with the most status. As a result, this highest-status man has the greatest number of dominating traits and the fewest expressive traits of all the officers in our sample. Because dominating traits are socially undesirable and expressive traits are socially desirable, the highest-status man has the fewest positive traits. Because he has so many undesirable personality traits, he has the poorest self-esteem. The more experienced man's low self-esteem has wide-ranging effects on his self-image. For example, he sees himself as less intelligent than do other police officers even though, by all indications, he is just as bright as they.[11]

A number of anecdotal accounts have suggested that as male police officers gain in experience, their self-esteem may actually show a decrease (Adlam, 1982; Bonifacio, 1991; Doerner, 1985). The present findings indicate that the critical variable—at least among male police officers who work as partners—is not overall experience, but an officer's experience relative to the partner, which can determine the officer's status in relation to the partner.[12]

Low self-esteem has been linked with a variety of personal and interpersonal difficulties, including depression and even suicide (Abramson, Metalsky, & Alloy, 1989; Baumeister, 1990; Beck, 1975); thus, the present findings highlight the importance of further research on police officers' global self-esteem.[13] They also point to a subgroup of police officers—the more experienced men in all-male teams—who appear to be most at risk for personal and interpersonal difficulties.

Police organizations as a whole and the immediate supervisors who work most closely with police officers need to be especially attuned to the problems of low self-esteem that can confront these senior men. They need to be alerted to the potentially serious personal and interpersonal difficulties often associated with low self-esteem and intervene with senior officers who appear to need assistance. Such interventions can take the form of a quiet word of advice or a referral for psychological counseling for those whose problems appear to be more severe.

But efforts by police organizations need to go beyond simply focusing on the high-status man as an individual. The difficulties faced by the high-status man in the all-male team cannot be ameliorated by focusing on him alone because they are rooted in the very ideals that govern many police organizations. A "real cop" is defined as a highly aggressive officer, indicating that he exemplifies an ideal toward which all police officers should strive (Herbert, 1997). Thus, these very high-status male officers who manifest extreme dominance and minimal expressiveness exemplify the personality attributes of the ideal police officer.

When police organizations define highly aggressive, dominating attributes as the ideal, they implicitly disparage the expressive skills involved in managing interpersonal disputes (Herbert, 1997). Perhaps the issue for police organizations is one of redefining the ideal police officer to include some expressive attributes, in addition to more positive instrumental attributes such as assertiveness. Dominance still would be considered necessary under certain circumstances but no longer viewed as the sole defining characteristic of the ideal police officer (Hollander & Offermann, 1990). If the definition of the ideal police officer were expanded to include some expressive qualities, officers would gain the flexibility to deal more effectively with interpersonal disputes and the communities in which they work. Further, senior men in all-male police teams could draw on the socially desirable expressive personality attributes to help maintain their self-esteem.[14]

Thus far, we have focused on the senior men in all-male police teams. But what about the junior men in these teams? They also can experience problems in their work. Even though the low-status man is in the highest status team in the police department, he is expected to be more accommodating than his partner and manifest more expressive and fewer dominating attributes. In other words, he is expected to exhibit more "feminine-typed" characteristics in comparison to his partner. Unless he demonstrates that he is "masculine" on other characteristics, known as the bipolar traits,[15] the supervisor downgrades his performance evaluations. He must show that he is aggressive, nonemotional, and able to handle crises effectively or be rated less competent.[16]

Because the low-status man is unaware that his bipolar characteristics are related to the way his supervisor evaluates his competence, he must feel perplexed by his evaluations. From his perspective, these assessments are unrelated to his job performance. He is not aware that his supervisor rewards masculine-typed bipolar characteristics and penalizes him when he manifests feminine-typed bipolar traits. Some important issues thus need to be addressed, especially the failure of the supervisor to explain his competence evaluations to the low-status man, which occurs most probably because the supervisor does not realize the true basis for that assessment. In addition, the question of whether masculine-typed bipolar characteristics are at all relevant to the low-status man's effectiveness in police work needs to be addressed. Theses characteristics may in fact promote the development of "emotional hardening," which can be associated with personal and interpersonal problems in police officers (Yarmey, 1990).

All-Female Police Teams

All-female teams are relatively new within the police department, and initially many supervisors were reluctant to let two women work together as a team. Supervisors were concerned about the women's safety and questioned whether they could win the respect of the public and effectively enforce the law. In more recent years, supervisors have allowed female officers to work together as partners. But the number of all-female teams in the NYPD is still very small, comprising only 4 percent of the teams that work on patrol.[17]

Because all-female police teams are still quite rare and because they work in such a highly masculine-typed occupational field, it must be hard for supervisors to know how to supervise them effectively. In addition, police departments often subscribe to traditional values, especially with respect to gender. As a result, supervisors may feel caught between the desire to encourage the members of all-female police teams to be more authoritative and the expectation that they should meet at least some of the traditional norms for women. In an attempt to resolve this dilemma, supervisors may pressure all-female police teams to act differently from the other kinds of teams because throughout the study, we see repeatedly that all-female teams are characterized by deviant patterns in relation to other kinds of police teams. And over and over again, we see that these deviant patterns are associated with pressures that come from the immediate supervisor.

Let us first examine the status of all-female teams within the police department as a whole. These teams have the lowest status in comparison to other kinds of police teams; consequently, the members are expected to manifest more expressive attributes and fewer dominating attributes than members of other teams. As expected, the officers' self-ratings on these traits are consistent with their low status. But contrary to prediction, their combined ratings of *one another* show much more dominance and much less expressiveness than predicted by the theory.[18] When we explore this unexpected finding further, we find that these deviant ratings are correlated with the supervisor's evaluations of the team. In other words, when both members of all-female teams rate one another as being more like members of higher-status police teams—as being more dominant and less expressive—the supervisor gives more favorable performance ratings to the team.

These findings are consistent with other research showing that external pressures—such as those from a supervisor—can bias the perceptions of another person, but not the self (Jones & Nisbett, 1972). The supervisor may urge the members of these all-female teams to be more dominating and less expressive, but only in a limited number of enforcement situations. In most other situations, the members of these teams still would be expected to behave in the low-status, less dominating, and more expressive way that is consistent with their low status.

The kind of discrepancy that we see between the way members of all-female teams rate themselves and the way they rate the partner often can give rise to internal conflict and personal distress (Higgins, 1987). But most important, this discrepancy appears to be due, in large part, to pressures from the immediate supervisor.

The supervisor puts pressure on members of all-female police teams in other ways as well. The more experienced woman in these teams is expected to have higher status and to possess more dominating and fewer expressive characteristics than her partner. But in doing so, she manifests personality characteristics that conflict with cultural norms for women. The supervisor, as outside observer, is particularly sensitive to this conflict and looks to other characteristics to determine whether she conforms with at least some of the cultural expectations for women. As a result, the supervisor's evaluations of the high-status woman are dependent on the way she portrays herself on the bipolar traits—characteristics that reflect idealized qualities associated with femininity versus masculinity. When the high-status woman describes herself as "feminine-typed" on the bipolar traits, such as being overly emotional and having difficulty handling major crises, the supervisor gives more favorable competence evaluations to her and to her team. But when she describes herself as "masculine-typed" on the bipolar traits, the supervisor downgrades her and her team's performance evaluations.[19] These findings highlight the necessity of providing better training for supervisors to enable them to base their evaluations on job-relevant criteria instead of gender-based norms.

The high-status woman herself is unaware of the basis for the supervisor's evaluations. She thinks that her supervisor is just like her and values the more masculine-typed bipolar characteristics, such as being nonemotional and able to handle crises effectively. The discrepancy between her own expectations and the way the supervisor actually evaluates her must be very confusing for her. Further confusion must arise from the fact that she is penalized for the traits that are generally valued in police officers (Manning, 1997).

What of the low-status woman in the all-female team? Again, the supervisor rewards personal attributes that appear likely to promote personal conflict—and also dissension within the team. Perhaps in an attempt to induce the low-status woman to be more authoritative, the supervisor encourages her to manifest the apparently conflicting personality attributes of dominance, verbal-aggression, and submissiveness by giving more favorable performance evaluations to her team.[20] But these traits are associated with the low-status woman's use of a unilateral form of power. Perhaps in an effort to help the low-status woman exercise more authority, the supervisor encourages her to use a form of power that ignores the wishes of the partner and may very well undermine the effective functioning of the partnership as a whole (Morey & Gerber, 1995; Raven & Kruglanski, 1970). In addition, by rewarding this constellation of socially undesirable personality traits, the supervisor encourages the low-status woman to manifest a patterning of personality traits that is deviant in comparison with other police teams.

The supervisor is the agent of the police organization as a whole and transmits the values and attitudes of the organization to the officers under his or her supervision (Ilgen, 1999). Perhaps what is needed is for police organizations to examine their implicit expectations involving members of all-female police teams. They need to decide which is more important—for members of these teams to function as effective police officers or for them to manifest the behaviors and personality attributes traditionally associated with women. The current solution appears to be to encourage them to do both; at the same time that they manifest authoritative personality attributes, they are expected to exhibit submissive or compliant attributes. The question for police departments is whether these conflicting patterns facilitate the performance of all-female police teams or whether they make it more difficult for them to function in their work.

BIASES THAT AFFECT SUPERVISORS' EVALUATIONS

Throughout the study, we have seen how society's expectations involving gender impinge on police organizations and the supervisors who work within these organizations. Most probably unknowingly, the supervisor frequently applies society's biases in evaluating and assessing the performances of both female and male police officers. Our focus should concentrate, however, not on the supervisor per se, but on the process. No blame should be assigned. Instead, all those in policing, from the highest to the lowest rank, need to be apprised of the biases that can influence their perceptions and the appropriate criteria by which the performance and effectiveness of police officers should be evaluated. The same evaluation criteria need to be used for every police officer, male and female. Evaluating police officers based on job-related criteria that are unaffected by gender prescriptions will result in more effective police officers and more effective supervision.

The supervisor is the member of management who is directly and regularly in contact with the police officers who do the work of the organization (Peak, Glensor, & Gaines, 1999). The supervisor's role is to motivate his or her subordinates to do their very best. As part of this role, the supervisor needs to define good performance, evaluate the performance of each officer and the police team as a whole, and provide feedback. Hence, it is of crucial importance that the supervisor be helped to become aware of any biases that could affect his or her evaluations and take measures to correct for them.

The biases that affect supervisors' evaluations are not unique to policing; similar kinds of biases distort the evaluations of women and men in other settings as well (Costrich, Feinstein, Kidder, & Maracek, 1975; Cowen & Kosiej, 1979; Dimitrovsky, Singer, & Yinon, 1989; Heilman, 1995).[21] The supervisor's evaluations simply reflect biases that pervade other occupational fields and society as a whole.

In police partnerships, we find that the most evident form of bias involves the high-status woman in the all-female partnership and the low-status man in the all-male partnership.[22] Because of their respective statuses, both officers manifest personality attributes that deviate from the cultural norms for their sex: The high-status woman is more dominating than her partner, and the low-status man is more expressive.

A considerable amount of research has shown that characteristics such as these occur in most work groups and enable team members to perform their assigned tasks most effectively (Berger, Wagner, & Zelditch, 1985). Hence, it is of crucial importance that police organizations be educated about work-oriented partnerships and how they function. It is especially important for supervisors to learn about the biases that can affect their perceptions of the police officers they oversee. They need to know that behaviors that deviate from expectations involving gender may actually be important for the effective functioning of the partnership as a whole. Further, they need training that will enable them to base their evaluations on job-relevant criteria, not on the extent to which individuals conform with traditional beliefs about masculinity and femininity. When supervisors use gender norms as the basis for their job performance evaluations, they make it more difficult for the officers to function effectively.

One way to minimize the effect of gender-related expectations on supervisors' competence evaluations is to develop measures that rely on very specific and direct information about job performance. Such specific behavioral measures should not require inference or interpretation, because it is only in very specific circumstances that stereotypes fade (Heilman, Block, & Martell, 1995; Nieva & Gutek, 1980; Tosi & Einbender, 1985). The measures used by supervisors to evaluate police officers' competence should involve concrete behavioral information about their performance in particular areas relevant to their job.[23]

We know from this police study that the officers themselves are unaware of the basis for the supervisor's evaluations—the high-status woman in the all-female team and the low-status man in the all-male team have no awareness of the way they are actually evaluated by their supervisors. As a result, the officers probably feel confused and are unable to relate their evaluations to their actual work performances.

Supervisors need to be especially attuned to problems in overseeing all-female police teams. Although initially reluctant, many supervisors now permit women officers to work together as a team. The task for police organizations is to determine what kind of supervision is most effective with these teams.

Ultimately, the issue is not whether women and men need to be "feminine" or "masculine" in policing. The question is: What kinds of behaviors and personal attributes will enable men and women to be most effective in their work? Supervisors and police organizations as a whole need to determine what behaviors and personality attributes enable men and women police officers to do their very best (Denmark, 1993; Hollander & Offermann, 1990). To achieve this goal, police organizations need to reexamine their expectations involving gender and change these expectations to be more relevant to a world that includes female officers, as well as men (Offermann, 1997).

A FINAL NOTE

The traditional approach to studying "police personality" has focused on the uniqueness of police officers. By contrast, the status approach described here shows that police officers and their supervisors are subject to the same kinds of processes that affect individuals in other work settings. Police personnel can be understood in terms of the same psychological and sociological principles that affect members of other occupational groups.

The relationship between police partners seldom has been studied empirically. As we have shown throughout the book, however, this relationship can influence almost every aspect of the partners' functioning, including how they perceive their personality attributes, their sense of competence, their ability to make decisions, and their self-esteem.

In addition, we have seen how the organization of the police department and the expectations that govern that system help perpetuate apparent sex differences in personality. These expectations are often unexamined, but have important implications for policing because they can have a major impact on the functioning of female and male police officers.

Most important, we have seen that police officers are not a homogeneous entity. Future research needs to move beyond studying police officers as a group, or even comparing men and women officers, to examine the particular situational demands that affect the individuals who work in policing.

Appendix A: Procedure

THE SAMPLE OF POLICE TEAMS

The New York City Police Department (NYPD) agreed to help with the data collection and surveyed all 75 police precincts throughout the five boroughs of New York City. For each precinct, every steady radio motor patrol (RMP) team was listed along with the sex of both partners, the length of time they had worked together, and the tour (shift) they worked (tour 1, midnight to 8:00 a.m.; tour 2, 8:00 a.m. to 4:00 p.m.; tour 3, 4:00 p.m. to midnight).

Because there were numerically few all-female teams, every all-female team that was listed was selected for the study. This group of all-female teams was matched as closely as possible with the groups of all-male and male–female teams on the amount of time the partners had worked together and the tour worked. In addition, all-male and male–female teams were selected from the same precinct, if possible, or from a neighboring precinct within the same borough.

A total of 289 RMP teams were initially selected (all-male = 112, male–female = 112, all-female = 65) from 53 precincts. Each RMP team currently working together when the questionnaires were distributed by the NYPD was asked to participate in the study. If members of a team were no longer working together, they were *not* asked to participate. Instead, they were listed on a form that also stated why they were no longer together. This form was returned with the completed question-naires for each precinct.

Because the NYPD had been transferring many officers into the new Community Policing program, it was anticipated that a number of teams would no longer be working together for reasons external to the partnership. As expected, the primary reason given for the breakup of teams was that one or both partners had been transferred to another program, such as Community Policing (33%), or to another tour, squad, or precinct (28%). Other reasons were: vacation (9%), sickness (7%), conflict between the partners (6%), promotion (4%), pregnancy (3%), or other (10%), for example, restricted duty.

Since information from seven precincts was incomplete, the following statistics are based on 46 precincts (246 teams). At the time the questionnaires were distributed (two to four months after the initial survey had been completed), 90 teams were no longer working together and were not asked to participate in the study (the numbers of teams still working together were: all-male = 65, male–female = 59, all-female = 32). A chi-square test showed no significant differences among the three partner types in the number of teams that were no longer working together versus those that were still together, $\chi^2(2, N = 246) = 1.26$, n.s. Of the 156 teams in which the partners were together when the questionnaires were distributed, 141 teams, or 90%, volunteered for the study.

An additional 13 questionnaires with incomplete information on participation were received from the seven precincts. Thus, the final sample comprised 154 teams (all-male = 66, male–female = 59, all-female = 29), or 308 officers. Statistical analyses showed that in the final sample, the three partner types were matched on the length of time they had worked together and their tour. There were no significant differences among the three partner types in the tour they worked, $\chi^2(4, N = 154) = 1.86$, n.s. (percentages of teams in the three tours: tour 1 = 22%, tour 2 = 40%, tour 3 = 38%). In addition, no significant differences among the three partner types were found in the length of time they had worked together, $F(2, 144) = 1.79$, n.s. (overall $M = 20.11$ months, $SD = 14.43$).

POLICE PARTNERS' QUESTIONNAIRE

The operations coordinator at each precinct (ranking officer in charge of the day-to-day operations of the precinct) described the study to both members of each team that were currently working together. Partners were informed that the study had no connection with the Police Department, participation was voluntary, information would be anonymous and confidential, and they would be given time on the job to fill out the questionnaires.

When both partners agreed to participate, the operations coordinator gave each partner a questionnaire to fill out and ensured that confidentiality was maintained. Each partner sealed his or her completed questionnaire in the envelope that was provided. The operations coordinator then sealed both partners' envelopes in a larger envelope that was returned to me through Police Headquarters.

SUPERVISOR'S QUESTIONNAIRE

The immediate supervising officer (squad sergeant) was asked to fill out a questionnaire for all teams whose members had been working together when the partners' questionnaires had been sent to the precincts. If the squad sergeant was unavailable, then another supervisor who had worked with the team on a regular basis completed the questionnaire. Again, the operations coordinator at each precinct explained the study and supervised the administration of the questionnaires. Each questionnaire was sealed in an envelope that was returned to me through Police Headquarters.

Since the partners' and supervisor's questionnaires had been filled out at different times and were both anonymous, it was necessary to match them using demographic and other data. Matching was done within each precinct, using information about the partners (sex category, age, race/ethnic group, and years as a police officer), as well as information about the team (months they had worked together and tour). (Partners' questionnaires returned without a precinct number could not be used for matching.)

Three research assistants and I worked together in pairs to do the matching. Overall agreement between the pairs was 94%, and differences were resolved through discussion. The total number of teams for which partners' and supervisor's questionnaires were matched was 125.

Appendix B: Development of Measures

SELF-EVALUATION SCALE

In previous research, self-esteem has been found to be substantially correlated with the instrumental traits, but only marginally correlated with the expressive traits (Whitley, 1983). These studies have been criticized because sometimes the items used to measure self-esteem overlap the items used to measure instrumentality (Nicholls, Licht, & Pearl, 1982). This suggests that the high correlation of self-esteem with instrumentality may be an artifact of the self-esteem measures used. To remedy this problem, a new measure of self-esteem was developed for the present study, the Self-Evaluation Scale. This scale was designed to be a "gender-neutral" measure of self-esteem that eliminates any item overlap between self-esteem and the instrumental (or expressive) traits.

Preliminary Study

To develop an initial item pool, adjectives from the Adjective Check List were selected that had been rated low on sex-stereotyping (degree to which the adjective was judged to be male-associated or female-associated), and either very high or very low on overall "favorability" (an item must either be very positive or very negative in order to evoke an evaluative response set) (Edwards, 1964). The specific criteria used for selection were: (a) sex-stereotyping rating between 450 and 550 (scale mean is 500) and (b) favorability rating below 400 or above 600 (Williams & Best, 1982).

In previous research (Williams & Best, 1982), these adjectives had been rated for overall favorability. But overall favorability can differ from an adjective's favorability for one sex or the other. For example, an adjective that is given a high rating on overall favorability might be considered to be less favorable for women than for men (Spence, Helmreich, & Stapp, 1974).

Since it was important that the adjectives be equally desirable for both sexes, a study was done in which female ($N = 44$) and male ($N = 42$) college students rated both the "ideal man" and the "ideal woman" on each adjective (Spence et al., 1974), using a seven-point scale with end points labeled "not at all" and "very" (for example, not at all responsible—very responsible). The order of rating the man and the woman was counterbalanced so that half the students rated the man first and half rated the woman first.

An adjective was selected for the Self-Evaluation Scale (a) if the overall desirability of that trait was judged by both male and female raters to be no more desirable for one sex than for the other, using a very strict criterion ($p > .20$; see Bem, 1974), (b) if ratings by female and male raters of the ideal woman (and the ideal man) did not differ significantly ($p < .05$), and (c) if the order of rating the ideal woman and man was not significantly different for female raters or for male raters ($p > .05$). Of the adjectives satisfying the criteria, 14 were selected for the Self-Evaluation Scale; these included seven positive and seven negative adjectives; they are presented in Table I.

Further tests were done to determine whether the items on the final scale were equally desirable for both sexes. After the individual items had been selected, mean desirability scores were computed for each of the 86 judges. The mean desirability scores for the positive and negative items, as well as for the 14 items individually, are presented in Table II. The mean desirability of the items did not differ significantly for women and men—as rated by female judges and by male judges—both ts (dfs = 43 and 41, respectively) < 1.00, $n.s.$ Thus, the scale satisfied the criterion that the traits be equally desirable for both sexes.

Police Partners Study

In the police partners study, each officer rated the self (and partner) on the 14 items comprising Self-Evaluation Scale. The instructions for rating the self were as follows:

> The following items inquire about what kind of a person you think you are. Each item consists of a *pair* of characteristics, with the numbers 1 – 7 on the scale in between. For example: [a 7-point scale with poles labeled "not at all healthy" and "very healthy" was presented here].

TABLE I
Items on the Self-Evaluation Scale with Item-Total Correlations

Item	Item-Total Correlations
Positive Items	
Responsible	.53
Fair-minded	.49
Relaxed	.46
Versatile	.45
Generous	.36
Original	.34
Witty	.30
Negative Items	
Dull	.50
Irritable	.42
Careless	.37
Conceited	.32
Immature	.32
Pessimistic	.28
Unfriendly	.24

Each pair describes contradictory characteristics—that is, you cannot be both at the same time, such as very healthy and not very healthy.

The numbers form a scale between the two extremes. You are to place an "X" to describe where *you* fall on the scale. For example, if you think you are not at all healthy, you would place an "X" above the 1. If you think you are pretty healthy, you would place an "X" above the 6. If you are only moderately healthy, you might place an "X" above the 4, and so forth.

Now go ahead and answer the questions on the following pages. For each characteristic, *place an "X" above the number* that best describes *you*. Please place your "X" *between* the vertical lines marked on the scale. Be sure to answer *every* question, even if you're not sure.

TABLE II
Mean Desirability of Items on the Self-Evaluation Scale

	Female Judges		Male Judges	
Item	For a Man	For a Woman	For a Man	For a Woman
Positive Items	5.84	5.86	5.77	5.77
Negative Items	2.33	2.29	2.45	2.48
All Items	4.09	4.08	4.11	4.13

The order of presentation for positive and negative items was randomized. Each item was rated from "not at all" to "very" on seven-point scales, counterbalanced so that for half the items the desirable pole was on the left and for half the items the desirable pole was on the right. These ratings were averaged to obtain a "self-evaluation score."

The self-evaluation score was correlated with the instrumental and expressive traits—for male police officers, for female police officers, and for the total sample. As can be seen from Table III, these correlations were highly significant ($p < .01$), indicating that the Self-Evaluation Scale was substantially correlated with both the instrumental and expressive traits. Further tests showed that there were no significant differences between the correlations involving the instrumental and expressive traits (Cohen & Cohen, 1983). These tests were performed separately for male and female officers—male officers t (176) = 1.37, n.s.; female officers t (105) < 1.00, n.s., total sample t (286) < 1.00, n.s.

Thus, the Self-Evaluation Scale was found to be a "gender-neutral" measure of self-esteem. The items on the scale were equally desirable for both women and men. Most critically, the scale was substantially correlated with both the instrumental and expressive traits. Item-total correlations for the police sample are presented in Table I. Coefficient alpha was computed and was equal to .76.

THE POLICE DECISION SCALE

This scale measures perceptions of the relative influence of each police partner in making decisions; it was developed using a procedure similar to that employed for a widely used decision scale for married couples (Blood & Wolfe, 1960; Centers, Raven & Rodrigues, 1971). The majority of the decisions included in the scale were rated as: (a) important, (b) made by most partners in the course of their work, and (c) affecting the partnership as a whole.

TABLE III
Correlations of the Self-Evaluation Scale with the Instrumental and Expressive Traits

Traits	Male Officers	Female Officers	Total Sample
Instrumental	.49**	.42**	.46**
Expressive	.38**	.49**	.41**

Note. For male officers, N = 179; for female officers, N = 108; for the total sample, N = 287.
**$p < .01$.

Preliminary Study

To develop an initial item pool, 20 police officers were interviewed and asked to describe the decisions made by police partners in their work together. Based on these interviews, a 40-item pool of decisions was created. These items were then rated by samples of police officers during "unit-training sessions" at one of the NYPD precincts.

First, a sample of 31 police officers rated all 40 items on the importance of the decision (importance), using a seven-point scale varying from "never or almost never . . . " to "always or almost always important for job functioning." The 20 items with the highest ratings on importance were then selected for additional ratings. In addition, two items with lower ratings were included in order to represent more "feminine-typed" areas of decision (family dispute, victim of crime). Researchers who have studied other kinds of dyadic relationships, such as marriage, have recommended that "feminine-typed" areas of decision be included to provide a range of the kinds of decisions that are made (Centers et al., 1971).

Second, another sample of 36 police officers rated the 22 items on the number of partners who make the decision (number of partners) and the effect of the decision on the partnership as a whole (effect on partnership). Number of partners was rated on a seven-point scale varying from "none or very few partners make this decision" to "all or almost all partners make this decision." Effect on partnership was rated on a seven-point scale varying from "never or almost never affects the partnership as a whole" to "always or almost always affects the partnership as a whole."

Items were selected on the basis of the following criteria: (a) the average rating on importance was 4.0 or higher (highest average rating was 6.0), (b) the average rating on number of partners was 4.0 or higher (highest average rating was 5.1), and (c) the average rating for effect on partnership was 2.4 or higher (highest average rating was 3.5). Note: The average ratings for effect on partnership are relatively low compared to similar ratings obtained earlier in studies of married couples (Blood & Wolfe, 1960; Centers et al., 1971). However, the decisions used in marriage studies, such as where the family will live, are more likely to have an impact on the marriage than the kinds of decisions that are relevant to the day-to-day work relationship between police partners.

Two additional items involving the use of force (deadly physical force, physical force) were included even though the ratings for number of partners were relatively low. Many partners are never faced with the decision to use force, but the items are important for police work. The two items representing more "feminine-typed" areas of decision were also included even though all these ratings were relatively low. A total of 15 items were selected for the police partners' questionnaire.

Police Partners Study

In the present study with police partners, each officer rated all 15 items. The instructions stated:

> In every partnership, somebody has to decide such things as to whether or not to call for emergency services in a particular situation, and so on. Many partners talk things over first, but the *final* decision has to be made by one or the other partner. For each of the following decisions, place an "X" in the appropriate column to indicate who makes the final decision.

All 15 items were then listed, as in Table IV, and officers indicated "which partner makes the final decision" for each item. Column headings were: myself always, myself more than my partner, myself and my partner exactly the same, my partner more than myself, my partner always. Items were scored from 1 to 5, with 1 indicating that the self makes most of the decisions and 5 indicating that the partner makes most of the decisions.

Item-total correlations were computed for all 15 items; as correlations showed that four of the items had very low item-total correlations (less than .09), these items were dropped. The final scale included eleven items that were averaged to obtain a "relative decision score." These items are presented in Table IV. Ratings of these items on importance,

TABLE IV
Items on the Police Decision Scale

Which partner makes the *final* decision about—

The kinds of tactics to use in a life-threatening situation?

Whether or not to use DPF (deadly physical force) in a particular situation?

Whether or not to separate on a particular job?

Whether or not to retreat in a particular situation?

Whether or not to use physical force in a particular situation (for example, a nightstick or physical restraint)?

Whether or not to call for backup assistance in a particular situation?

Whether or not to arrest a particular person?

Whether or not to answer the radio if the tour is almost ended?

Whether or not to investigate a suspicious situation?

Who will do the talking in a family dispute?

Who will talk to the victim of a crime?

---

number of partners, and effect on the partnership are shown in Table V; the item-total correlations for these items are presented in Table VI. Coefficient alpha was computed and was equal to .61.

TABLE V
Ratings of Items on the Police Decision Scale for Importance, Number of Partners, and Effect on the Partnership

Item	Importance	Number of Partners	Effect on Partnership
Life-threatening situation	6.0	5.1	3.5
Deadly physical force	5.9	2.9	2.9
Separate on job	5.4	4.3	2.7
Retreat in situation	5.1	4.0	2.5
Physical force	5.0	3.0	2.6
Backup assistance	4.9	4.2	2.5
Whether to arrest	4.7	4.8	2.6
Answer radio	4.1	4.4	2.5
Investigate situation	4.0	4.3	2.4
Family dispute	3.5	3.4	1.9
Victim of crime	3.3	3.8	1.8

TABLE VI
Item-Total Correlations for Items on the Police Decision Scale

Item	Item-Total Correlations
Life-threatening situation	.43
Deadly physical force	.30
Separate on job	.27
Retreat in situation	.20
Physical force	.27
Backup assistance	.30
Whether to arrest	.27
Answer radio	.18
Investigate situation	.25
Family dispute	.36
Victim of crime	.20

Appendix C: Further Statistical Analyses

ANALYSES OF THE EPAQ TRAITS

It was predicted that high-status police officers would be perceived as having relatively more dominating and instrumental traits; low-status police officers would be perceived as having relatively more expressive traits. In addition, it was predicted that the level of dominating, instrumental, and expressive traits in the partnership as a whole would vary with each partnership's group status. Since the all-male partnership had the highest group status, the male–female partnership had intermediate group status, and the all-female partnership had the lowest group status, the instrumental and dominating traits would be highest in the all-male partnership and would decrease linearly across the male–female and all-female partnerships. The level of expressive traits was expected to be lowest in the all-male partnership and to increase linearly across the male–female and all-female partnerships.

Each of the EPAQ scores for the self-perceptions and perceptions of the partner was analyzed in a 2 by 3 analysis of variance (ANOVA) with factors for individual status (high-status officer, low-status officer) and group status (highest-status all-male team, intermediate-status male–female team, lowest-status all-female team). In the analyses of the self-perceptions, high- and low-status officers referred to the perceiver; in the analyses of the partner-perceptions, they designated the person being perceived (target person). Since high- and low-status officers were both members of the same partnership, the factor for individual status was analyzed as a repeated measure.

Dominating Traits

In the ANOVA for the self-perceptions, the main effect for individual status tended toward significance, $F(1, 138) = 2.78, p < .10$. As predicted, the high-status officer perceived himself or herself as having somewhat more dominating traits than did the low-status officer (see Table 4.1 in Chapter 4 for means; SDs for high- and low-status officers were 4.18 and 4.31, respectively).

Also as predicted, for the self-perceptions, the main effect for group status was significant, $F(2, 138) = 5.48, p < .005$. Here, the score represents the combined self-perceptions of both partners. A linear trend analysis (Keppel, 1973) showed that the scores varied as expected, $F(1, 138) = 6.04, p < .01$ (see Table 4.2 in Chapter 4 for means; SDs for all-male, male–female, and all-female teams were 4.26, 3.98, and 4.41, respectively). The level of dominating traits within the partnership as a whole was highest in the all-male team, which had the highest group status; it then decreased linearly across the intermediate-status male–female and lowest-status all-female teams.

In the ANOVA for the perceptions of the partner, group status was again significant, $F(2, 138) = 3.34, p < .05$. Here, the score represents both dyad members' combined perceptions of the partner. A linear trend analysis was done, but was not significant, $F(1, 138) = 1.00$, n.s. There were differences between the means, but contrary to prediction, they did not decrease linearly across all three partnerships according to their group status (see Table 4.2 in Chapter 4 for means; SDs for all-male, male–female, and all-female teams were 4.76, 5.53, and 5.89, respectively).

As hypothesized, individual status and group status were found to be independent dimensions that had separate effects on trait ratings, as indicated by the finding that the interactions between individual status and group status did not approach significance in either ANOVA, both $Fs (2, 138) < 1.00$, n.s.

Expressive Traits

In the ANOVAs for both the self-perceptions and the partner-perceptions, the main effects for individual status were significant—self-perceptions, $F(1, 138) = 12.86, p < .001$; partner-perceptions, $F(1, 138) = 6.59, p < .01$. As predicted, the high-status officer was perceived as having fewer of the expressive traits than the low-status officer in both analyses (see Table 4.1 in Chapter 4 for means; SDs for the self-perceptions of high- and low-status officers were 3.85 and 3.55, and for the partner-perceptions were 4.87 and 4.89, respectively).

For the self-perceptions, the main effect for group status was significant, as predicted, $F(2, 138) = 7.81$, $p < .001$. This score represents the combined self-perceptions of both officers. A linear trend analysis (Keppel, 1973) showed that the expressive traits in the partnership as a whole varied with each partnership's group status, as expected. The level of expressive traits was lowest in the highest-status all-male partnership and increased linearly across the male–female and all-female partnerships, $F(1, 138) = 6.04$, $p < .01$. (See Table 4.2 in Chapter 4 for means; SDs for all-male, male–female, and all-female teams were 3.55, 3.74, and 3.41, respectively).

For the partner-perceptions, the main effect for group status was again significant, $F(2, 138) = 4.80$, $p < .01$. However, contrary to prediction, the linear trend analysis did not reach significance, $F(1, 138) = 2.20$, $n.s.$ There were differences between the means, but they did not increase linearly across partner types according to their group status. (See Table 4.2 in Chapter 4 for means; SDs for all-male, male–female, and all-female teams were 4.24, 5.07, and 5.40, respectively).

As hypothesized, individual status and group status were found to be independent dimensions with separate effects on trait ratings, as indicated by the finding that the interactions between individual status and group status did not approach significance in either ANOVA—both Fs $(2, 138) < 1.00$, $n.s.$

Instrumental Traits

It had been expected that the socially desirable instrumental traits would vary as a function of status. However, none of the effects was significant for either the self-perceptions or the partner-perceptions. The overall means for the self-perceptions ($M = 23.60$, $SD = 3.90$) and partner-perceptions ($M = 23.37$, $SD = 4.57$) were compared with the norm for college males (Spence & Helmreich, 1975, p. 50). Statistical tests showed that the means for police officers were significantly higher than the norm—self-perceptions, $z = 7.69$, $N = 282$, $p < .001$; partner-perceptions, $z = 6.73$, $N = 282$, $p < .001$. Thus, the group of police officers, regardless of their status, perceived themselves and their partner as being extremely high on these desirable, self-assertive attributes.

Verbal-Aggressive Traits

The purpose of these analyses was to explore whether the verbal-aggressive traits were related to status. In the ANOVAs for the self-perceptions and partner-perceptions, the interactions between individual status and group status were significant—self-perceptions, F (2, 138) = 6.38, $p < .005$; partner-perceptions, F (2, 138) = 5.15, $p < .01$. (See Table 5.1 in Chapter 5 for means. SDs for the self-perceptions by high-status officers in all-male, male–female, and all-female teams were 3.08, 2.60, and 2.98, and for low-status officers were 3.03, 2.39, and 3.26, respectively; SDs for perceptions by the partner of the high-status officers were 3.07, 3.38, and 3.86, respectively, and for low-status officers were 3.08, 4.20, and 3.42, respectively.)

Whether members of mixed-sex groups manifest more (or less) highly differentiated characteristics than members of same-sex groups is important for status characteristics theory (Lockheed & Hall, 1976; Ridgeway, 1988). To explore this issue, post hoc comparisons were made between the means for high- and low-status officers within each of the three partnership types using Fisher's modified LSD test (Cohen & Cohen, 1983; Winer, 1971). The comparison in the male–female partnership was significant for both the perceptions of the self ($p < .001$) and partner ($p < .01$). The low-status female officer was perceived as significantly more verbally aggressive than the high-status male officer was perceived. Thus, significant differences between the two sexes were found when they worked together in the male–female partnership. This finding was consistent for both the self-perceptions and the partner-perceptions.

An additional comparison was significant, but just for the partner-perceptions: in the all-male partnership, the low-status male officer was perceived by the partner as being more verbally aggressive than the high-status male officer ($p < .01$).

Submissive Traits

The purpose of these analyses was to explore whether the submissive traits were related to status. In the ANOVA for the perceptions of the partner, the interaction between individual status and group status was significant, F (2, 138) = 3.42, $p < .05$. (See Table 5.3 in Chapter 5 for means; SDs for perceptions by the partner of high-status officers in all-male, male–female, and all-female teams were 2,55, 2.17, and 2.80, and for low-status officers were 2.45, 2.74, and 3.06, respectively.)

As with the verbal-aggressive traits, post hoc comparisons were made between the means for high- and low-status officers within each partnership type using Fisher's modified LSD test. The comparison in the male–female partnership was significant ($p < .05$). The low-status female officer was perceived as significantly more submissive than the high-status male officer was perceived. None of the other comparisons were significant.

The results for the submissive traits, in which a significant difference between the male and female officers in the male–female partnership was found, are similar to those for the verbal-aggressive traits. However, in contrast to the previous findings for verbal aggression, in which male–female differences were found for both the self- and partner-perceptions, here they were found only for the perceptions of the partner (for the self-perceptions, the overall mean for all officers = 4.36, SD = 2.09). Unlike the findings for verbal aggression (see Chapter 5), the difference in partner-perceptions of the submissive traits in the male–female partnership was unrelated to other status differences involving work experience, education, or age.

Bipolar Traits

These analyses explored whether the bipolar traits were related to status. In the ANOVA for the self-perceptions, the main effect for group status tended toward significance, F $(1, 138)$ = 2.76, $p < .07$. Means for the combined self-perceptions of both officers in each police team were: all-male, 18.35; male–female, 17.91; all-female, 16.87 (SDs = 3.80, 3.76, and 3.51, respectively).

No prediction had been made for the bipolar traits in which the ideal female is rated with a low score and the ideal male is rated with a high score. Based on an examination of the means, a post hoc linear trend analysis was performed, which tended toward significance, F $(1, 138)$ = 3.07, $p < .09$. The results for the self-perceptions were consistent with those reported previously for the dominating (and expressive) traits. Members of the highest-status all-male partnership tended to perceive themselves as most similar to the ideal male, members of the intermediate-status male–female partnership tended to perceive themselves as intermediate in similarity, and members of the lowest-status all-female partnership tended to perceive themselves as least similar.

CONSISTENT VERSUS INCONSISTENT STATUS INFORMATION

In a field study such as this, people cannot be randomly assigned to conditions, and sometimes status information is inconsistent (see Norman, Smith, and Berger, 1988). When seniority designates high- and low-status officers in the same-sex partnerships, for example, their relative education may be inconsistent with seniority. Similarly, when sex category designates high- and low-status officers in the mixed-sex partnership, other status characteristics may be inconsistent. To test whether these inconsistencies affected perceptions, each of the EPAQ scores for the self- and partner-perceptions was analyzed in a 2 by 3 by 2 ANOVA with factors for individual status (high-status officer, low-status officer), group status (highest-status all-male team, intermediate-status male–female team, lowest-status all-female team), and consistency of status characteristics (all consistent, some inconsistent). Equality between the two dyad members on a particular characteristic was considered to be "consistent," since characteristics that do not differentiate individuals are not salient in the determination of the power and prestige order (Webster, 1977). Three relevant statuses were recorded in same-sex partnerships (experience, education, age), and four (sex category, experience, education, age) in the mixed-sex partnership. None of the main effects or interactions involving consistency of status characteristics was significant in any of these ANOVAs; thus, consistency did not affect any reported results.

GENDER-SPECIFIC MODEL VERSUS STATUS MODEL OF GENDER STEREOTYPING: DOMINATING AND EXPRESSIVE TRAITS

The previously described analyses of the EPAQ traits showed that the two status variables explained all of the variance in the dominating and expressive traits. The correlations presented here demonstrate that if the data had been analyzed without taking into account the two status variables, the results would have appeared to support the gender-specific model of gender stereotyping. Even when statistically significant, most of these results would have been misleading. As we see in the following multiple regression analyses, the critical dimension is status (individual status and group status), which accounts for more of the variance than does sex category.

Correlations of Sex of Officer with the Dominating and Expressive Traits

To test whether male and female officers appear to differ in stereotypic ways, sex of officer (male = 1, female = 2) was correlated with the dominating and expressive traits (see Table 4.4 in Chapter 4). All of the results were in the predicted direction, and all but one were highly significant (all $ps < .001$ or .01, with the exception of the correlation for the partner-perceptions of the dominating traits, which tended toward significance, $p < .10$). Male officers were perceived as higher on the dominating traits and women officers were seen as higher on the expressive traits—for both the self-perceptions and the partner-perceptions. Thus, the findings appear to support the gender-specific model.

Hierarchical Multiple Regression Analyses of the Dominating and Expressive Traits

These analyses tested whether the status model of gender stereotyping better represents how people perceive their own and their partners' personality traits than does the gender-specific model. To determine whether the two status variables, individual status and group status, better account for the variance in the ratings of the dominating and expressive traits than does the variable of sex of officer, hierarchical multiple regression analyses were performed.

Two analyses were performed for the self-perceptions and for the partner-perceptions. In one analysis the dependent variable was the score on the dominating traits, and in the other analysis the dependent variable was the score on the expressive traits. Sex of officer was entered on the first step of each analysis, and individual status and group status were entered on the second step. The independent variables were coded as follows: sex of officer: male = 1, female = 2; individual status: high-status officer = 1, low-status officer = 2; group status: highest-status all-male team = 1, intermediate-status male–female team = 2, lowest-status all-female team = 3.

As the previous correlations had shown, sex of officer was either significant or tended toward significance when it was entered into the equation on the first step of each multiple regression analysis ($ps < .001$, .01, or .10; see Table 4.5 in Chapter 4).

The changes in the beta weights for sex of officer when individual status and group status were entered into the equation were the critical results. As can be seen in Table 4.5 (Chapter 4), the beta weights for sex of officer were no longer significant in any of the four analyses. Sex of officer did not account for any of the variance once the two status variables were brought into the equation. Further, individual status and group status accounted for an additional portion of the variance when they were brought into the equation. For the dominating traits, this was significant ($p < .05$); for the expressive traits, this tended toward significance ($p < .10$).

In a second set of hierarchical multiple regression analyses, the regression was reversed so that the two status variables were entered first and sex of officer was entered second. As can be seen from Table VII, the portion of the variance accounted for by the two status variables was highly significant in the analyses involving the self-perceptions of both the dominating and expressive traits (both $ps < .001$). In the partner-perceptions analyses, it tended toward significance in the analysis of the dominating traits ($p < .10$) and was significant in the analysis of the expressive traits ($p < .01$). When sex of officer was entered on the second step, it did not account for any of the variance in any of the four

TABLE VII
Standardized Beta Weights from Hierarchical Multiple Regression Analyses of the Dominating and Expressive Traits: Status Variables Entered First

Step	Variable	Dominating Traits			Expressive Traits		
		R	R^2 Change	Beta	R	R^2 Change	Beta
		Perceptions of the Self					
1	Individual Status	.23	.05****	−.11[a]	.31	.10****	.22****
	Group Status			−.20****			.22****
2	Sex of Officer	.23	.00	.06	.32	.00	.14
		Perceptions of the Partner					
1	Individual Status	.13	.02[a]	.02	.20	.04**	.13*
	Group Status			−.12*			.16**
2	Sex of Officer	.13	.00	−.03	.20	.00	.05

Note. In Step 1, $df = 2/284$; in Step 2, $df = 3/283$.
[a]$p < .10$. *$p < .05$. **$p < .01$. ****$p < .001$.

analyses. (These results are similar to those for the ANOVAs of the dominating and expressive traits.)

In summary, the initial correlations of sex of officer with the dominating and expressive traits seemed to support the gender-specific model of gender stereotyping. However, the multiple regression analyses showed that the two status variables accounted for all of the variance in the ratings, and none of the variance was accounted for by sex of officer.

Sex of officer was initially correlated with the dominating and expressive traits because sex-related variables were associated in some way with both individual status and group status. With respect to individual status, sex category was used to designate status in one of the police teams—the male–female police team. Even though seniority was used to designate status in the other two police teams, the use of sex category as a status variable in the male–female team meant that, within the sample as a whole, males were more often given a high individual status and females a low individual status. A male was in the high-status position in two of the three police teams—the all-male and male–female teams; a female was in the low-status position in two of the three police teams—the male–female and all-female teams.

With respect to group status, the proportion of males and females in the three police teams was used to designate group status, so that the all-male team had higher status than the male–female team, which in turn had higher status than the all-female team. Thus, in the overall sample, two males were in the highest-status police team and one male was in the intermediate-status police team; two females were in the lowest-status police team and one female was in the intermediate-status police team. In other words, within the overall sample, male officers were in teams with greater group status than were female officers.

As we have shown here, status was the critical variable in accounting for the perceptions of male and female officers on the dominating and expressive traits. But because sex-related variables were associated in some way with both individual status and group status, males in the overall sample held higher-status positions than did females.

LOW-STATUS MAN IN THE ALL-MALE PARTNERSHIP: CORRELATIONS WITH HIS PERCEIVED VERBAL AGGRESSION

In the analyses of the verbal-aggressive traits, described previously, the low-status man in the all-male partnership was perceived as being significantly higher on verbal aggression than the high-status man— but just for the analysis of the partner-perceptions ($p < .01$), not for the analysis of the self-perceptions. Because this finding was not consistent for both the self- and partner-perceptions, it is somewhat tentative. However, it was decided to explore it further to see whether the low-status man's verbal aggression was associated with an increase in his influence (as it had been for the low-status woman in the male–female team).

Correlations were computed between the partner's perception of the low-status man's verbal-aggressive traits and both officers' scores on the Police Decision Scale. Neither of these correlations was significant, indicating that the low-status man's perceived verbal aggression was not associated with any increased influence—low-status man r (58) = .06, *n.s.*; high-status man r (60) = .18, *n.s.*

An additional correlation was computed using the supervisor's rating of individual performance. Results showed that when the low-status man was perceived as verbally aggressive, the supervisor rated him as being significantly less competent, r (48) = –.40, $p < .005$. This finding suggests that verbal aggression was associated with adverse consequences for the low-status man—not only did it fail to gain him any influence, but he was rated by his supervisor as being less competent in his work. It also suggests that verbal aggression may be effective only when status is designated by an ascribed characteristic such as sex category and there is a potential conflict with another status characteristic such as seniority, as it was for the low-status woman in the male–female police team. By contrast, verbal aggression may not be effective when status is designated by an achieved characteristic such as seniority, as it was for the low-status man in the all-male police team.

OFFICERS IN ROLES CONSISTENT WITH GENDER NORMS: CORRELATIONS BETWEEN THE SUPERVISOR'S EVALUATIONS AND OFFICERS' BIPOLAR TRAITS

The supervisor's evaluations were predicted to be unrelated to how officers in roles consistent with gender norms perceived themselves on the bipolar traits. In same-sex police teams, these "gender-normative" officers were the low-status woman in the all-female police team and the high-status man in the all-male police team—the low-status woman was in a traditionally "feminine-typed" follower role and the high-status man was in a traditionally "masculine-typed" leader role. In the male–female police team, both officers were in roles consistent with gender norms—the man was in the high-status role of leader and the woman was in the low-status role of follower.

Correlations were computed between the supervisor's performance ratings and each gender-normative officer's self-perceptions on the bipolar traits (see Tables VIII and IX). The supervisor's performance ratings included the evaluations of the gender-normative officer, the partner, and the team as a whole.

None of the correlations involving gender-normative officers in same-sex or male–female police teams reached statistical significance, as predicted. (In the male–female team, one correlation tended toward significance, $p < .10$.) Thus, all of the results were consistent with the hypothesis.

ANALYSES OF THE SELF-EVALUATION, PERCEIVED INTELLIGENCE, EDUCATION, FEMALE COWORKERS, AND MALE COWORKERS SCALES

The Self-Evaluation Scale and the perceived intelligence, education, female coworkers, and male coworkers scales were each analyzed in a 2 by 3 ANOVA with factors for individual status (high-status officer, low-status officer) and group status (highest-status all-male team, intermediate-status male–female team, lowest-status all-female team). Since high- and low-status officers were both

TABLE VIII
Gender-Normative Officers in Same-Sex Police Teams and Their Bipolar Traits: Correlations with the Supervisor's Evaluations

Supervisor's Evaluations	Low-Status Woman in All-Female Team	High-Status Man in All-Male Team
Team as a Whole		
Competence	−.16	−.15
Handling Service-Oriented Calls	−.08	.06
Handling Enforcement Situations	−.13	.12
Working with the Public	−.01	.01
Gender-Normative Officer		
Competent on the Job	−.07	−.02
Highly Regarded by Superiors	−.13	−.19
Gender-Distinct Partner		
Competent on the Job	−.05	.14
Highly Regarded by Superiors	−.07	.08

Note. The gender-normative officer's bipolar traits are correlated with the supervisor's evaluations of the team, the gender-normative officer, and the gender-distinct partner. On the bipolar traits, a low score is "feminine" and a high score is "masculine." For the low-status woman, $df = 20$; for the high-status man, $df = 48$.

TABLE IX
Gender-Normative Officers in Male–Female Police Teams and Their Bipolar Traits: Correlations with the Supervisor's Evaluations

Supervisor's Evaluations	High-Status Man	Low-Status Woman
Team as a Whole		
Competence	.03	.15
Handling Service-Oriented Calls	.00	.25[a]
Handling Enforcement Situations	.02	.02
Working with the Public	−.21	.21
Officer Being Studied		
Competent on the Job	.00	.17
Highly Regarded by Superiors	−.14	.10
Partner		
Competent on the Job	.01	.09
Highly Regarded by Superiors	−.20	.16

Note. The "officer being studied" refers to the officer whose bipolar traits are correlated with the supervisor's evaluations of the team as a whole, the officer being studied, and the partner. On the bipolar traits, a low score is "feminine" and a high score is "masculine." For all correlations, $df = 46$.
[a]$p < .10$.

members of the same partnership, individual status was analyzed as a repeated measure.

Self-Evaluation Scale

In the ANOVA of the Self-Evaluation Scale, the interaction between individual status and group status was significant, F (2, 138) = 4.80, $p <$ .01. Means are presented in Table 7.1 in Chapter 7 (SDs for high-status officers in all-male, male–female, and all-female teams were .78, .61, and .58, and for low-status officers were .62, .62, and .73, respectively).

To test whether low self-esteem was associated with status position, comparisons were made between high- and low-status officers within each of the three police teams using the Fisher LSD test. Results showed that the high-status man in the all-male partnership perceived himself as having significantly lower self-esteem than did the low-status man ($p <$ .01). Comparisons between high- and low-status officers in the male–female and all-female teams were not significant.

Additional comparisons were performed in order to explore this finding further. These showed that the high-status man in the all-male team had significantly lower self-esteem in comparison to all but one of the other four officers (all $ps <$ .01, except for the comparison with the low-status officer in the all-female team, which tended in the predicted direction, $p <$ .25). Thus, the high-status man in the all-male police team perceived himself as having significantly lower self-esteem than almost everyone else.

Perceived Intelligence

In the ANOVA of the perceived intelligence score, the interaction of individual status and group status was significant, F (2, 138) = 3.81, $p <$ .05. Means are presented in Table 7.3 in Chapter 7 (SDs for the high-status officer in all-male, male–female, and all-female teams were 1.31, .96, and 1.16, and for the low-status officer were .85, 1.01, and 1.51, respectively).

As in the analysis of the Self-Evaluation Scale, comparisons were made between high- and low-status officers within each of the three police teams. The comparison for the all-male team was significant ($p <$ .01). The high-status man perceived himself as having significantly lower intelligence than the low-status man perceived himself as having. The comparisons for the male–female and all-female teams were not significant.

To explore this finding further, the perceptions on intelligence score for the high-status man in the all-male team was compared with all other officers. The comparisons with both officers in the male–female team were significant (both $ps < .01$). For comparisons with the officers in the all-female team, one comparison (with the high-status officer) tended in the predicted direction ($p < .20$); the other (with the low-status officer) did not approach significance.

Education

To examine whether there could be any basis for the high-status man's perceived low intelligence, an ANOVA was done using the education score. None of the effects was significant, indicating that the high-status man did not have a significantly lower educational level than other officers. Thus, his low self-rating on intelligence could not be explained by deficiencies in his educational level, compared with other officers.

Female Coworkers Scale

In the ANOVA for the female coworkers scale, the main effect for group status was significant, F (2, 138) = 6.93, $p < .001$. This main effect was examined in light of the significant individual status by group status interaction, F (2, 138) = 4.79, $p < .01$. Means are presented in Table 7.3 in Chapter 7 (SDs for high-status officers in all-male, male–female, and all-female teams were 1.84, 1.53, and 1.35, and for low-status officers were 1.63, 1.48, and 1.64, respectively).

Comparisons between high- and low-status officers within each police team showed that in the all-male partnership, the high-status man perceived himself as being significantly less able to work effectively with female coworkers than the low-status man perceived himself ($p < .01$). Comparisons between high- and low-status officers in the male–female and all-female teams were not significant.

Additional comparisons showed that the mean for the high-status man in the all-male team was significantly lower than the means for all other officers ($ps < .001$ or $.01$), indicating that the high-status man in the all-male partnership perceived himself as having significantly less ability to work with females than did everyone else (see Table 6.2 in Chapter 6).

Thus, the pattern of results for the female coworkers scale is similar to that described previously for the Self-Evaluation Scale and perceived intelligence scale—the high-status man in the all-male partnership perceived himself as having lower self-esteem, less intelligence, and more difficulty working with females than did the other officers.

Male Coworkers Scale

In the ANOVA for the male coworkers scale, none of the effects were statistically significant. No differences were found between high- and low-status officers in their perceived ability to work effectively with males. Thus, the high-status man in the all-male team's perceived difficulty in working with coworkers was restricted to females; it did not include males.

MULTIPLE REGRESSION ANALYSES FOR THE SELF-EVALUATION SCALE AND DEMOGRAPHIC VARIABLES: SENIOR MAN IN ALL-MALE POLICE TEAM VERSUS OTHER OFFICERS

Self-Evaluation Scale

Previous analyses found that the senior male in the all-male police team had the lowest score obtained on the Self-Evaluation Scale—a score significantly lower than his partner's and significantly lower than all but one of the scores for the other four officers.

The senior man's perception of himself as having fewer positive personality traits (more of the undesirable dominating traits and less of the desirable expressive traits) in comparison with other officers might account for his low Self-Evaluation Score (self-esteem). To test this hypothesis, analyses of covariance were performed using hierarchical multiple regression analyses with the Self-Evaluation Score as the dependent variable (Cohen & Cohen, 1983). In one analysis, the senior man in the all-male team was compared with his junior male partner (partner analysis); and in another analysis, he was compared with all other officers including his partner (all officers analysis).

The covariates were the scores on the dominating and expressive traits. Status of officer was coded as a dummy variable, with the senior man in the all-male partnership = 0 and the officer(s) with whom he was being compared = 1.

For these regression analyses, the dominating traits (A) and expressive traits (B) were entered into the equation on the first step, and status of officer (C) was entered on the second step. The requirement for homogeneity of regression between groups was assessed by entering the interactions—dominating traits × status of officer (A × B), expressive traits × status of officer (A × C)—on the third step.

In both analyses, the dominating and expressive traits accounted for a highly significant proportion of the variance in the Self-Evaluation Score when entered into the equation on the first step (partner analysis 29%, all officers analysis 30%; both $ps < .001$; see Table 7.4 in Chapter 7). No additional variance was accounted for by status of officer when it was entered into the equation on the second step, or by the interaction terms when they were entered on the third step.

These results are consistent with the interpretation that the differences in the Self-Evaluation Score (self-esteem) found in the previous ANOVAs were due to differences between the levels of dominating and expressive traits associated with the senior man in the all-male team in comparison to his partner, and in comparison with all other officers. In other words, the senior man perceived himself as having the greatest amount of negative personality traits in comparison with all other officers—as having more undesirable dominating traits and fewer desirable expressive traits—and, as a result, he had lower self-esteem.

These results suggest that even though other officers had varying amounts of negative traits (see Tables 4.1 and 4.2 in Chapter 4), they all had some positive traits to draw on to maintain their self-esteem (see Blaine & Crocker, 1993). They also suggest there is a critical level of negative traits. Once this critical level is reached, as it was for the most senior man, people are no longer able to maintain their self-esteem through various compensatory mechanisms.

Work Experience, Education, and Age

These analyses examined the possibility that the senior man in the all-male police team had lower self-esteem than his junior male partner because he was still a police officer, like his lower-status partner, and had not been promoted to a higher rank. Analyses of covariance using hierarchical multiple regression analysis were performed using work experience, education, and age as covariates and the Self-Evaluation Score as the dependent variable. In one analysis, the senior man was compared with his junior partner; in another analysis, he was compared with all other officers including his partner.

The three covariates—years of work experience, education, and age—were entered into the equation on the first step, status of officer was entered on the second step, and the interaction terms were entered on the third step. The results did not support this alternate explanation—the covariates failed to account for a significant proportion of the variance in the Self-Evaluation Score.

MULTIPLE REGRESSION ANALYSES FOR PERCEIVED INTELLIGENCE: SENIOR MAN IN ALL-MALE POLICE TEAM VERSUS OTHER OFFICERS

Individuals' perceptions of their intelligence differ from their global self-esteem because intelligence is a very specific attribute. It is possible that differences in the levels of dominating and expressive traits associated with the senior man in the all-male team in comparison with other officers lead to differences in global self-esteem, which then lead to differences in specific attributes such as the self-perceptions on intelligence (see Wyer & Srull, 1989).

To test this hypothesis, hierarchical multiple regression analyses were performed in which the dependent variable was the perceived intelligence score (Cohen & Cohen, 1983). In one analysis, the senior man in the all-male team was compared with his junior male partner (partner analysis), and in another analysis, he was compared with all other officers, including his junior partner (all officers analysis). For these analyses, status of officer was entered into the equation first, the dominating and expressive traits were entered second, and the Self-Evaluation Score was entered third (see Table 7.4 in Chapter 7). Status of officer was coded as a dummy variable with the senior man in the all-male partnership = 0 and the officer(s) with whom he was being compared = 1.

In both multiple regression analyses, status of officer accounted for a significant proportion of the variance in the perceived intelligence score when it was entered into the equation on the first step (partner analysis 6%, all officers analysis 3%; $ps < .01$ and $.001$, respectively). As expected, the senior male officer perceived himself as having lower intelligence in comparison to his junior male partner, and in comparison with all other officers.

On the second step of the analyses, the dominating and expressive traits accounted for an additional proportion of the variance, which was statistically significant (partner analysis 5%, all officers analysis 4%; $ps < .05$ and $.005$, respectively). On the third step, the Self-Evaluation Score accounted for a substantial additional portion of the variance, which was highly significant in both analyses (partner analysis 31%, all officers analysis 15%; both $ps < .001$). An examination of the standardized beta weights showed that status of officer, as well as the dominating and expressive traits, were no longer significantly related to the dependent variable when the Self-Evaluation Score was brought into the equation.

Thus, the results from both analyses were consistent with the hypothesis that differences in the levels of dominating and expressive traits associated with the senior man in the all-male team in comparison with his partner and all other officers led him to develop a more globally negative view of himself (lower self-esteem), which then led him to perceive himself as less intelligent (Wyer & Srull, 1989).

PARTIAL CORRELATIONS BETWEEN THE BIPOLAR TRAITS AND OTHER EPAQ TRAITS FOR OFFICERS IN DIFFERENT POLICE TEAMS

The bipolar traits differ from all the other EPAQ traits because one pole is desirable for women and the other pole is desirable for men

(Spence, Helmreich, & Stapp, 1974, 1975). By contrast, for all of the other EPAQ traits, the same pole is desirable for both sexes. Because of this difference between the bipolar traits and the other EPAQ traits, it is difficult to interpret any partial correlations between them. Consequently, these partial correlations were not included in Chapter 8 and instead are presented here.

Partial correlations between the bipolar traits and all of the other EPAQ traits were computed for high and low-status officers within each of the three police teams—all-male, male–female, and all-female. Each officer's score on the Self-Evaluation Scale was used to control for the desirability of that officer's personality traits. The results are presented in Table X.

TABLE X
Partial Correlations Between the Bipolar Traits and the Other EPAQ Traits for High- and Low-Status Officers in Different Police Teams

| Police Team and Status of Officer | Personality Traits | | | | |
	Instrumental	Expressive	Dominating	Submissive	Verbal-Aggressive
All-Male					
High Status	.25*	.11	−.07	−.23[a]	−.30*
Low Status	.42****	−.25[a]	.00	−.60****	−.15
Male–Female					
High Status	.44****	−.38**	.17	−.34**	−.24[a]
Low Status	.55****	−.26[a]	.29*	−.21	−.22
All-Female					
High Status	.47*	−.23	−.17	−.14	−.32
Low Status	.46*	−.14	.05	−.21	.10

Note. These partial correlations control for self-evaluation or the overall desirability of an officer's personality. For the all-male, male–female, and all-female teams, *df*s = 57, 54, and 24, respectively.
[a]$p < .10$. *$p < .05$. **$p < .01$. ****$p < .001$.

Notes

INTRODUCTION: WOMEN AND MEN IN POLICING

1. Throughout the book, the terms "sex" or "sex category" refer to the appearance of an individual that results in the categorization and labeling of that individual as "female" or "male" and is the basis of most social organization; "gender" refers to judgments or inferences about the sexes, such as stereotypes, roles, and masculinity and femininity (Deaux, 1993; Unger, 1979; Wiley, 1995). These terms do not imply anything about biological or sociocultural causes (Deaux, 1993).

2. Police officers work together as partners more frequently in large, urban areas, as compared with other locations (Department of Justice, 1992).

3. Both the female and the male police officer had seven years' experience as police officers.

4. It should be noted that most of the research on the modal police personality has used self-report personality measures (see, for example, Lefkowitz, 1975; Niederhoffer, 1967); in other words, previous research has measured officers' perceptions of their own personality traits, as will be studied here.

5. One study (Davis, 1984) purports to find female police officers to be more authoritarian and more cynical than male officers. Findings from this study need to be taken with caution, however, because a brief two-item scale was used to measure authoritarianism instead of the standard 30-item California F scale (Christie, 1991). Furthermore, cynicism was measured by a single item instead of the standard 20-item scale used in most research (Niederhoffer, 1967).

6. The NYPD did a preliminary survey for this study of all police teams working together in radio motor patrol cars throughout the 75 precincts of New York City.

The survey showed that 84% of the teams were all-male, 12% were male–female, and 4% were all-female.

7. The preliminary survey by the NYPD of all police teams throughout New York City found that 10% of the officers were women and 90% were men.

8. The expectation that men act as leader and women as follower in male–female police teams is consistent with research on other populations. For example, research with college students has found that a woman who is paired with a man defers to the man as leader when the task is "masculine-typed" (Carbonell, 1984; Megargee, 1969).

CHAPTER 1: THE STATUS MODEL OF GENDER STEREOTYPING

1. The gender-specific model is also called the "essentialist" model (Bohan, 1993).

2. More recently, in personality theory, psychological traits have been used less frequently to refer to inherent characteristics of an individual's personality that predict and explain the person's behavior. Instead, they refer to concepts used by both lay people and psychologists to describe clusters of semantically or functionally related characteristics (Wyer & Lambert, 1994).

3. Gender stereotypes are more or less accurate judgments of the probability that a man or a woman will manifest instrumental or expressive traits (Fiske & Taylor, 1991; McCauley et al., 1980).

4. In a highly masculine-typed occupation such as policing, sex category is highly salient and generally supersedes all other status characteristics. Even if a female officer has more seniority or education, the male officer still has the higher status (Martin, 1990). The mechanisms by which sex category comes to operate as a status characteristic in work organizations have been discussed elsewhere (Acker, 1999; Heilman, 1995; Ridgeway, 1997; Webster & Hysom, 1998).

5. The NYPD's preliminary survey of all police teams working together in radio motor patrol cars throughout New York City showed that only a minority (10%) of the officers were women; the majority (90%) were men. These percentages are comparable to ones found in other police departments (Martin, 1990).

6. Most of the research in laboratory settings has been carried out with college students who were not previously acquainted with one another (Berger et al., 1977; Buss & Craik, 1984).

7. The sample of police partners selected for the present study was comprised of partners who were presently working together. At the time they participated in the study, they had worked together for an average of one year and eight months. Based on this average, we would assume that many partners work together for more than a year.

8. The masculinity and femininity scales have also been called "agency" and "communion," respectively (Spence et al., 1979).

9. The instrumental traits have shown higher correlations with self-esteem than the expressive traits (Spence et al., 1979; Whitley, 1983). However, this may be because of overlap between some of the items on the instrumental and self-esteem scales (Nicholls, Licht, & Pearl, 1982).

10. The Geis and associates (1984) masculinity–femininity scale contains items that overlap with the EPAQ bipolar, instrumental, dominating, and submissive scales; it also includes an item that relates to roles ("leader" versus "follower").

11. Because research has shown that, in addition to the socially desirable instrumental and expressive traits, both sexes have other undesirable traits (Spence et al., 1979), the argument still holds that they would have similar levels of self-esteem.

CHAPTER 2: STATUS CHARACTERISTICS THEORY AND THE GENDER-STEREOTYPED PERSONALITY TRAITS

1. See Chapter 1, Note 4.

2. The task-related behaviors described by status characteristics theory consist of: (a) performance outputs—attempts to solve the problem of the group, as well as giving opinions, suggestions, and information; (b) action opportunities—being encouraged to talk, asked questions, and asked for suggestions; (c) influence—acceptance of suggestions by others when there is disagreement (Berger et al., 1977, p. 19).

3. A key concept of status characteristics theory is that status is *relational*. An individual's status position is always designated with reference to the interaction partner (Berger et al., 1977).

4. In the field of policing, sex category is a highly salient status characteristic. However, in other situations, status characteristics such as race or educational level could also be used to designate group status.

5. It is important to note that group status is dependent on the *proportion* of men and women in different types of police teams. This differs from the way sex category is used to designate the individual status of officers in male–female police teams: In these teams, an individual officer's status is determined by his or her sex category, with the male high and the female low in individual status. Thus, a male–female police team would have an intermediate group status; however, within this team, the male officer would have a high individual status and the female officer would have a low individual status. Sex category is not relevant to the designation of the officers' individual status in same-sex police teams; instead, work experience is most relevant.

6. Individual status is designated by the most salient status characteristic. In a same-sex police team, work experience is primarily used, and in a male–female police team, sex category is used. By contrast, group status is designated in the same way in all police teams—by the proportion of men and women in the team. For example, an all-male police team would have a high group status; however, within this team, the less-experienced male officer would have a low individual status.

The statistical analyses, described later, test the postulate that individual status and group status are independent variables that have separate and independent effects on personality trait ratings. In the analyses of variance performed on the data, two main effects are predicted: one for individual status and another for group status. If these predictions are incorrect, then the interactions of individual status and group status should be statistically significant.

7. Although task-related behaviors generally are viewed in a positive light (Berger et al., 1977), some of the high-status group leader's task-related behaviors can appear to be "aggressive," leading to diminished liking by other group members (Bales, 1958).

CHAPTER 3: DESCRIPTION OF THE STUDY: THE SAMPLE OF POLICE PARTNERS AND MEASURES

1. Most sergeants are male, and few are female.

2. Because some of the police partners' questionnaires did not indicate the officers' precinct, they had to be excluded from the matching process.

3. In a field study such as this, people cannot be randomly assigned to conditions, and sometimes status information is inconsistent (see Norman, Smith, & Berger, 1988). For example, relative education might be inconsistent with seniority in same-sex police teams—the officer with more seniority might have less education than his or her partner. Because none of the main effects or interactions involving consistency of status characteristics was significant in any of the analyses of variance of the EPAQ traits, consistency did not affect any reported results (see Appendix C).

4. One same-sex team could not be categorized because all three characteristics were the same for both partners.

5. As discussed previously, sex category is such a highly salient status characteristic in male–female police teams that it generally supercedes all other status characteristics. It is interesting to note, however, that if status had been designated by seniority/education/age in male–female teams (as it was in same-sex teams) the man would have been high status in 59% of the teams, and the woman would have been high status in 41%.

6. It is important to note that group status is determined separately from individual status. Sex category is used to designate individual status in the male–female partnership, but this is a separate determination from overall group status that depends on the *proportion* of males and females in different types of police partnerships.

As indicated in Chapter 2, group status can be designated on the basis of other types of status characteristics, such as race. Because sex category is so highly salient within the masculine-typed police department, it is most relevant to the overall group status of different kinds of police partnerships.

7. The items on each of the EPAQ scales are presented here (Spence et al., 1974, 1979). With some exceptions, each item is labeled with the end points "very" and "not at all"—for example, "very independent" and "not at all independent." For traits with different end points, both labels are given. For each of the bipolar traits, the first-listed label is feminine-typed and the second-listed label is masculine-typed.

Instrumental traits are: independent, very active—very passive, competitive, can make decisions easily—has difficulty making decisions, never gives up easily— gives up very easily, self-confident, feels very superior—feels very inferior, stands up well under pressure—goes to pieces under pressure. Dominating traits are: arrogant, boastful, egotistical, greedy, dictatorial, cynical, hostile, looks out only for self; unprincipled—does not look out only for self; principled. Expressive traits are: emotional, able to devote self completely to others—not at all able to devote self completely to others, very gentle—very rough, helpful to others, kind, aware of feelings of others, understanding of others, very warm in relations with others— very cold in relations with others. Verbal-aggressive traits are: whiny, complaining, nags a lot—doesn't nag, fussy. Submissive traits are: spineless, subordinates oneself to others—never subordinates oneself to others, servile, gullible. Bipolar traits are:

very home-oriented—very worldly, very strong need for security—very little need for security, highly needful of others' approval—indifferent to others' approval, feelings easily hurt—feelings not easily hurt, cries very easily—never cries, very excitable in a major crisis—not at all excitable in a major crisis, not at all aggressive—very aggressive, very submissive—very dominant.

The order of rating items from different scales is randomized, and "masculine" and "feminine" poles are counterbalanced between left and right.

8. The bipolar traits are also called the "sex-specific" traits (Spence et al., 1975).

9. Each item on the unilateral power scale is rated: all the time, most of the time, more often than not, occasionally, rarely, or never.

10. The control over team activities scale asks, "To what extent do you exert control over the activities in your partnership?" This is rated as follows: none or not at all, very little, moderate amount, substantial amount, or extreme amount.

11. On the perceived intelligence scale, the end points are labeled: not at all (very) intelligent. On the perceived job success scale, the end points are labeled: not at all (very) highly regarded by superiors.

On the male and female coworkers scales, the end points are labeled: "does not work effectively with male (female) coworkers" and "works effectively with male (female) coworkers."

12. For the team competence scales, the supervisor was asked to "describe the way both partners work together as a team" on items with end points labeled: the team is not at all (very) competent in their work together; the team is not (very) effective in handling service-oriented calls (e.g., lost child or accident cases); the team is not (very) effective in handling enforcement situations (e.g., arrests or summons); the team is not (highly) effective in working with the public.

For the individual performance items, the end points are labeled: not at all (very) competent on the job; not at all (very) highly regarded by superiors.

For the leadership scale, the end points are labeled: "In the partnership, the partner never (always) acts as the leader."

13. Race/ethnic group was categorized as follows: white, black, Hispanic, Asian, American Indian, or other. Education was categorized as follows: 1 = college MA degree, 2 = some graduate work in college, but no degree, 3 = college BA degree, 4 = associate college degree (2 years of college), 5 = some college, but no degree, 6 = high school graduate, 7 = some high school, but not a graduate.

14. For example, officers were asked to rate who made the final decisions in the partnership—"myself" or "my partner"—on a five-point scale. Officers were then asked to illustrate the way in which decisions were usually made by describing an incident in detail. They were asked to include a description of the situation, what was said and done by both partners, and what happened afterward. Officers were also asked to describe situations in which decisions were made in a different way.

CHAPTER 4: STATUS AND PERSONALITY: THE DOMINATING, INSTRUMENTAL, AND EXPRESSIVE TRAITS

1. The dominating and expressive traits were analyzed separately in a 2 (individual status) by 3 (group status) analysis of variance. The factor for individual status

included the high- and low-status officers; the factor for group status included the highest-status (all-male), intermediate-status (male–female), and lowest-status (all-female) partnerships. Because high- and low-status officers were members of the same partnership, the factor for individual status was analyzed as a repeated measure.

According to the status model, individual status and group status are independent dimensions that should both affect trait ratings. Thus, it is predicted that there will be two main effects in the analyses of variance: one for individual status and another for group status. If these predictions are incorrect and both sexes are rated in stereotypic ways, then the interactions of individual status and group status should be significant.

Eight police teams were not included in these analyses because of discrepancies or the absence of information about critical variables.

2. The effects for group status in the analyses of the dominating and expressive traits are both significant—$ps < .05$ and $.01$, respectively. However, the linear trend analyses fail to reach significance, indicating that the means do not vary linearly across the three partnership types.

3. The instrumental traits were analyzed in a 2 (individual status) by 3 (group status) repeated measures analysis of variance. None of the main effects or interaction effects were significant. The overall means for the entire sample of police officers were: self-perceptions $M = 23.60$, partner-perceptions $M = 23.37$.

4. The concept of "instrumentality" (or "agency" as it is sometimes called) contains two types of attributes—highly directive, dominant attributes and self-directive, goal-oriented attributes (Spence, Deaux, & Helmreich, 1985). Sometimes both types of attributes are included in a single scale, but the EPAQ measures them as two separate aspects of instrumentality—the "dominating" traits and the "instrumental" traits.

Previous studies that have found connections among status, power, and instrumentality have used measures containing both types of attributes (Conway et al., 1996; Gerber, 1988, 1991; Smoreda, 1995). The short form of the S. L. Bem (1981) scale used in some of these studies (Conway et al., 1996; Gerber, 1991) contains highly directive, dominant attributes, such as "dominant," "strong personality," "forceful," and "aggressive," in addition to more self-directive, goal-oriented attributes, such as "independent," "willing to take a stand," and "defends own beliefs." The Gerber (1988) study used a 14-item version of the Bem scale, and the Smoreda (1995) study used an 11-item French version of the Bem scale. Again, however, both scales included highly dominant traits in addition to more self-directive instrumental traits. In two of the studies reported in the Conway and associates (1996) paper, attributes drawn from the EPAQ were used—these included items from the standard EPAQ "instrumental" scale, such as "independent" and "never gives up easily," in addition to highly dominant items from the EPAQ "bipolar" scale, such as "aggressive" and "dominant."

All of the just-cited studies involve the perceptions of hypothetical situations. In addition, results from studies of interactions between people, some of which took place in actual work situations, are consistent with the argument that status is related to dominating characteristics, not self-directive, goal-oriented instrumental characteristics (Johnson, 1993; Moskowitz, Suh, & Desaulniers, 1994). In these studies, status was found to be related to dominating behaviors, but the more task-oriented instrumental behaviors were unrelated to status.

5. In the preliminary survey for this study by the NYPD, only 4% of the police teams in precincts throughout New York City were all-female.

6. To explore this hypothesis, correlations were computed between the supervisor's rating of team competence and the dominating traits, as well as the expressive traits. The score for each of the traits was the combined (or averaged) score for both dyad members' perceptions of the partner.

7. The correlations between the supervisor's rating of the all-female team's competence and the combined self-perceptions for the dominating and expressive traits are: rs (20) = .29 and −.05, $n.s.$, respectively.

8. None of the correlations involving the perceptions of the self are significant for the all-male and male–female partnerships. The correlations between supervisor's ratings of team competence and the self-perceptions on the dominating and expressive traits for the all-male and male–female teams range from r (48) = −.14 to r (44) = .11, $n.s.$ In addition, none of the correlations involving the perceptions of the partner reaches significance (see Table 4.3).

9. If the results had reflected sex-typed personality differences with women perceived as having more expressive traits and men perceived as having more dominating traits, then the interaction terms in the analyses of variance would have been significant. However, the interaction terms do not even approach significance in the analyses of variance of the dominating and expressive traits—both Fs (2, 138) < 1.00, $n.s.$

10. Selection bias could not account for the observed effect of status on personality dispositions. If a supervisor formed same-sex teams based on the supervisor's accurate estimates of complementary personalities, then experience presumably would be independent of the personality measure. The only reason to expect that experience would affect perceived personality traits is the theoretical link that has been elaborated here. In addition, any selection bias would have had to involve different supervisors in 53 precincts throughout the five boroughs of New York City.

11. For the self-perceptions, when the two status variables are entered into the equation, the increase in R^2 is statistically significant ($p < .05$) in the analysis of the dominating traits; it tends toward significance ($p < .10$) in the analysis of the expressive traits (see Table 4.5).

12. The final equations in the analyses of the self-perceptions are: dominating traits, $R = .23$, $p < .01$; expressive traits, $R = .32$, $p < .001$. The final equations in the analyses of the partner-perceptions are: dominating traits, $R = .13$, $p = .20$; expressive traits, $R = .20$, $p < .01$.

If we reverse the regressions and enter the status variables first, we find significant effects for the beta weights that parallel those from the previously reported analyses of variance—and again, no effects for sex of officer (see Appendix C). These analyses demonstrate once more that all of the variance in personality attributions is accounted for by the two status variables.

CHAPTER 5: COPING WITH LOW STATUS: THE VERBAL-AGGRESSIVE AND SUBMISSIVE TRAITS

1. Verbal aggressiveness and submissiveness might also be used by low-status individuals when relative status is designated by other diffuse status characteristics, such as race.

2. The verbal-aggressive and submissive traits were each analyzed in a 2 by 3 repeated measures analysis of variance with factors for individual status and group status. Separate analyses were performed for the perceptions of the self and the perceptions of the partner. No significant main effects were found for either individual status or group status, but the interactions between individual status and group status were significant in both analyses of the verbal-aggressive traits and in the partner-perceptions analysis of the submissive traits. Further statistical tests showed that these significant interactions primarily resulted from differences between high- and low-status officers in the male-female police team. For a more extensive description of the results, see Appendix C.

3. In the all-male partnership, the low-status man is perceived as significantly more verbally aggressive than the high-status man ($p < .01$). However, this result is found only in the analysis of the partner-perceptions, not the analysis of the self-perceptions (see Appendix C). In contrast to the results for the low-status woman in the male–female partnership, the low-status man's verbal aggression does not gain him any increased influence (see Appendix C), suggesting that verbal aggression is only effective when an ascribed status characteristic, such as sex category, is used to designate low status. To test this hypothesis, future research might explore whether verbal aggression is effective when another ascribed status characteristic, such as race, is used to designate status.

In addition, it appears from the means in Table 4.5 that the high-status woman in the all-female partnership is perceived (by herself and her partner) as high on verbal aggression. However, the comparisons between high- and low-status officers do not approach significance—perhaps because of the relatively small number of all-female police teams.

4. As can be seen in Table 5.2, the female officer's self-ratings on the verbal aggressive traits are correlated with her relative work experience ($p < .005$), her own and her partner's scores on the Police Decision Scale ($ps < .06$ and $.05$, respectively), as well as her own and her partner's self-ratings on the job success scales ($ps < .05$ and $.005$, respectively).

5. As can be seen in Table 5.2, the male officer's self-rating on the verbal-aggressive traits tends to be negatively correlated with his female partner's perception of her job success ($p < .10$).

6. For the correlation between the male officer's verbal aggression and the supervisor's rating of his female partner's individual performance, $r (45) = -.11$, n.s.

7. For the correlation between the male officer's verbal aggression and the supervisor's rating of his individual performance, $r (45) = 39, p < .01$.

It is interesting to note that the correlation between the female officer's verbal aggression and the supervisor's evaluation of her individual performance is not significant, $r (44) = .02$, n.s., indicating that the female officer's verbal aggression is unrelated to the way the supervisor evaluates her job performance. Perhaps because the supervisor sees the woman's verbal aggression simply as typical of women in general, it has no impact on his assessment of her job performance.

8. The woman's perceived submissiveness is not associated with her increased influence: in the male–female partnership, the correlation between the partner's perception of the woman's submissive traits and his perception of her influence, as measured by the Police Decision scale, is not significant $r (52) = .17$, n.s.). Further, in contrast to the findings for verbal aggression, the partner's perception of the

woman's submissive traits is unrelated to other status differences involving relative work experience, education, or age.

9. As described in the chapter, low-status women in male–female police teams are perceived as more verbally aggressive than their male partners in both the analyses of the self-perceptions and the partner-perceptions. The low-status man in the all-male team is also perceived as more verbally aggressive than his partner, but only in the analysis of the partner-perceptions; thus this finding is not consistent for both analyses.

CHAPTER 6: POLICE OFFICERS WHO VIOLATE GENDER NORMS: THE BIPOLAR TRAITS

1. Even though female police officers are often stereotyped as being highly emotional, in actuality, they can develop the same emotional guardedness as do male officers (McElhinny, 1993).

2. For example, in the Carbonell (1984) study, dominant women were less likely to be the leader when paired with a man on masculine-typed tasks. However, when performing a feminine-typed task, dominant women were able to take a leadership role—probably because the feminine-typed nature of the task validated their gender identity.

3. Gender-stereotyped traits on which the same pole is desirable for both sexes are the instrumental and expressive traits; those on which the same pole is undesirable for both sexes are the dominating, submissive, and verbal-aggressive traits (Spence et al., 1979).

4. As with many assumptions about gender, research has shown that different gender-related characteristics have little to do with an individual's actual gender identity (Spence & Sawin, 1985).

5. It is important to note that the supervisor's evaluations are based exclusively on the way police officers in gender-deviant roles describe themselves on the bipolar traits. The supervisor's evaluations are not based on these officers' self-descriptions on the dominating and expressive traits because there were no statistically significant correlations found between the officers' self-ratings on the dominating and expressive traits and the supervisor's competence evaluations.

CHAPTER 7: SELF-ESTEEM: THE IMPACT OF STATUS AND PERSONALITY TRAITS

1. Maccoby and Jacklin (1974) report that men and women are similar in global self-esteem. In subsequent meta-analytic studies comparing men's and women's global self-esteem, small effect sizes are found favoring males. The Kling and associates (1999) study reports an overall effect size of .21, and the Major and associates (1999) study reports an overall effect size of –.14. However, an effect size of .21 is considered small (Cohen, 1977), and an overall effect size of –.14 "could be considered so small as to be of little meaning or practical significance, even if it did attain statistical significance" (Major et al., 1999, p. 245).

2. In addition, people often have assumed that blacks would have lower self-esteem than whites because blacks have lower status within our society. However, research has shown that, contrary to people's assumption, blacks generally score

higher on self-esteem than whites (Rosenberg, 1979; Wylie, 1979), suggesting that status is not the critical factor in determining self-esteem.

3. Also see Paula Caplan (1984), who argues against theories postulating that women are "naturally" masochistic. She shows how women's so-called masochistic behavior can be explained by societal pressures, social survival, and a wish to maintain a positive view of the self.

4. A 2 by 2 ANOVA was used with factors for individual status (high-status and low-status officers) and group status (highest-status all-male, intermediate-status male–female, and lowest-status all-female partnerships). The factor for individual status was analyzed as a repeated measure because high- and low-status officers were members of the same partnership.

5. The comparison with the low-status woman in the all-female team is in the predicted direction ($p < .25$).

6. It is conceivable that the high-status man in the all-male police team perceives himself as having less desirable attributes than the low-status man because he is still a police officer, like his lower-status partner, and has not been promoted to a higher rank. To examine this possibility, analyses of covariance using hierarchical regression analysis were performed using work experience, education, and age as covariates. The results do not support this alternate explanation—the covariates fail to account for a significant proportion of the variance in the self-esteem score (see Appendix C).

7. Fenster and Locke (1973) found that college students as a group, whether police or civilians, did not differ from one another in IQ scores. However, college students as a group were superior to non–college-educated police and civilians. In addition, and perhaps most germane, non–college-educated police had significantly higher IQs than non–college-educated civilians.

8. In this case illustration, even though the senior officer feels bad about himself, he is perceived by his junior partner in a positive light. This is consistent with the statistical findings from the present study. As described previously, senior officers in all-male police teams perceive themselves as being relatively low in self-esteem. However, an additional analysis of variance of the partners' perceptions of the other officers' self-esteem show that the junior officer does not perceive the senior officer in the all-male team as having low self-esteem in comparison to other officers (none of the effects in the analysis of variance of partners' perceptions of the other officers' self-esteem score reached statistical significance).

9. A number of research studies have found self-esteem to be correlated substantially with the instrumental traits but only correlated marginally with the expressive traits (Whitley, 1983). Further investigation showed that many of the scales used to measure self-esteem in these studies were biased in favor of the instrumental traits (Nicholls et al., 1982). When an unbiased, gender-neutral Self-Evaluation Scale is used, as it is here, self-esteem is found to be substantially correlated with both the instrumental and expressive traits, indicating that they both enhance self-esteem, just as we would expect (see Appendix B).

CHAPTER 8: THE PATTERNING OF TRAITS WITHIN INDIVIDUAL PERSONALITY

1. Bakan's (1966) concept of "agency" contains elements of the positive aspects of instrumentality in addition to the negative aspects that are of concern here.

"Self-assertion" is included in both the socially desirable instrumental traits and the socially undesirable, instrumentally oriented dominating traits; the "urge to master" is included only in the undesirable dominating traits.

2. Authentic mastery experiences (enactive attainments) are not the only source of judgments of self-efficacy. Other sources include: vicarious experiences, seeing others similar to oneself perform successfully, verbal persuasion, and information from one's physiological state (Bandura, 1982).

3. Results from the analyses of variance for the perceptions of the self on the instrumental traits and on the submissive traits (see Appendix C) show no significant differences as a function of status of individual police officer (individual status) or partnership type (group status) indicating that, as a group, police officers have similar levels of these traits.

The overall means for police officers on the instrumental and submissive traits were compared with the norms for college males. College males were used for the comparisons because they are more extreme than college females on these traits—they are higher on the instrumental traits and lower on the submissive traits. For the instrumental traits, the standard deviation was available in the normative sample (Spence & Helmreich, 1975, p. 50), and so a z test was used for the comparison. For the submissive traits, the standard deviation was not given in the normative sample (Spence et al., 1979), and so a t test was used.

For the instrumental traits, the overall mean for police officers (M = 23.60) is significantly higher than the norm for college males, z = 7.69, N = 282, p < .001. For the submissive traits, the overall mean for police officers (M = 6.39) is significantly lower than the norm for college males, t (281) = 16.32, p < .001. These results indicate that, as a group, police officers perceive themselves as being extremely high on the instrumental traits and extremely low on the submissive traits, regardless of their status.

4. The partial correlations between the bipolar traits and all of the other personality traits on the EPAQ can be found in Appendix C. The bipolar traits differ from the other traits in that one pole is desirable for women and the other pole is desirable for men (for all of the other traits, the same pole is desirable for both sexes). Because of this, partial correlations involving the bipolar traits are difficult to interpret and are not included in the tables in this chapter.

5. Previous research (Helmreich et al., 1981; Spence et al., 1979) used zero-order correlations to examine the interrelatedness of personality traits, which meant that the correlations were affected by the social desirability of traits. The present procedure extends the earlier research by using partial correlations to remove the effects due to social desirability.

6. As shown in Table 8.1, the partial correlation involving the high-status officer in the all-male partnership tends toward significance (p < .10).

7. As shown in Table 8.1, the partial correlation involving the low-status officer in the all-male team tends toward significance (p < .10).

8. See Note 3.

9. None of the members of all-male and male–female police teams show positive correlations between pairs of all three socially undesirable traits. However, significant positive partial correlations between the dominating and verbal-aggressive traits are found for the high- and low-status officers in the all-male team and for the low-status officer in the male–female team (see Tables 8.1 and 8.2). In addition, the

partial correlation between the submissive and verbal-aggressive traits (but not the dominating traits) is significant for the high-status officer in the all-male team.

10. As Table 8.4 shows, the correlations of the supervisor's rating of the junior woman's leadership ability with her dominance is significant ($p < .05$), with her submissiveness is in a significant direction ($p < .20$), and with her verbal aggressiveness is not significant. Correlations of the supervisor's evaluation of team competence with all three of the junior woman's undesirable traits are in a significant direction ($ps < .20$).

11. Another possibility is that status is reflected in the dominating–expressive dimension within personality as well as the instrumental–submissive dimension. If so, one would expect positive correlations between the dominating and instrumental traits and between the expressive and submissive traits, as we find in the male–female partnership. However, this raises the question of why status would have been reflected in these two personality dimensions for officers in the male–female partnership but not for those in same-sex partnerships.

12. It is interesting to note that the dominant–submissive dimension of personality proposed by Leary (1957) was based primarily on research with samples of people in psychotherapy (Freedman, Leary, Ossorio, & Coffey, 1951). There very well may have been negative correlations between the dominating and submissive traits in these samples, but they are not representative of the population as a whole nor of samples involving work partners.

CHAPTER 9: STATUS, GENDER, AND PERSONALITY: TOWARD AN INTEGRATED THEORY

1. See Chapter 4.

2. See Chapter 8.

3. Leary (1957), for example, developed a circumflex model of personality in which the dominating and submissive traits formed a basic dimension within individual personality. However, the samples he used to develop the model were composed predominantly of psychotherapy patients, who might be expected to manifest deviant patterns of personality traits.

4. The EPAQ used in this study is the most extensive instrument for measuring the gender-stereotyped personality traits and contains scales for six different traits.

5. See Chapters 5 and 8.

6. If we simply compare women and men police officers on their EPAQ traits, as is done in most studies of men's and women's personalities, for the most part we find differences. But as we have shown throughout the book, these results obscure the more complex status processes in interactions that affect the personalities of women and men.

To illustrate this phenomenon, simple t tests were performed on the self-ratings by the male and female police officers in our sample for all of the EPAQ scales (all $dfs = 285$). Significant differences in the predicted direction are found on four of the six EPAQ scales—all of the scales on which we had previously found status differences: dominating traits, $t = 3.10$, $p < .01$ (male $M = 10.80$, female $M = 9.28$); expressive traits, $t = -5.20$, $p < .001$ (male $M = 22.48$, female $M = 24.72$); verbal-aggressive traits, $t = -3.09$, $p < .01$ (male $M = 4.76$, female $M = 5.84$); bipolar traits, $t = 3.01$, $p < .01$ (male $M = 18.40$, female $M = 17.04$).

The two EPAQ scales, which had not shown any differences related to status, do not show sex differences either: instrumental traits, $t < 1.00$, *n.s.* (male $M = 23.76$, female $M = 23.44$); submissive traits, $t < 1.00$, *n.s.* (male $M = 4.28$, female $M = 4.48$).

CHAPTER 10: IMPLICATIONS FOR POLICING

1. See Chapter 4.

2. To say that policing is a masculine-typed field and requires masculine-typed personality traits is to subscribe to the erroneous notion that all men are character-ized by instrumental traits, regardless of their status or role (Denmark, 1977). It simply begs the question: What is the function of these traits for individuals who work as police officers?

3. See Chapter 4.

4. In male–female police teams, sex category is used to designate status. This means that the male officer has high status and the woman is restricted to a low-status role. The only time women are able to assume a senior role is when they work in an all-female team—because, in this case, status is designated by seniority.

The initial survey by the NYPD of all police teams throughout New York City found that 4% were all-female, 12% were male–female, and 84% were all-male. Thus, all-female teams comprise only a very small percentage of teams within the police department, so very few women ever are able to assume a senior position. (Based on the percentages of police teams in the initial survey, only 21% of female officers were in high-status roles and 79% were in low-status roles.) Consequently, only a small minority of women ever manifest more dominating personality characteristics and fewer expressive characteristics in comparison to their partners. By contrast, because a majority of male police officers are in high-status roles, a majority of them appear to be more dominant and less accommodating than their partners. (Based on the initial survey, 53% of male officers were in high-status roles, and 47% were in low-status roles.)

In addition, and perhaps even more importantly, the proportion of men and women in different kinds of teams is also related to status. This proportion serves to designate the overall status of the team as a whole. All-male teams have the highest status, male–female teams have intermediate status, and all-female teams have the lowest status within the organization of the police department. Because the overwhelming majority of police teams are ones in which two men work together, most men work in the very highest-status teams.

5. See Chapter 4.

6. See Chapter 5.

7. See Chapter 5.

8. On the other hand, a woman who works with a man experiences an increase in her team status—as compared with a situation in which she is partnered with a woman.

9. The overall status of each team is dependent on the proportion of women versus men who work in the team. Male–female teams have a lower team status than all-male teams because the male officer has high status and the female officer

has low status, resulting in a lowered overall team status in comparison to the all-male police teams in which both officers are male and both have high status.

10. The original survey of all police teams throughout New York City found that 84% of the teams were all-male, 12% were male–female, and 4% were all-female. Given the percentages of male officers (90%) and female officers (10%) in police teams, if the choice of male or female partner were random, 80% would be all-male, 19% male–female, and 1% all-female police teams. A chi-square test showed that the difference between the actual and expected frequencies for different police teams was highly significant (the actual frequencies for different types of police teams were used for the chi square test, not the percentages given here), χ^2 (2, $N = 1502$) = 186.47, $p < .001$. These results show that the number of male-female teams was less than would be expected by chance; by contrast, there were more all-female and all-male teams. These results suggest that not only are male officers reluctant to work with women, but women officers may also be reluctant to work with men.

11. See Chapter 7.

12. The primary variable that is used to designate individual status in all-male police teams is the officer's experience relative to his partner.

13. Although some research has indicated that male police officers do not have a higher suicide rate than a matched group of males from the general population (Stack & Kelley, 1999), the low self-esteem found here may be relevant to the high suicide rate among police officers that has been reported in a variety of newspaper articles (Allen, 1995; Forrest, 1994).

Very few empirical studies of police officers have dealt with global self-esteem; the studies that have done so have found that police officers with low self-esteem suffer from increased stress and an increased number of physical and mental health symptoms (Lester, 1986; Rosse, Boss, Johnson, & Crown, 1991).

14. Additional reasons for redefining the characteristics of the ideal police officer to incorporate expressive attributes include facilitating the officer's ability to manage interpersonal disputes and establishing cooperative relations with the community (Herbert, 1997).

15. The bipolar traits include characteristics in which one pole is socially desirable for women and the other pole is desirable for men (Spence, Helmreich, & Stapp, 1979).

16. See Chapter 6.

17. Although there were numerically few all-female teams throughout New York City, this number was greater than would have been expected by chance (see Note 10).

18. See Chapter 4.

19. See Chapter 6.

20. See Chapter 8.

21. Consistent with the present findings, training officers in the Israeli military give higher course grades to male and female soldiers who describe themselves as having sex-typed personality attributes on the Bem Sex-Role Inventory (S. L. Bem, 1974), as compared with those who describe themselves as having "androgynous" or "undifferentiated" personality attributes (Dimitrovsky et al., 1989).

Other evidence that administrators and supervisors are especially attuned to sex-typed personal attributes comes from the military. When women first were admitted to West Point, administrators established a rule that women cadets were required to wear skirts, not trousers, if they wished to participate in dances held at the school (Barkalow & Raab, 1990). In addition, women recruits in the U.S. Marine Corps are required to wear makeup and take classes in makeup, hair care, and etiquette (Williams, 1989).

22. See Chapter 6.

23. In the present police study, the measures used by supervisors to evaluate the performance of each police officer and the team as a whole were very general. For example, supervisors evaluated the overall competence of each officer, overall team competence, and the overall effectiveness of the team in various situations.

References

Abramson, L. Y., Metalsky, G. I., & Alloy, L. B. (1989). Hopelessness depression: A theory-based subtype of depression. *Psychological Review, 96,* 358–372.

Acker, J. (1999). Gender and organizations. In J. S. Chafetz (Ed.), *Handbook of the sociology of gender* (pp. 177–194). New York: Kluwer Academic/Plenum.

Adlam, K. R. (1982). The police personality: Psychological consequences of being a police officer. *Journal of Police Science and Administration, 10,* 344–349.

Adler, L. L., & Denmark, F. L. (Eds.). (1995). *Violence and the prevention of violence.* Westport, CT: Praeger.

Adorno, T. W. (1950). *The authoritarian personality.* New York: Harper and Brothers.

Allen, A. C. (1995, November 2). New hot line for suicidal cops. *New York Post,* p. 28.

Allport, G. W. (1954). *The nature of prejudice.* Garden City, NY: Doubleday.

Allport, G. W. (1961). *Pattern and growth in personality.* New York: Holt, Rinehart & Winston.

Antill, J. K. (1983). Sex role complementarity versus similarity in married couples. *Journal of Personality and Social Psychology, 45,* 145–155.

Arcuri, A. F. (1976). Police pride and self-esteem: Indications of future occupational changes. *Journal of Police Science and Administration, 4,* 436–444.

Austin, T. L., & O'Neill, J. J. (1985). Authoritarianism and the criminal justice student: A test of the predispositional model. *Criminal Justice Review, 10,* 33–40.

Bakan, D. (1966). *The duality of human existence: Isolation and communion in Western man.* Boston, MA: Beacon Press.

Baker, Mark. (1985). *Cops: Their lives in their own words.* New York: Pocket Books.

Balch, R. W. (1972). The police personality: Fact or fiction. *Journal of Criminal Law, Criminology and Police Science, 63,* 106–119.

Baldwin, M. W. (1992). Relational schemas and the processing of social information. *Psychological Bulletin, 112,* 461–484.

Baldwin, M. W. (1999). Relational schemas; Research into social-cognitive aspects of interpersonal experience. In D. Cervone & Y. Shoda (Eds.), *The coherence of personality: Social-cognitive bases of consistency, variability, and organization* (pp. 127–154). New York: Guilford Press.

Bales, R. F. (1951). *Interaction process analysis: A method for the study of small groups.* Cambridge, MA: Addison-Wesley.

Bales, R. F. (1958). Task roles and social roles in problem-solving groups. In E. E. Maccoby, T. M. Newcomb, & E. L. Hartley (Eds.), *Readings in social psychology* (3rd ed., pp. 437–447). New York: Henry Holt.

Bales, R. F., & Slater, P. E. (1955). Role differentiation in small decision-making groups. In T. Parsons & R. F. Bales, *Family, socialization and interaction process* (pp. 259–306). Glencoe, IL: Free Press of Glencoe

Balkwell, J. W. (1994). Status. In M. Foschi & E. J. Lawler (Eds.), *Group processes: Sociological analyses* (pp. 119–148). Chicago: Nelson-Hall.

Banaji, M. R., & Prentice, D. A. (1994). The self in social contexts. *Annual Review of Psychology, 45,* 297–332.

Bandura, A. (1977). Self-efficacy: Toward a unifying theory of behavioral change. *Psychological Review, 84,* 191–215.

Bandura, A. (1982). Self-efficacy mechanism in human agency. *American Psychologist, 37,* 122–147.

Barkalow, C., & Raab, A. (1990). *In the men's house.* New York: Poseidon Press.

Baumeister, R. F. (1990). Suicide as escape from the self. *Psychological Review, 97,* 90–113.

Baumeister, R. F. (1998). The interface between intrapsychic and interpersonal processes: Cognition, emotion, and self as adaptations to other people. In J. M. Darley & J. Cooper (Eds.), *Attribution and social cognition: The legacy of Edward E. Jones* (pp. 201–223). Washington, DC: American Psychological Association.

Beck, A. T. (1975). *Depression: Causes and treatments.* Philadelphia: University of Pennsylvania Press.

Bem, D. J. (1972). Self-perception theory. In L. Berkowitz (Ed.), *Advances in experimental social psychology, Vol. 6* (pp. 1–62). New York: Academic Press.

Bem, S. L. (1974). The measurement of psychological androgyny. *Journal of Consulting and Clinical Psychology, 42,* 155–162.

Bem, S. L. (1981). *Bem Sex-Role Inventory: Professional Manual.* Palo Alto, CA: Consulting Psychologists Press.

Berg, B. L., & Budnick, K. J. (1986). Defeminization of women in law enforcement: A new twist in the traditional police personality. *Journal of Police Science and Administration, 14,* 314–319.

Berger, J., & Conner, T. L. (1974). Performance expectations and behavior in small groups: A revised formulation. In J. Berger, T. L. Conner, & M. H. Fisek (Eds.), *Expectation states theory: A theoretical research program* (pp. 85–109). Washington, DC: University Press of America.

Berger, J., Fisek, M. H., Norman, R. Z., & Zelditch, M., Jr. (1977). *Status characteristics and social interaction: An expectation states approach.* New York: Elsevier.

Berger, J., Rosenholtz, S. J., & Zelditch, M., Jr. (1980). Status organizing processes. *Annual Review of Sociology, 6,* 479–508.

Berger, J., Wagner, D. G., & Zelditch, M., Jr. (1985). Introduction: Expectation states theory: Review and assessment. In J. Berger & M. Zelditch, Jr. (Eds.), *Status, rewards, and influence* (pp. 1–72). San Francisco, CA: Jossey-Bass.

Berger, J., Webster, M., Jr., Ridgeway, C., & Rosenholtz, S. J. (1986). Status cues, expectations, and behavior. In E. J. Lawler (Ed.), *Advances in group processes: A research annual, Vol. 3* (pp. 1–22). Greenwich, CT: JAI Press.

Berger, J., & Zelditch, M., Jr. (Eds.). (1993). *Theoretical research programs: Studies in the growth of theory.* Stanford, CA: Stanford University Press.

Berscheid, E. (1994). Interpersonal relationships. *Annual Review of Psychology, 45,* 79–129.

Blaine, B., & Crocker, J. (1993). Self-esteem and self-serving biases in reactions to positive and negative events: An integrative review. In R. F. Baumeister (Ed.), *Self-esteem: The puzzle of low self-regard* (pp. 55–85). New York: Plenum Press.

Blascovich, J., & Tomaka, J. (1991). Measures of self-esteem. In J. P. Robinson, P. R. Shaver, & L. S. Wrightsman (Eds.), *Measures of personality and social psychological attitudes* (Vol. 1, pp. 115–160). New York: Academic Press.

Blood, R. O., Jr., & Wolfe, D. M. (1960). *Husbands and wives: The dynamics of married living.* New York: Free Press.

Blumberg, A. S. (1985). The police and the social system: Reflections and prospects. In A. S. Blumberg & E. Niederhoffer (Eds.), *The ambivalent force: Perspectives on the police* (3rd ed., pp. 3–26). Fort Worth: Holt, Rinehart and Winston.

Blumberg, A. S., & Niederhoffer, E. (Eds.). (1985). *The ambivalent force: Perspectives on the police* (3rd ed.). Fort Worth: Holt, Rinehart & Winston.

Bohan, J. S. (1993). Regarding gender: Essentialism, constructionism, and feminist psychology. *Psychology of Women Quarterly, 17,* 5–21.

Bonifacio, P. (1991). *The psychological effects of police work: A psychodynamic approach.* New York: Plenum Press.

Briggs, J. (1992). *Fractals: The patterns of chaos.* New York: Touchstone, Simon & Schuster.

Burbeck, E., & Furnham, A. (1985). Police officer selection: A critical review of the literature. *Journal of Police Science and Administration, 13,* 58–69.

Buss, D. M., & Craik, K. H. (1983). The act frequency approach to personality. *Psychological Review, 90,* 105–126.

Buss, D. M., & Craik, K. H. (1984). Acts, dispositions, and personality. In B. A. Maher & W. B. Maher (Eds.), *Progress in experimental personality research, Vol. 13* (pp. 241–301). San Diego, CA: Academic Press.

Caplan, P. J. (1984). The myth of women's masochism. *American Psychologist, 39,* 130–139.

Carbonell, J. L. (1984). Sex roles and leadership revisited. *Journal of Applied Psychology, 69,* 44–49.

Carli, L. L. (1990). Gender, language, and influence. *Journal of Personality and Social Psychology, 59,* 941–951.

Carpenter, B. N., & Raza, S. M. (1987). Personality characteristics of police applicants: Comparisons across subgroups and with other populations. *Journal of Police Science and Administration, 15,* 10–17.

Centers, R., Raven, B. H., & Rodrigues, A. (1971). Conjugal power structure: A re-examination. *American Sociological Review, 36,* 264–278.

Cervone, D. (1991). The two disciplines of personality psychology. *Psychological Science, 2,* 371–377.

Cervone, D., & Shoda, Y. (1999). Social-cognitive theories and the coherence of personality. In D. Cervone & Y. Shoda (Eds.), *The coherence of personality: Social-cognitive bases of consistency, variability, and organization* (pp. 3–33). New York: Guilford Press.

Christie, R. (1991). Authoritarianism and related constructs. In J. P. Robinson, P. R. Shaver, & L. S. Wrightsman (Eds.), *Measures of personality and social psychological attitudes, Vol. 1* (pp. 501–571). New York: Academic Press.

Cohen, J. (1977). *Statistical power analysis for the behavioral sciences* (Rev. ed.). New York: Academic Press.

Cohen, J., & Cohen, P. (1983). *Applied multiple regression/correlation analysis for the behavioral sciences* (2nd ed.). Hillsdale, NJ: Erlbaum.

Collins, P. H. (1990). *Black feminist thought: Knowledge, consciousness, and the politics of empowerment.* New York: Routledge.

Connell, R. W. (1987). *Gender and power: Society, the person and sexual politics.* Stanford, CA: Stanford University Press.

Constantinople, A. (1979). Sex-role acquisition: In search of the elephant. *Sex Roles, 5,* 121–133.

Constantinople, A. (1973). Masculinity-femininity: An exception to the famous dictum? *Psychological Bulletin, 80,* 389–407.

Conway, M., Pizzamiglio, M. T., & Mount, L. (1996). Status, communality, and agency: Implications for stereotypes of gender and other groups. *Journal of Personality and Social Psychology, 71,* 25–38.

Costrich, N., Feinstein, J., Kidder, L., & Maracek, J. (1975). When stereotypes hurt: Three studies of penalties for sex-role reversals. *Journal of Experimental Social Psychology, 11,* 520–530.

Cowen, G., & Koziej, J. (1979). The perception of sex-inconsistent behavior. *Sex Roles, 5,* 1–10.

Davis, J. A. (1984). Perspectives of policewomen in Texas and Oklahoma. *Journal of Police Science and Administration, 12,* 395–403.

Deaux, K. (1985). Sex and gender. *Annual Review of Psychology, 36,* 49–81.

Deaux, K. (1993). Commentary: Sorry, wrong number—A reply to Gentile's call. *American Psychologist, 4,* 125–126.

Deaux, K., & LaFrance, M. (1998). Gender. In D. T. Gilbert, S. T. Fiske, & G. Lindzey (Eds.), *The handbook of social psychology* (4th ed., Vol. 1, pp. 788–827). New York: McGraw-Hill.

Deaux, K., & Lewis, L. (1984). Structure of gender stereotypes: Interrelationships among components and gender label. *Journal of Personality and Social Psychology, 46,* 991–1004.

Denmark, F. L. (1977). Styles of leadership. *Psychology of Women Quarterly, 2,* 99–113.

Denmark, F. L. (1980). Psyche: From rocking the cradle to rocking the boat. *American Psychologist, 35,* 1057–1065.

Denmark, F. L. (1993). Women, leadership, and empowerment. *Psychology of Women Quarterly, 17,* 343–356.

Department of Justice. (1992). *Sourcebook of criminal justice statistics, 1991*. Washington, DC: U.S. Government Printing Office.

Dimitrovsky, L., Singer, J., & Yinon, Y. (1989). Masculine and feminine traits: Their relation to suitedness and success in training for traditionally masculine and feminine army functions. *Journal of Personality and Social Psychology, 57*, 839–847.

Dion, K. L. (1985). Sex, gender, and groups: Selected issues. In V. E. O'Leary, R. K. Unger, & B. S. Wallston (Eds.), *Women, gender, and social psychology* (pp. 293–347). Hillsdale, NJ: Erlbaum.

Doerner, W. G. (1985). I'm not the man I used to be: Reflections on the transition from prof to cop. In A. S. Blumberg & E. Niederhoffer (Eds.), *The ambivalent force: Perspectives on the police* (3rd ed., pp. 394–399). Chicago: Holt, Rinehart & Winston.

Dorsey, R. R., & Giacopassi, D. J. (1987). Demographic and work-related correlates of police officer cynicism. In D. B. Kennedy & R. J. Homant (Eds.), *Police and law enforcement, Vol. 5* (pp. 173–188). New York: AMS Press.

Eagly, A. H. (1983). Gender and social influence: A social psychological analysis. *American Psychologist, 38*, 971–981.

Eagly, A. H. (1987). *Sex differences in social behavior: A social-role interpretation*. Hillsdale, NJ: Erlbaum.

Eagly, A. H., & Karau, S. (1991). Gender and the emergence of leaders: A meta-analysis. *Journal of Personality and Social Psychology, 60*, 685–710.

Eagly, A. H., & Wood, W. (1982). Inferred sex differences in status as a determinant of gender stereotypes about social influence. *Journal of Personality and Social Psychology, 43*, 915–928.

Eagly, A. H., & Wood, W. (1985). Gender and influenceability: Stereotype versus behavior. In V. O'Leary, R. Unger, & B. Wallston (Eds.), *Sex, gender and social psychology* (pp. 225–256). Hillsdale, NJ: Erlbaum.

Edwards, A. L. (1964). The measurement of human motives by means of personality scales. In D. Levine (Ed.), *Nebraska symposium on motivation: 1964*. Lincoln: University of Nebraska Press.

Egan, T. (1991, April 25). Police officer's role changes with times. *New York Times*, pp. A1, B10.

Ellyson, S. L., & Dovidio, J. F. (1985). Power, dominance, and nonverbal behavior: Basic concepts and issues. In S. L. Ellyson & J. F. Dovidio (Eds.), *Power, dominance, and nonverbal behavior* (pp. 1–28). New York: Springer-Verlag.

Epstein, C. F. (1988). *Deceptive distinctions: Sex, gender, and the social order*. New Haven, CT: Yale University Press.

Erickson, E. H. (1959). Identity and the life cycle: Selected papers. *Psychological Issues, 1*(1).

Eysenck, H. J. (1990). Biological dimensions of personality. In L. A. Pervin (Ed.), *Handbook of personality: Theory and research* (pp. 244–276). New York: Guilford Press.

Falbo, T., Hazen, M. D., & Linimon, D. (1982). The costs of selecting power bases or messages associated with the opposite sex. *Sex Roles, 8*, 147–157.

Falbo, T., & Peplau, L. A. (1980). Power strategies in intimate relationships. *Journal of Personality and Social Psychology, 38*, 618–628.

Fenster, C. A., & Locke, B. (1973). "The dumb cop": Myth or reality? An exami-
    nation of police intelligence. *Journal of Personality Assessment, 37,* 276–281.
Fenster, C. A., Wiedemann, C. F., & Locke, B. (1978). Police personality—Social
    science folklore and psychological measurement. In B. D. Sales (Ed.), *Psy-
    chology in the legal process* (pp. 89–109). New York: SP Books Division of
    Spectrum Publications.
Fiske, S. T., & Taylor, S. E. (1991). *Social cognition* (2nd ed.). New York: McGraw-
    Hill.
Forest, S. (1994, July 26). 2 more officers in suicides. *New York Newsday,* p. 10.
Foschi, M. (1992). Gender and double standards for competence. In C. Ridgeway
    (Ed.), *Gender, interaction, and inequality* (pp. 181–207). New York: Springer-
    Verlag.
Foschi, M. (1997). On scope conditions. *Small Group Research, 28,* 535–555.
Foschi, M. (1998). Double standards: Types, conditions, and consequences. *Ad-
    vances in Group Processes, 15,* 59–80.
Freedman, M. B., Leary, T. F., Ossorio, A. G., & Coffey, H. S. (1951). The interper-
    sonal dimension of personality. *Journal of Personality, 20,* 143–161.
French, J. R. P., Jr., & Raven, B. (1968). The bases of social power. In D. Cartwright
    & A. Zander (Eds.), *Group dynamics* (pp. 259–269). New York: Harper & Row.
Fromm, E. (1941). *Escape from freedom.* New York: Avon Books.
Fromm, E. (1951). *The forgotten language.* New York: Grove Press.
Gecas, V. (1982). The self-concept. *Annual Review of Sociology, 8,* 1–33.
Geis, F. L., Brown, V., Jennings, J., & Corrado-Taylor, D. (1984). Sex vs. status in
    sex-associated stereotypes. *Sex Roles, 11,* 771–785.
Gerber, G. L. (1973). Psychological distance in the family as schematized by
    families of normal, disturbed, and learning-problem children. *Journal of
    Consulting and Clinical Psychology, 40,* 139–147.
Gerber, G. L. (1987). Sex stereotypes among American college students: Im-
    plications for marital happiness, social desirability and marital power.
    Genetic, Social, and General Psychology Monographs, 113, 413–431.
Gerber, G. L. (1988). Leadership roles and the gender stereotype traits. *Sex Roles,
    18,* 649–668.
Gerber, G. L. (1990). Social acceptability of hypothetical married couples and
    their relationships. *Journal of Psychology, 124,* 575–586.
Gerber, G. L. (1991). Gender stereotypes and power: Perceptions of the roles in
    violent marriages. *Sex Roles, 24,* 439–458.
Gerber, G. L. (1993). The instrumental and expressive traits in social cognition:
    Parallels with social interaction. *Genetic, Social, and General Psychology
    Monographs, 119,* 99–123.
Gerber, G. L. (1996). Status in same-gender and mixed-gender police dyads:
    Effects on personality attributions. *Social Psychology Quarterly, 59,* 350–
    363.
Gerber, G. L., & Kaswan, J. (1971). Expression of emotion through family group-
    ing schemata, distance, and interpersonal focus. *Journal of Consulting and
    Clinical Psychology, 36,* 370–377.
Gergen, K. J. (1991). *The saturated self.* New York: Basic Books.
Goffman, E. (1976). Gender display. *Studies in the Anthropology of Visual Commu-
    nication, 3,* 69–77.

Gold, M., & Yanof, D. S. (1985). Mothers, daughters, and girlfriends. *Journal of Personality and Social Psychology, 49,* 654–659.

Goldstein, H. (1990). *Problem-oriented policing.* New York: McGraw-Hill.

Greenberg, J. R., & Mitchell, S. A. (1983). *Object relations in psychoanalytic theory.* Cambridge, MA: Harvard University Press.

Hare-Mustin, R. T., & Maracek, J. (1990). Gender and the meaning of difference. In R. T. Hare-Mustin & Jeanne Maracek (Eds.), *Making a difference: Psychology and the construction of gender* (pp. 22–64). New Haven, CT: Yale University Press.

Hare-Mustin, R. T., & Marecek, J. (1994). Asking the right questions: Feminist psychology and sex differences. *Feminism and Psychology, 4,* 531–537.

Heilman, M. E. (1995). Sex stereotypes and their effects in the workplace: What we know and what we don't know. In N. J. Struthers (Ed.), Gender in the workplace (Special issue). *Journal of Social Behavior and Personality, 10,* 3–26.

Heilman, M. E., Block, C. J., & Martell, R. F. (1995). Sex stereotypes: Do they influence perceptions of managers? In N. J. Struthers (Ed.), Gender in the workplace [Special issue]. *Journal of Social Behavior and Personality, 10,* 237–252.

Helmreich, R. L., Spence, J. T., & Wilhelm, J. A. (1981). A psychometric analysis of the personal attributes questionnaire. *Sex Roles, 7,* 1097–1108.

Henley, N. M. (1977). *Body politics: Power, sex, and nonverbal communication.* Englewood Cliffs, NJ: Prentice-Hall.

Herbert, S. (1997). *Policing space: Territoriality and the Los Angeles Police Department.* Minneapolis: University of Minnesota Press.

Higbie, D. (1995, January 19). New York forum: About cops. *New York Newsday,* pp. A28, A30.

Higgins, E. T. (1987). Self-discrepancy: A theory relating self and affect. *Psychological Review, 94,* 319–340.

Hogg, M. A., & Abrams, D. (1988). *Social identifications: A social psychology of intergroup relations and group processes.* New York: Routledge.

Hollander, E. P. (1985). Leadership and power. In G. Lindzey & E. Aronson (Eds.), *Handbook of social psychology: Special fields and applications* (3rd ed., Vol. 2, pp. 485–537). New York: Random House.

Hollander, E. P. (1992). The essential interdependence of leadership and followership. *Current Directions in Psychological Science, 1,* 71–75.

Hollander, E. P., & Offermann, L. R. (1990). Power and leadership in organizations: Relationships in transition. *American Psychologist, 45,* 179–189.

Howard, J. A. (1990). A sociological framework of cognition. *Advances in Group Processes, 7,* 75–103.

Howard, J. A. (1995). Social cognition. In K. S. Cook, G. A. Fine, & J. S. House (Eds.), *Sociological perspectives on social psychology* (pp. 90–117). Needham Heights, MA: Allyn and Bacon.

Hunt, J. (1984). The development of rapport through the negotiation of gender in field work among police. *Human Organization, 43,* 283–296.

Hunt, J. (1990). The logic of sexism among police. *Women and Criminal Justice, 1,* 3–30.

Ilgen, D. R. (1999). Teams embedded in organizations. *American Psychologist, 54,* 129–139.

Jacobs, P. (1987). How female police officers cope with a traditionally male position. *Sociology and Social Research, 72,* 4–6.

James, J. B. (Ed.). (1997). The significance of gender: Theory and research about difference [Special issue]. *Journal of Social Issues, 53*(2).

James, W. (1890). *The principles of psychology.* Cambridge, MA: Harvard University Press.

Johnson, C. (1993). Gender and formal authority. *Social Psychology Quarterly, 56,* 193–210.

Johnson, P. (1976). Women and power: Toward a theory of effectiveness. *Journal of Social Issues, 32,* 99–110.

Johnston, J. R. (1985). How personality attributes structure interpersonal relations. In J. Berger & M. Zelditch, Jr. (Eds.), *Status, rewards, and influence* (pp. 317–349). San Francisco: Jossey-Bass.

Jones, E. E., & Davis, K. E. (1965). From acts to dispositions: The attribution process in person perception. In L. Berkowitz (Ed.), *Experimental social psychology, Vol. 2* (pp. 219–266). New York: Academic Press.

Jones, E. E., & Harris, V. A. (1967). The attribution of attitudes. *Journal of Experimental Social Psychology, 3,* 1–24.

Jones, E. E., & Nisbett, R. E. (1972). The actor and the observer: Divergent perceptions of the causes of behavior. In E. E. Jones, D. E. Kanouse, H. H. Kelley, R. E. Nisbett, & S. Valins (Eds.), *Attribution: Perceiving the causes of behavior* (pp. 79–94). Morristown, NJ: General Learning Press.

Jourard, S. M. (1974). Some lethal aspects of the male role. In J. H. Pleck & J. Sawyer (Eds.), *Men and masculinity* (pp. 21–29). Englewood Cliffs, NJ: Prentice-Hall.

Jurik, N. C., & Martin, S. (2000). Femininities, masculinities, and organizational conflict: Women in criminal justice occupation. In L. Goodstein & C. Renzetti (Eds.), *Women, crime and justice.* Los Angeles, CA: Roxbury Press.

Kanter, R. M. (1977). *Men and women of the corporation.* New York: Basic Books.

Kelley, H. H. (1983). Epilogue: An essential science. In H. H. Kelley, E. Berscheid, A. Christensen, H. H. Harvey, T. L. Huston, G. Levinger, E. McClintock, L. A. Peplau, & D. R. Peterson (Eds.), *Close relationships* (pp. 486–503). San Francisco: Freeman.

Kelly, J. A., Caudill, M. S., Hathorn, S., & O'Brien, C. G. (1977). Socially undesirable sex-correlated characteristics: Implications for androgyny and adjustment. *Journal of Consulting and Clinical Psychology, 45,* 1185–1186.

Kennedy, D. B., & Homant, R. J. (1981). Nontraditional role assumption and the personality of the policewoman. *Journal of Police Science and Administration, 9,* 346–355.

Kenney, D. J., & McNamara, R. P. (1999). *Police and policing: Contemporary issues,* (2nd ed.). Westport, CT: Praeger.

Keppel, G. (1973). *Design and analysis: A researcher's handbook.* Englewood Cliffs, NJ: Prentice-Hall.

Kernberg, O. (1976). *Object relations theory and clinical psychoanalysis.* New York: Jason Aronson.

Kipnis, D., & Goodstadt, B. (1970). Character structure and friendship relations. *British Journal of Social and Clinical Psychology, 9,* 201–211.

Kohut, H. (1977). *The restoration of the self.* New York: International Universities Press.

Kristen, K. C., Hyde, J. S., Showers, C. J., & Buswell, B. N. (1999). Gender differences in self-esteem: A meta-analysis. *Psychological Bulletin, 125*, 470–500.

Langworthy, R. H. (1987). Police cynicism: What we know from the Niederhoffer scale. *Journal of Criminal Justice, 15*, 17–35.

Leary, T. (1957). *Interpersonal diagnosis of personality: A functional theory and methodology for personality evaluation.* New York: Ronald Press.

Lefkowitz, J. (1975). Psychological attributes of policemen: A review of research and opinion. *Journal of Social Issues, 31*, 3–26.

Lefkowitz, J. (1977). Industrial-organizational psychology and the police. *American Psychologist, 32*, 346–364.

Lester, D. (1986). Subjective stress and self-esteem of police officers. *Perceptual and Motor Skills, 63*, 1334.

Lewin, M. (1984a). "Rather worse than folly?" Psychology measures femininity and masculinity, 1: From Terman and Miles to the Guilfords. In M. Lewin (Ed.), *In the shadow of the past: Psychology portrays the sexes: A social and intellectual history* (pp. 155–178). New York: Columbia University Press.

Lewin, M. (1984b). Psychology measures femininity and masculinity, 2: From "13 gay men" to the instrumental-expressive distinction. In M. Lewin (Ed.), *In the shadow of the past: Psychology portrays the sexes: A social and intellectual history* (pp. 179–204). New York: Columbia University Press.

Lockheed, M. E., & Hall, K. P. (1976). Conceptualizing sex as a status characteristic: Applications to leadership training strategies. *Journal of Social Issues, 32*, 111–124.

Locksley, A., Borgida, E., Brekke, N., & Hepburn, C. (1980). Sex stereotypes and social judgment. *Journal of Personality and Social Psychology, 38*, 36–49.

Lorber, J. (1994). *Paradoxes of gender.* New Haven, CT: Yale University Press.

Lunneborg, P. W. (1989). *Women police officers: Current career profile.* Springfield, IL: Charles C. Thomas.

Maccoby, E. E., & Jacklin, C. N. (1974). *The psychology of sex differences.* Stanford, CA: Stanford University Press.

Major, B., Barr, L., Zubek, J., & Babey, S. H. (1999). Gender and self-esteem: A meta-analysis. In W. B. Swann, Jr., J. H. Langlois, & L. A. Gilbert (Eds.), *Sexism and stereotypes in modern society: The gender science of Janet Taylor Spence.* Washington, DC: American Psychological Association.

Manning, P. K. (1997). *Police work: The social organization of policing* (2nd ed.). Prospect Heights, IL: Waveland Press.

Markus, H., & Cross, S. (1987). The dynamic self-concept: A social psychological perspective. *Annual Review of Psychology, 38*, 299–337.

Markus, H., & Cross, S. (1990). The interpersonal self. In L. A. Pervin (Ed.), *Handbook of personality: Theory and research* (pp. 576–608). New York: Guilford Press.

Markus, H., & Kunda, Z. (1986). Stability and malleability of the self-concept. *Journal of Personality and Social Psychology, 35*, 858–866.

Martin, S. E. (1990). *On the move: The status of women in policing.* Washington, DC: Police Foundation.

Martin, S. E., & Jurik, N. C. (1996). *Doing justice, doing gender: Women in law and criminal justice occupations.* Thousand Oaks, CA: Sage.

McCauley, C., Stitt, C. L., & Segal, M. (1980). Stereotyping: From prejudice to prediction. *Psychological Bulletin, 87,* 195–208.

McCrae, R. R., & Costa, P. T., Jr. (1994). The stability of personality: Observations and evaluations. *Current Directions in Psychological Science, 3,* 173–175.

McCrae, R. R., & Costa, P. T., Jr. (1996). Toward a new generation of personality theories: Theoretical contexts for the five-factor model. In J. S. Wiggins (Ed.), *The five-factor model of personality: Theoretical perspectives* (pp. 51–87). New York: Guilford Press.

McCrae, R. R., & Costa, P. T., Jr. (1997). Personality trait structure as a human universal. *American Psychologist, 52,* 509–516.

McElhinny, B. (1993). An economy of affect: Objectivity, masculinity and the gendering of police work. In A. Cornwall & N. Lindisfarne (Eds.), *Dislocating masculinity: Comparative ethnographies* (pp. 158–171). New York: Routledge.

McNamara, R. P. (1999). The socialization of the police. In D. J. Kenney & R. P. McNamara (Eds.), *Police and policing: Contemporary issues* (2nd ed., pp. 1–12). Westport, CT: Praeger.

Mead, G. H. (1934). *Mind, self, and society.* Chicago: University of Chicago Press.

Meeker, B. F., & Weitzel-O'Neill, P. A. (1977). Sex roles and interpersonal behavior in task oriented groups. *American Sociological Review, 42,* 92–105.

Megargee, E. I. (1969). Influence of sex roles on the manifestation of leadership. *Journal of Applied Psychology, 53,* 377–382.

Mills, C. J., & Bohannon, W. E. (1980). Personality characteristics of effective state police officers. *Journal of Applied Psychology, 65,* 680–684.

Mischel, W. (1990). Personality dispositions revisited and revised: A view after three decades. In L. A. Pervin (Ed.), *Handbook of personality theory and research* (pp. 111–134). New York: Guilford Press.

Morash, M., & Haar, R. N. (1995). Gender, workplace problems, and stress in policing. *Justice Quarterly, 12,* 113–138.

Morey, N., & Gerber, G. L. (1995). Two types of competitiveness: Their impact on the perceived interpersonal attractiveness of women and men. *Journal of Applied Social Psychology, 25,* 210–222.

Morgan, D. L., & Schwalbe, M. L. (1990). Mind and self in society: Linking social structure and social cognition. *Social Psychology Quarterly, 53,* 148–164.

Moskowitz, D. S., Suh, E. J., & Desaulniers, J. (1994). Situational influences on gender differences in agency and communion. *Journal of Personality and Social Psychology, 66,* 753–761.

Nicholls, J. G., Licht, B. G., & Pearl, R. A. (1982). Some dangers of using personality questionnaires to study personality. *Psychological Bulletin, 92,* 572–580.

Niederhoffer, A. (1967). *Behind the shield: The police in urban society.* Garden City, NY: Doubleday.

Nieva, V. F., & Gutek, B. A. (1980). Sex effects on evaluation. *Academy of Management Review, 5,* 267–276.

Norman, R. Z., Smith, R., & Berger, J. (1988). The processing of inconsistent status information. In M. Webster, Jr., & M. Foschi (Eds.), *Status general-*

ization: New theory and research (pp. 169–187). Stanford, CA: Stanford University Press.

Norvell, N. D., Hills, H. A., & Murrin, M. R. (1993). Understanding stress in female and male law enforcement officers. *Psychology of Women Quarterly, 17*, 289–301.

Offermann, L. R. (1997, July). Leading and empowering diverse followers. In Leadership and Followership Focus Group, *The balance of leadership and Followership.* College Park, MD: Kellogg Leadership Studies Project.

Ogilvie, D. M., & Ashmore, R. D. (1991). Self-with-other representation as a unit of analysis in self-concept research. In R. C. Curtis (Ed.), *The relational self* (pp. 282–314). New York: Guilford Press.

Parsons, T., & Bales, R. F. (1955). *Family, socialization and interaction process.* Glencoe, IL: Free Press of Glencoe.

Peak, K. J., Glensor, R. W., & Gaines, L. K. (1999). Supervising the police. In D. J. Kenney & R. P. McNamara (Eds.), *Police and policing: Contemporary issues* (pp. 37–56). Westport, CT: Praeger.

Pedhazur, E. J., & Tetenbaum, T. J. (1979). Bem's Sex Role Inventory: A theoretical and methodological critique. *Journal of Personality and Social Psychology, 37,* 996–1016.

Pervin, L. A. (1990). A brief history of modern personality theory. In L. A. Pervin (Ed.), *Handbook of personality: Theory and research* (pp. 3–18). New York: Guilford Press.

Planalp, S. (1987). Interplay between relational knowledge and events. In R. Burnett, P. McGhee, & D. D. Clarke (Eds.), *Accounting for relationships: Explanation, representation and knowledge* (pp. 175–191). New York: Methuen.

Price, B. R. (1974). A study of leadership strength of female police executives. *Journal of Police Science and Administration, 2,* 219–226.

Raven, B. H., & Kruglanski, A. W. (1970). Conflict and power. In P. Swingle (Ed.), *The structure of conflict* (pp. 69–109). New York: Academic Press.

Reinisch, J. M., Rosenblum, L. A., Rubin, D. B., & Schulsinger, M. F. (1997). Sex differences emerge during the first year of life. In M. R. Walsh (Ed.), *Women, men, and gender: Ongoing debates* (pp. 37–43). New Haven, CT: Yale University Press.

Ridgeway, C. L. (1982). Status in groups: The importance of motivation. *American Sociological Review, 47,* 76–88.

Ridgeway, C. L. (1988). Gender differences in task groups: A status and legitimacy account. In M. Webster, Jr., & M. Foschi (Eds.), *Status generalization: New theory and research* (pp. 188–206). Stanford, CA: Stanford University Press.

Ridgeway, C. L. (1997). Interaction and the conservation of gender inequality: Considering employment. *American Sociological Review, 62,* 218–235.

Ridgeway, C. L., & Berger, J. (1988). The legitimation of power and prestige orders in task groups. In M. Webster, Jr., & M. Foschi (Eds.), *Status generalization: New theory and research* (pp. 207–231). Stanford, CA: Stanford University Press.

Ridgeway, C. L., & Diekema, D. (1992). Are gender differences status differences? In C. L. Ridgeway (Ed.), *Gender, interaction and inequality* (pp. 157–180). New York: Springer-Verlag.

Ridgeway, C. L., & Smith-Lovin, L. (1999). Gender and interaction. In J. S. Chafetz (Ed.), *Handbook of the sociology of gender* (pp. 247–274). New York: Kluwer Academic/Plenum.

Robins, R. W., Norem, J. K., & Cheek, J. M. (1999). Naturalizing the self. In L. A. Pervin & O. P. John (Eds.), *Handbook of personality: Theory and research* (2nd ed., pp. 443–477). New York: Guilford Press.

Rosenberg, M. (1979/1986). *Conceiving the self.* Malabar, FL: Robert E. Krieger.

Rosse, J. G., Boss, R. W., Johnson, A. E., & Crown, D. F. (1991). Conceptualizing the role of self-esteem in the burnout process. *Group and Organization Studies, 16,* 428–451.

Scanzoni, J. (1979). Social processes and power in families. In W. R. Burr, Jr., R. Hill, F. I. Nye, & I. L. Reiss (Eds.), *Contemporary theories about the family, Vol. 1* (pp. 295–316). New York: Free Press.

Scheibe, K. E. (1995). *Self studies: The psychology of self and identity.* Westport, CT: Praeger.

Sherman, L. J. (1973). A psychological view of women in policing. *Journal of Police Science and Administration, 1,* 383–394.

Sherman, L. W. (1985). Causes of police behavior: The current state of quantitative research. In A. S. Blumberg & E. Niederhoffer (Eds.), *The ambivalent force: Perspectives on the police* (3rd ed., pp. 3–26). Fort Worth, TX: Holt, Rinehart and Winston.

Skolnick, J. H. (1994). *Justice without trial: Law enforcement in democratic society.* New York: Macmillan College.

Smoreda, Z. (1995). Power, gender stereotypes and perceptions of heterosexual couples. *British Journal of Social Psychology, 34,* 421–435.

Spence, J. T., Deaux, K., & Helmreich, R. L. (1985). Sex roles in contemporary American society. In G. Lindzey & E. Aronson (Eds.), *Handbook of social psychology: Special fields and applications* (3rd ed., Vol. 2, pp. 149–178). New York: Random House.

Spence, J. T., & Helmreich, R. L. (1975). *Masculinity and femininity: Their psychological dimensions, correlates, and antecedents.* Austin: University of Texas Press.

Spence, J. T., Helmreich, R. L., & Holahan, C. K. (1979). Negative and positive components of psychological masculinity and femininity and their relationships to self-reports of neurotic and acting out behaviors. *Journal of Personality and Social Psychology, 37,* 1673–1682.

Spence, J. T., Helmreich, R., & Stapp, J. (1974). The Personal Attributes Questionnaire: A measure of sex role stereotypes and masculinity-femininity. Abstracted in the *JSAS Catalog of Selected Documents in Psychology, 4,* 43. (Ms. No. 617)

Spence, J. T., Helmreich, R. L., & Stapp, J. (1975). Ratings of self and peers on sex-role attributes and their relation to self-esteem and conceptions of masculinity and femininity. *Journal of Personality and Social Psychology, 32,* 29–39.

Spence, J. T., & Sawin, L. L. (1985). Images of masculinity and femininity. In V. O'Leary, R. Unger, & B. Wallston (Eds.), *Sex, gender and social psychology* (pp. 35–66). Hillsdale, NJ: Erlbaum.

Spencer, S. J., Josephs, R. A., & Steele, C. M. (1993). Low self-esteem: The uphill struggle for self-integrity. In R. M. Baumeister (Ed.), *Self-esteem: The puzzle of low self-regard* (pp. 21-36). New York: Plenum Press.

Stack, S., & Kelley, T. (1999). Police suicide. In D. J. Kenney & R. P. McNamara (Eds.), *Police and policing: Contemporary issues* (pp. 94–107). Westport, CT: Praeger.

Storms, L. H., Penn, N. F., & Tenzell, J. H. (1990). Policemen's perception of real and ideal policemen. *Journal of Police Science and Administration, 17*, 40–43.

Strodtbeck, F. L. (1951). Husband-wife interaction over revealed differences. *American Sociological Review, 16*, 468–473.

Stryker, S. (1987). Identity theory: Developments and extensions. In K. Yardley & T. Honess (Eds.), *Self and identity: Psychosocial perspectives* (pp. 89–103). New York: Wiley.

Stryker, S. (1989). The two psychologies: Additional thoughts. *Social Forces, 68*, 45–54.

Stryker, S., & Gottlieb, A. (1981). Attribution theory and symbolic interactionism: A comparison. In J. H. Harvey, W. Ickes, & R. F. Kidd (Eds.), *New directions in attribution research, Vol. 3*. Hillsdale, NJ: Erlbaum.

Swann, W. B., Jr. (1990). To be adored or to be known: The interplay of self-enhancement and self-verification. In R. M. Sorrentino & E. T. Higgins (Eds.), *Motivation and cognition, Vol. 2* (pp. 408–448). New York: Guilford Press.

Swim, J. K. (1994). Perceived versus meta-analytic effect sizes: An assessment of the accuracy of gender stereotypes. *Journal of Personality and Social Psychology, 66*, 21–36.

Tajfel, H. (1982). Social psychology of intergroup relations. *Annual Review of Psychology, 33*, 1–39.

Terry, W. C., III. (1981). Police stress: The empirical evidence. *Journal of Police Science and Administration, 9*, 61–75.

Terry, W. C., III. (1985). Police stress: The empirical evidence. In A. S. Blumberg & E. Niederhoffer (Eds.), *The ambivalent force: Perspectives on the police* (3rd ed., pp. 357–370). Chicago: Holt, Rinehart & Winston.

Thurstone, L. L. (1922). The intelligence of policemen. *Journal of Personnel Research, 1*, 64–74.

Tosi, H. L., & Einbender, S. W. (1985). The effects of the type and amount of information in sex discrimination research: A meta-analysis. *Academy of Management Journal, 32*, 662–669.

Turner, J. C. (1987). *Rediscovering the social group: A self-categorization theory*. New York: Basil Blackwell.

Unger, R. K. (1979). Toward a redefinition of sex and gender. *American Psychologist, 34*, 1085–1094.

van Wormer, K. (1981). Are males suited for patrol work? *Police Studies, 3*, 41–44.

Violanti, J. M., Marshall, J. R., & Howe, B. (1985). Stress, coping, and alcohol use: The police connection. *Journal of Police Science and Administration, 13*, 106–110.

Wagner, D. G. (1984). *The growth of sociological theories*. Beverly Hills, CA: Sage.

Wagner, D. G., & Berger, J. (1997). Gender and interpersonal task behaviors: Status expectation accounts. *Sociological Perspectives, 40*, 1–32.

Webster, M., Jr. (1977). Equating characteristics and social interaction. *Sociometry, 40*, 41–50.

Webster, M., Jr., & Foschi, M. (1988). Overview of status generalization. In M. Webster, Jr. & M. Foschi (Eds.), *Status generalization: New theory and research* (pp. 1–20). Stanford, CA: Stanford University Press.

Webster, M., Jr., & Hysom, S. (1998). Creating status characteristics. *American Sociological Review, 63*, 351–378.

Webster, M., Jr., & Sobieszek, B. (1974a). *Sources of self-evaluation: A formal theory of significant others and social influence.* New York: Wiley.

Webster, M., Jr., & Sobieszek, B. I. (1974b). Sources of evaluations and expectation states. In J. Berger, T. L. Conner, & M. H. Fisek (Eds.), *Expectation states theory: A theoretical research program* (pp. 115–158). Washington, DC: Winthrop.

West, C., & Zimmerman, D. H. (1987). Doing gender. *Gender and Society, 1,* 125–151.

Wexler, J. G., & Logan, D. D. (1983). Sources of stress among women police officers. *Journal of Police Science and Administration, 11,* 49–53.

Whitley, B. E., Jr. (1983). Sex role orientation and self-esteem: A critical meta-analytic review. *Journal of Personality and Social Psychology, 44,* 765–778.

Wiggins, J. S. (1982). Circumplex models of interpersonal behavior in clinical psychology. In P. C. Kendall & J. N. Butcher (Eds.), *Handbook of research methods in clinical psychology* (pp. 183–221). New York: Wiley.

Wiley, M. G. (1995). Sex category and gender in social psychology. In K. S. Cook, G. A. Fine, & J. S. House (Eds.), *Sociological perspectives on social psychology* (pp. 362–386). Boston: Allyn and Bacon.

Wiley, M. G., & Alexander, C. N. (1987). From situated activity to self-attribution: The impact of social structural schemata. In K. Yardley & T. Honess (Eds.), *Self and identity: Psychosocial perspectives* (pp. 105–117). New York: Wiley.

Williams, C. L. (1989). *Gender differences at work: Women and men in nontraditional occupations.* Berkeley: University of California Press.

Williams, J. E., and Best, D. L. (1982). *Measuring sex stereotypes: A thirty-nation study.* Beverly Hills, CA: Sage.

Wilson, C., & Braithwaite, H. (1995). Police patrolling, resistance, and conflict resolution. In N. Brewer & C. Wilson (Eds.), *Psychology and policing* (pp. 5–29). Hillsdale, NJ: Erlbaum.

Winer, B. J. (1971). *Statistical principles in experimental design.* New York: McGraw-Hill.

Worell, F. (1996). Opening doors to feminist research. *Psychology of Women Quarterly, 20,* 469–485.

Wyer, R. S., Jr., & Lambert, A. J. (1994). The role of trait constructs in person perception: A historical perspective. In P. G. Devine, D. L. Hamilton, & T. L. Ostrom (Eds.), *Social cognition: Impact on social psychology* (pp. 113–143). New York: Academic Press.

Wyer, R. S., Jr., & Srull, T. K. (1989). *Memory and cognition in its social context.* Hillsdale, NJ: Erlbaum.

Wylie, R. (1979). *The self-concept: Theory and research on selected topics* (Vol. 2, Rev. ed.). Lincoln: University of Nebraska Press.

Yarmey, A. D. (1990). *Understanding police and police work: Psychosocial issues.* New York: New York University Press.

Yoder, J. D. (1989). Women at West Point: Lessons for token women in male-dominated occupations. In J. Freeman (Ed.), *Women: A feminist perspective.* Mountain View, CA: Mansfield.

Yoder, J. D. (1996). Undergraduates regard deviation from occupational gender stereotypes as costly for women. *Sex Roles, 34,* 171–188.

Name Index

Abrams, D., 23, 25
Abramson, L. V., 86, 148
Adlam, K. R., xviii, xxi, 84, 86, 131, 147
Adler, L. L., 146
Adorno, T. W., xvii
Alexander, C. N., 122, 140
Alloy, L. B., 86, 148
Allport, G. W., 48, 84, 99, 126, 132, 143
Antill, J. K., 7
Arcuri, A. F., 86
Ashmore, R. D., 122
Austin, T. L., xix

Babey, S. H., 13, 83, 138
Bakan, D., 104
Baker, M., 65
Balch, R. W., xxii, 50
Baldwin, M. W., 115, 122, 124, 126
Bales, R. F., 3, 19–22, 26, 65, 95–96, 101, 115, 117, 126
Balkwell, J. W., 18
Banaji, M. R., 121
Bandura, A., 100, 104–6, 127
Barr, L., 13, 83, 138
Baumeister, R. F., 85–86, 96, 132, 148

Beck, A. T., 86, 148
Bem, D. J., 4, 18, 20, 23, 26–27
Bem, S. L., 1, 6, 9, 21, 99, 129, 138, 160
Berg, B. L., xix
Berger, J., xv, xxii, 1, 3–5, 8, 10–11, 17–21, 23, 26–27, 54–55, 62–63, 68–69, 72, 120, 123, 128, 135–36, 153, 171
Berscheid, E., 115, 121–26, 130, 140
Best, D. L., 159–60
Blaine, B., 88, 181
Blascovich, J., 35, 84
Block, C. J., 153
Blood, R. O., Jr., 22, 36, 162–63
Blumberg, A. S., 32, 60
Bohan, J. S., 1–3
Bohannon, W. E., 43
Bonifacio, P., xx, 69, 81, 83, 86, 147
Borgida, E., 8, 23
Braithwaite, H., xviii
Brekke, N., 8, 23
Briggs, J., 127
Brown, V., 8
Budnick, K. J., xix
Burbeck, E., xvii–xviii, 142
Buss, D. M., 4, 20, 27, 70–71, 76, 86, 96, 100, 104, 107, 117, 126, 129

Buswell, B. N., 13, 83, 138

Carbonell, J. L., 68
Carli, L. L., 10, 55, 60, 63, 68, 111, 125
Carpenter, B. N., 50
Caudill, M. S., 7
Centers, R., 162–63
Cervone, D., 117, 120, 131, 138
Cheek, J. M., 130
Cohen, J., 162, 170, 180, 182
Cohen, P., 162, 170, 180, 182
Collins, P. H., 136
Connell, R. W., 136
Conner, T. L., 20
Constantinople, A., 6, 138
Conway, M., 9, 43, 136–37
Corrado-Taylor, D., 8
Costa, P. T., Jr., 117, 131
Costrich, N., 11, 67, 133–35, 152
Cowen, G., 67, 70, 133–35, 152
Craik, K. H., 4, 20, 27, 70–71, 76, 86, 96, 100, 104, 107, 117, 126, 129
Crocker, J., 88, 181
Cross, S., 117, 120, 122, 130–31, 140
Crowne, D. F. 86

Davis, J. A., 94
Davis, K. E., 4, 20, 23, 27
Deaux, K., xiii, 6–7, 21, 65, 67, 72, 120, 127, 133, 141
Denmark, F. L., 139, 143, 146, 153
Department of Justice, 142
Diekama, D., 19–20
Dimitrovsky, L., 152
Dion, K. L., 19, 23–24, 47–48
Doerner, W. G., xviii, xxi, 84, 86, 92, 147
Dorsey, R. R., xx
Dovidio, J. F., 100, 102, 127

Eagly, A. H., 2, 7, 10, 19, 21, 136
Edwards, A. L., 35, 159
Egan, T., 144
Einbender, S. W., 153
Ellyson, S. L., 100, 102, 127
Epstein, C. F., 4, 7–8, 50, 138
Erikson, Erik, 84, 105

Eysenck, H. J., 100, 126

Falbo, T., 11, 57, 61, 67, 70, 112
Feinstein, J., 11, 67, 133, 152
Fenster, C. A., xviii, 89
Fisek, M. H., xv, 3, 17, 54, 72
Fiske, S. T., 27, 44, 78, 81, 121–22, 125
Foschi, M., 4, 18, 72–73, 81, 121, 128, 133, 135
French, J. R. P., Jr., 102
Fromm, Erich, 105
Furnham, A., xvii–xviii, 142

Gaines, L. K., 152
Gecas, V., 100, 128
Geis, F. L., 8
Gerber, G. L., 3, 8–9, 11, 21–23, 25, 43, 67–68, 121–22, 134, 136–37, 143, 151
Gergen, K. J., 130
Giacopassi, D. J., xx
Glensor, R. W., 152
Goffman, E., 11, 71, 133
Gold, M., 36
Goldstein, H., 144
Goodstadt, B., 36
Gottleib, A., 8
Greenberg, J. R., 101–2, 104
Gutek, B. A., 153

Haar, R. N., xx
Hall, K. P., 19, 170
Hare-Mustin, R. T., 3, 138, 143
Harris, V. A., 44, 125
Hathorn, S., 7
Hazen, M. D., 11, 67
Heilman, M. E., 2–5, 10, 152–53
Helmreich, R. L., xiii, 1–2, 21, 26, 33, 53, 65, 68, 99–101, 107, 114, 120, 126, 129, 141, 160, 183
Henley, N. M., 7, 60, 100, 102, 127
Hepburn, C., 8, 23
Herbert, S., 147–48
Higbie, D., xvi, 1
Higgins, E. T., 150
Hills, H. A., xix, 94
Hogg, M. A., 23, 25
Holahan, C. K., 2, 26, 33, 53, 68, 100, 126

Hollander, E. P., 3, 21, 103, 145, 147–48, 153
Homant, R. J., xix, 146
Howard, J. A., 8, 14, 131
Howe, B., xix
Hunt, J., xix
Hyde, J. S., 13, 83, 138
Hysom, S., 144, 146

Ilgen, D. R., 151

Jacklin, C. N., 2, 13, 83, 138
Jacobs, P., xix
James, J. B., 2–3
James, W., 84, 132
Jennings, J., 8
Johnson, A. E., 86
Johnson, P., 10, 53, 55, 57, 61, 113
Johnston, J. R., 21, 50
Jones, E. E., 4, 20, 23, 26–27, 44–45, 125, 150
Josephs, R. A., 84
Jourard, S. M., 81
Jurik, N. C., xix, 60, 79, 143–44, 146

Kanter, R. M., 4–5, 7, 22, 24
Karau, S., 19
Kaswan, J., 23, 25, 121
Kelley, H. H., 121
Kelly, J. A., 7
Kennedy, D. B., xix, 146
Kenney, D. J., 106
Kernberg, O., 102
Kidder, L., 11, 67, 133, 152
Kipnis, D., 36
Kohut, H., 102, 104
Koziej, J., 67, 70, 133–35, 152
Kristen, K. C., 13, 83, 138
Kruglanski, A. W., 113, 151
Kunda, Z., 122

LaFrance, M., 65, 67, 133
Lambert, A. J., 3, 12–13
Langworthy, R. H., xviii
Leary, T., 101, 104, 115, 117, 126
Lefkowitz, J., xviii
Lester, D., 86
Lewin, M., 6, 99, 138

Lewis, L., 6, 72
Licht, B. G., 38, 87
Linimon, D., 11, 67
Locke, B., xviii, 89
Lockheed, M. E., 19, 170
Locksley, A., 8, 23
Logan, D. D., xix–xx
Lorber, J., 2, 10, 136
Lunneborg, P. W., xiii, xix, 47, 79, 94, 143–44

Maccoby, E. E., 2, 13, 83, 138
Major, B., 13, 83, 138
Manning, P. K., 43, 69–70, 79, 106, 141, 151
Maracek, J., 3, 11, 67, 133, 138, 143, 152
Markus, H., 117, 120, 122, 130–31, 140
Marshall, J. R., xix
Martell, R. F., 153
Martin, S. E., xiii, xix–xx, 4, 19, 24, 32, 56, 60, 79, 143–44, 146
McCauley, C., 3
McCrae, R. R., 117, 131
McElhinny, B., 66, 79–80
McNamara, R, P., xvii–xviii, 106, 131
Mead, G. H., 84
Meeker, B. F., 12, 60, 125, 132
Metalsky, G. I., 86, 148
Mills, C. J., 43
Mischel, W., 4, 50
Mitchell, S. A., 101–2, 104
Morash, M., xx
Morey, N., 151
Morgan, D. L., 2, 4, 14, 50, 115, 121, 126, 131
Mount, L., 9, 43, 136
Murrin, M. R., xix, 94

Nicholls, J. G., 35, 87, 97, 159
Niederhoffer, A., xvii–xviii, xx–xxi, 32, 56, 60, 83
Nieva, V. F., 153
Nisbett, R. E., 26–27, 44–45, 125, 150
Norem, J. K., 130
Norman, R. Z., xv, 3, 17, 54, 72, 171
Norvell, N. D., xix, 94

O'Brien, C. G., 7
Offermann, L. R., 145, 147–48, 153
Ogilvie, D. M., 122
O'Neill, J. J., xix

Parsons, T., 22, 65, 101, 115, 117, 126
Peak, K. J., 152
Pearl, R. A., 35, 87, 159
Penn, N. F., 43, 141
Pedhazur, E. J., 6
Peplau, L. A., 57, 61, 112
Pervin, L. A., 4, 8, 12, 14, 50, 99–101,
    126
Pizzamiglio, M. T., 9, 43, 136
Planalp, S., 122, 124
Prentice, D. A., 121
Price, B. R., 58

Raven, B., 102, 113, 151, 162
Raza, S. M., 50
Reinisch, J. M., 2
Ridgeway, C. L., 3, 12, 19–20, 23–24,
    47, 55, 60, 63, 68, 111, 113, 125, 129,
    135
Robins, R. W., 130–31
Rodrigues, A., 162
Rosenberg, M., 35, 84, 132
Rosenblum, L. A., 2
Rosenholtz, S. J., 1, 3, 18, 20
Rosse, J. G., 86
Rubin, D. B., 2

Sawin, L. L., 6, 66, 72, 79
Scanzoni, J., 3
Scheibe, K. E., 130
Schulsinger, M. F., 2
Schwalbe, M. L., 2, 4, 14, 50, 115, 121,
    126, 131
Segal, M., 3
Sherman, L. J., xix
Sherman, L. W., 32
Shoda, Y., 120, 131, 138
Showers, C. J., 13, 83, 138
Singer, J., 152
Skolnick, J. H., xvii–xviii, 142
Slater, P. E., 3, 19, 21, 95–96
Smith, R., 171
Smith-Lovin, L., 3

Smoreda, Z., 9, 43, 136–37
Sobieszek, B. I., 85, 95, 132
Spence, J. T., xiii, 1–2, 6–7, 9–10, 12,
    14, 21, 26, 33, 35, 53, 65–66, 68, 72,
    79, 99–101, 104, 107, 114, 117, 120,
    126, 129, 131, 136, 138–39, 141,
    160, 183
Spencer, S. J., 84–85
Srull, T. K., 13, 84, 96
Stapp, J., 1, 21, 33, 65, 99, 107, 129,
    150, 183
Steele, C. M., 84
Stitt, C. L., 3
Storms, L. H., 43, 141
Strodtbeck, F. L., 19
Stryker, S., 2, 4, 6, 8, 14, 50, 131
Swann, W. B., Jr., 85, 132
Swim, J. K., 48

Tajfel, H., 23, 25
Taylor, S. E., 27, 44, 78, 81, 121–22,
    125
Tenzell, J. H., 43, 141
Terry, W. C., xix–xx, 84
Tetenbaum, T. J., 6
Thurstone, L. L., 89
Tomaka, J., 35, 84
Tosi, H. L., 153

van Wormer, K., 47, 146
Violanti, J. M., xix

Wagner, D. G., xxii, 10–11, 18–19, 21,
    27, 55, 62–63, 68–69, 120, 123, 128,
    135–36, 153
Webster, M., Jr., 18, 20, 72, 85, 95,
    121, 128, 132, 144, 146, 172
Weitzel-O'Neill, P. A., 12, 60, 125, 132
West, C., 11, 72, 133
Wexler, J. G., xix–xx
Whitley, B. E., Jr., 7, 159
Wiedemann, C. F., xviii, 89
Wiggins, J. S., 101, 104, 117
Wiley, M. G., 122, 140
Wilhelm, J. A., 100
Williams, J. E., 159–60
Wilson, C., xviii
Winer, B. J., 170

Wolfe, D. M., 22, 36, 162–63
Wood, W., 2, 7, 10
Worell, F., 2
Wyer, R. S., Jr., 3, 12–13, 84, 96

Yanof, D. S., 36
Yarmey, A. D., 149

Yinon, Y., 152
Yoder, J. D., 144

Zelditch, M., Jr., xv, xxii, 1, 3, 11, 17–
   18, 21, 54, 72, 120, 128, 136, 153
Zimmerman, D. H., 11, 72, 133, 136
Zubek, J., 13, 83, 138

Subject Index

Agency, 186 n.8, 190 n.4, 194 n.1. *See also* Instrumental traits
Aggression, 24–25, 147
Alcoholism, 83; and low self-esteem, 86
All-female teams, xxi–xxii, 30, 109–10; and bipolar traits, 73–78, 134–35, 150–51; high-status woman in, 73–75, 77–78, 111; low-status woman in, 111–14, 128–29; negative traits in, 111–14, 128–29, 151; status and, 25, 149–52; supervisor's evaluations and, 43–46, 73–76, 79–81, 112–14, 149–52
All-male teams, xv–xvi, xx–xxi, 30, 147–49; and bipolar traits, 75, 78, 148–49; high-status man in, 87–94, 147–49, 180–82; low-status man in, 75, 78, 148–49; and self-esteem, 87–94, 147–48; status and, 147–49
Attribution theorists, 20
Autonomy, 105–106

Behaviors, and traits, 20–21
Biases: affecting schemas, 125–26; in supervisor's evaluations, 152–53

Bipolar traits, 10–12, 65–82, 134–35, 171, 176–77, 182–83, 188 n.7, 189 n.8; and behavior, 66–67

Cognitive representations, 128–29
Communion, 186 n.8. *See also* Expressive traits

Demographic and partnership information, 37
Depression, and low self-esteem, 86, 148
Dominating traits, 40–43, 107–113, 122–23, 128–29, 168, 172–75, 188 n.7, 194 n.1
"Dumb cop" stereotype, 89–91

Efficacy dimension, 100–1, 104–7, 110–11, 116, 127–28, 137
Empathy, 104
Essentialist model. *See* Gender-specific model
Expressive traits, xiv, 40–43, 107–110, 168–69, 172–75, 188 n.7; and status, 20–21

Extended Personal Attributes
  Questionnaire (EPAQ), 7, 10–11,
  33–35, 66, 107–13, 114–15, 167–78,
  180–83; comparing women and
  men, 196 n.6

Female police officers. *See* Women
  Police Officers
Femininity, xix

Gender, xiii–xiv, 137–136; definition
  of, 185 n.1; and outside observers,
  133–36; and personality, xxii–xxiii,
  119–140; salience of, 133–36; and
  self-esteem, 83–84, 97; and status,
  119–140
Gender-distinct officers: 73–78, 134–
  36; roles and behavior, 67–69; self-
  evaluations, 76–78; supervisor's
  evaluations, 73–76
Gender markers, 71–73, 76
Gender-normative officers,
  supervisor's evaluations, 75–76;
  176–77
Gender norms, 79–81; and personality, 10–12; violation of, 65–82
Gender-specific model, 2–4, 46, 119–
  20, 172–75; and essentialist model,
  186 n.1
Gender-stereotyped traits: desirable
  and undesirable, 26–27, 88–89,
  107–8; intercorrelations of, 99–101,
  107–5, 129–30; research on, 5–10.
  See also Gender stereotyping
Gender stereotyping, 1–16, 48–50,
  186 n.3; gender-specific model of,
  2–4, 46, 172–75; status model of, 1–
  4, 21–23, 46–48, 119–21, 172–75
Gender roles, xiii, 79–81
Group status, 23–26, 32–33, 41–43,
  146–47, 187 nn.5, 6; analysis of,
  189 n.1; schema, 123

High-status man: low self-esteem,
  87–89, 92–94, 147–48, 178, 180–82;
  perceived low intelligence, 89–91,
  92–94, 178–79; 181–82; problems
  with women officers, 90–94, 179

High-status woman: self-evaluations
  and bipolar traits, 77–78, 151;
  supervisor's evaluations and bipolar traits, 73–76, 150–51

Individual status, 23–26, 31–32, 40–
  41, 187 n.6; analysis of 189 n.1;
  schema, 123
Individuation, 105
Influence, relative, 77–78. *See also*
  Power
Influence schemas, 123–25
Instrumental traits, xiv, 43, 110–11,
  127–28, 137, 141–42, 169, 188 n.7,
  190 n.4, 194 n.1; and status, 20–21
Interviews, structured, 31, 37–38

Low status, 53–64; coping with, 10,
  53–64, 144–47
Low-status man: self-evaluations and
  bipolar traits, 77–78; supervisor's
  evaluations and bipolar traits, 75,
  78; verbal-aggression, 175–76
Low-status woman: in all-female
  team and undesirable traits, 111–
  14, 128–29; in male–female team
  and submissive traits, 59–60; in
  male–female team and verbal aggressive traits 56–63, 144–45

Male–female teams, xvi, xix–xx, 30,
  56–64, 144–47; high-status man
  in, 58–59, 61–62, 124–25, 144–45;
  low-status woman in, 56–61, 124–
  25, 144–45; sex-typing in, 114–15;
  status and, 144–47; submissive
  traits in, 59–60, 62, 125; verbal-aggressive traits in, 56–64, 124–25,
  144–45
Marital problems, 83; and low self-
  esteem, 86
Male police officers. *See* Men police
  officers
Men police officers, ix–x, xiii, 141–
  44; status effects on personalities
  of, 142–44; stresses on, xix–xxii,
  94; verbal aggression of, 58–59. *See
  also* All-male teams; High-status

man; Low-status man; Male–
female teams

Nagging, 62–63

Observers, perceptions by, 78–79,
    133–36

Partner, perceptions of, 41–43, 56–57,
    59–60, 167–71
Patterning of traits, 12–14, 99–117,
    126–30; external pressures and,
    128–29; and individual officers,
    107–15
Personality: dimensions, 101–11, 115–
    16; theories, x. See also Efficacy di-
    mension; Patterning of traits;
    Power dimension
Personality trait theory, and self-es-
    teem, 12–13, 85–86
Police, and gender norms, 65–82;
    macho image of, 47; personality
    traits of, 141–42; self-evaluation
    of, 76–78; stress and, 83, 86
Police Decision Scale, 35–36, 57–59,
    77–78, 162–65, 189 n.14
Police partners, relationship be-
    tween, xiv–xvii; and status, xv–
    xvii, 141–42; stresses on, xix–xxii;
    study of, 4–5, 29–38. See also All-
    female teams; Male–female teams;
    All-male teams
Police personality, x–xi, xvii–xix,
    xxii, 142–44, 154; female officers
    and, xviii–xix
Police teams: interview sample, 31;
    sample of, xv, 30–31, 155–56, 191
    n.10, 197 n.4, 198 n.10
Power, direct and indirect, 60–62
Power dimension, 100–4, 109, 115–
    16, 126–28

Questionnaire: police partners, 30,
    156–57; supervisor's, 31, 157

Research on gender–stereotyped
    traits, 5–10; measuring scales, 6–7;
    status and power, 7–10

Scales: education, 90, 176, 179, 189
    n.13; female coworkers, 36, 90–92,
    176, 179, 189 n.11; individual per-
    formance, 37, 58–59, 73–76, 189
    n.12; leadership, 37, 112–13; male
    coworkers, 36, 92, 176, 179–80, 189
    n.11; perceived intelligence, 36, 89–
    91, 176, 178–79, 181–82, 189 n.11;
    perceived job success, 36, 57–59,
    73–76; team competence, 37, 45,
    73–76, 189 n.12. See also Extended
    Personal Attributes Questionnaire;
    Self-Evaluation Scale; Unilateral
    power and control scales
Schemas, 122–25; biases affecting,
    125–26. See also Influence schemas;
    Status schemas
Self-efficacy, 127–28. See also Efficacy
    dimension
Self-esteem, 83–97, 131–32; and bipo-
    lar traits, 77–78; and competence
    evaluations, 95, 131–32; gender is-
    sues and, 83–84, 97; personality
    traits and, 85–89; status and, 87–
    89, 131
Self-Evaluation Scale, 35, 77–78, 87–
    89, 108, 159–62, 176, 178, 180–81
Self evaluations: by officers, 76–79,
    131–32; role of personality traits
    in, 12–13
Self, perceptions of, 40–42, 56–57,
    76–79; 130–32, 167–71. See also
    Observers
Sex. See Sex category
Sex category: definition of, 185 n.1;
    and sex, 185 n.1
Sex typing, 114–15
Social cognition, xi, 27–28, 120–21;
    and actor-observer effect, 45, 125;
    and external pressures, 43–46, 125–
    26; and social interaction, 120–22,
    139–40
Status, xxii–xxiii, 46–51, 175–76;
    adverse effects of, 92–94; consis-
    tent and inconsistent characteris-
    tics and, 171–72, 188 n.3;
    determination of, xix–xx, 18–20,
    145–46; and gender stereotyping,

1–16, 21–23, 119–40; individual
and group, 23–26, 31–33, 40–43,
123; in interactions, x, xiii–xiv;
low, 53–64; and personality, 39–51,
83–97; in police partnerships, xv–
xvii, xix–xxii; and self-esteem, 87–
88, 92–94, 96–97. *See also* Status
model; Status order; Status schemas
Status characteristics theory, xi, xv–
xvi; and gender-stereotyped personality traits, 17–28; implications
for, 81–82; and relational status,
187 n.3; and self-esteem, 95–96;
and social cognition, xi, 27–28, 81–
82; and task-related competence,
85, 95
Status model, 1–4, 10–12, 21–23, 46–
48, 119–21, 136–40, 172–75
Status order, xv–xvii, xix–xxii; and
conflict between sex category and
seniority, xix–xx, 60–64, 124–25,
144–45; violation of, xx
Status-related traits, 136–37
Status schemas, 122–123
Stress, and police partnerships, xix–
xxii. *See also* All-female teams; All-
male teams; Male–female teams
Submissive traits, 10, 53–64, 110–13,
128–29, 170–71, 188 n.7; and low-
status woman, 59–60
Suicide, 83, and low self-esteem, 86,
148
Supervisor: and all-female teams,
43–46, 112–14; biases in evaluations by, 152–53, 198 n.21; and
gender norms, 79–81; job perfor
mance evaluations by, 37, 45, 58–
59, 73–76, 78–79, 112–14, 152–53,

176; as observer, 70–71, 76; role of,
113–14. *See also* Scales: individual
performance; leadership; team
competence

Theory, status, gender, and personality, 119–140
Traits, xiii–xiv, 119–40, 142–44; desirable and undesirable, 26–27, 107–
8; female officers', xviii–xix;
organization of, 13–14, 99–117,
126–30; research on gender-stereotyped, 5–10; status and, 39–51, 83–
97, 137–39. See also Bipolar traits;
Dominating traits; Expressive
traits; Gender-stereotyped traits;
Instrumental traits; Status-related
traits; Submissive traits; Verbal-
aggressive traits

Unilateral power and control scales,
36, 112–13, 198 n n.9, 10

Verbal-aggressive traits, 10, 53–64, 111–
13, 123–25, 128–29, 169–70, 175–76,
188 n.7; and coping with low status,
54–56, 60–62; female officers', 56–58,
60–64, 124–25, 144–45; male
officers', 58–59, 144–45

Women police officers: behavior of,
66–67; personality traits of, ix–x,
xiii; xviii–xix, 10–16; and self-esteem, 94–95; and status, xix–xx;
status effects on personalities of,
142–44; stresses on, xix–xxii, 94;
verbal aggression of, 57–58. *See
also* All-female teams; High-status
woman; Low-status woman; Male–
female teams

ABOUT THE AUTHOR

GWENDOLYN L. GERBER is Professor of Psychology at John Jay College of Criminal Justice and the Graduate Center of the City University of New York. Professor Gerber has published extensively in journals such as *Sex Roles, Social Psychology Quarterly* and the *Journal of Applied Social Psychology* as well as in edited books. A Fellow in the American Psychological Association and The New York Academy of Sciences, she has received the Wilhelm Wundt and Kurt Lewin Awards from the New York State Psychological Association.